# More Nature Walks in Eastern Massachusetts

Michael Tougias

APPALACHIAN MOUNTAIN CLUB BOOKS
BOSTON, MASSACHUSETTS

Cover Photograph: Marny Ashburne
All photographs by the author unless otherwise noted
Cover Design: Elisabeth Leydon Brady
Book Design: Carol Bast Tyler

Distributed by The Globe Pequot Press, Inc.

*Library of Congress Cataloging-in-Publication Data*
*Tougias, Mike, 1955–*
*More nature walks in eastern Massachusetts: discover 47 new walks*
*including scenic Cape Cod / Michael Tougias.*
*p. cm.*
*Includes index.*
*ISBN 1-878239-67-8 (alk. paper)*
*1. Nature trails—Massachusetts—Boston Region—Guidebooks. 2. Natural history—Massachusetts—Boston Region—Guidebooks. 3. Wildlife viewing sites—Massachusetts—Boston Region—Guidebooks. 4. Wildlife watching—Massachusetts—Boston Region—Guidebooks. 5. Walking—Massachusetts—Boston Region—Guidebooks. 6. Boston Region (Mass.)—Guidebooks. I. Appalachian Mountain Club. II. Title.*
*QH105.M4T68   1998*
*508.744—dc21*
98-28882
CIP

The paper used in this publication meets the minimum requirements of the American National Standard for Information Sciences—Permanence of Paper for Printed Library Materials, ANSI Z39.48–1984.∞

**Due to changes in conditions,
use of the information in this book
is at the sole risk of the user.**

Printed on recycled paper using soy-based inks.
Printed in the United States of America.

10 9 8 7 6 5 4 3 2

00 01 02 03

# Contents

## Southeastern Massachusetts

*This book is dedicated to my old boyhood*
*friends: Dale, Cogs, Griff, and Opie,*
*who all helped in their own way.*
*And to all the readers who have offered kind*
*words and supported my work over the years.*

# Introduction

A weekend is just not a weekend without a walk in the woods. The physical joy of walking combined with the potential of seeing wildlife makes for a winning combination. A special day outdoors can make your spirits soar whether it's a walk on a crisp, colorful autumn day, a winter's trek just after a heavy snow, or the first hike of spring when the earth awakens.

Eastern Massachusetts affords a number of diverse pockets of wilderness where you can walk in solitude. Properties range in size from the 23 acres of Hemlock Gorge in Needham and Newton to the sprawling woods of Freetown State Forest in Freetown. One of my toughest challenges was deciding which of the one hundred or so properties I researched to include in the forty-seven reviewed in the book. Ultimately the selection was narrowed down to those properties with the most diversity. The walks in this book take you to hilltop overlooks, quaking cedar bogs, riverfront trails, glacial eskers and erratics, and lesser-known historic sites.

Each walk includes directions, suggested trails, a map, wildlife and plants to be seen, estimated hiking time, trail conditions, scenic views, and a brief description of any nearby points of interest. Also included is a level of difficulty for each walk. In general, I have rated walks under three miles on fairly level terrain as *easy,* walks of three miles or more as *medium,* and walks more than five miles or steep hills as *difficult.*

Henry David Thoreau viewed walking as a way to lose oneself: "What business have I in the woods, if I am thinking of something out of the woods." He walked often and far afield: "I think that I cannot preserve my health and spirits, unless I spend four hours a day at least—and it is commonly more than that—sauntering through the woods and over the hills and fields, absolutely free from all worldly engagements." And if Thoreau saw wildlife, all the better. It was not unusual for him to sit and wait patiently for some creature to appear or stop his walk to watch wildlife for the rest of the day. Your walks will be more enjoyable if you follow Thoreau's examples.

I wrote this book to share some of my special places with you, and because the feedback from readers for the original *Nature Walks in Eastern Massachusetts* book was so positive. I hope that by raising appreciation for nature we can protect more wild places before they are forever lost to development.

## A Few Suggestions

- For a more enjoyable hike, bring binoculars, a camera, and a snack (food tastes better in the outdoors).

- Bring extra film—don't run out when the best picture presents itself.

- Women should not hike alone. Ask a friend who shares your love of the outdoors, or better yet, pick a friend who spends more time in the malls than the woods, and introduce him or her to the joys of walking in the great outdoors.

- Bring a map and/or compass and make sure you know how to use these. There are several good introductory books and workshops available through the AMC and other organizations. Getting lost in the woods is no fun. If you are unfamiliar with an area, be sure you set out well before dark. Even at the smaller reservations it's possible to get lost. Always tell someone what reservations you plan to explore.

- The tiny ticks that can carry Lyme disease are spread throughout New England. Always wear long pants, preferably with the pants tucked beneath your socks. Avoid fields of tall grass during the warm weather months. And to be on the safe side, give yourself a "tick check" after every hike by examining yourself all over, especially the scalp, neck, armpits, groin, and ankles.

- Be on the lookout for poison ivy—identified by its three shiny leaves. Again, long pants are recommended.

- During warm weather months carry a small backpack or fanny pack with water and bug spray. (It's a good idea to have pack permanently loaded for nature walks, so that all you need do is fill the water bottle.)

- During cold weather months layer your clothes so that you can peel off or add items easily. The best layering is a moisture-wicking inner layer, a warm insulating layer, and waterproof/windproof outer layer. Be sure to wear warm, waterproof boots. Always bring a hat.

- Deer hunting season is in the fall. Wear a blaze orange hat to be on the safe side—even when in a no hunting area.

## Trail Courtesy

Respect for nature involves a few basic rules.

- Be sure to follow the "carry-in, carry-out" principle when it comes to trash.

- Do not remove any plants from the woods. Return logs and rocks that you have moved back to their original position.

- Keep to the established trails.

- Give wildlife a wide berth. Binoculars and a telephoto lens on your camera will allow you to view the wildlife without disturbing it.

Become involved in local conservation efforts. We can all help maintain our woods and waters in a clean, natural state where wildlife has a chance to flourish. Besides local conservation commissions and watershed associations, there are many statewide organizations such as the Appalachian Mountain Club, The Trustees of Reservations, and Massachusetts Audubon Society that have active conservation programs.

## How To Use This Book

The walks are grouped into four sections according to the regions they are in. (See the Map Locator after the Introduction.) Once you have selected the location you want to explore, and have read the property description, look up directions to the site under "Getting There" found at the end of each walk.

The approximate time for the recommended walk is given at the beginning of each entry, along with the level of difficulty. The time-to-mileage ratio used is about thirty minutes for each mile, but you may want to allow more time to enjoy the environment. This ratio was used in some cases to figure approximate trail mileage.

You might want to take the book with you to use the map if you are unfamiliar with the property. A bold letter "P" designates the parking area found at the entrance to each site. Each map shows north, and includes an approximate scale in either feet or miles. A heavy dashed line indicates the route described in the text, and the lighter dashed line indicates other trails in the area.

If you are walking with children, see the recommended walks for children found later in this introduction.

Conditions of trails do change from time to time and we would appreciate hearing about any changes you find. Address trail updates to: Appalachian Mountain Club Books, 5 Joy Street, Boston, MA 02108.

## Wildlife Watching

Walkers are often disappointed when they stroll through four or five miles of wooded terrain and see nothing of the area's wildlife but a chipmunk. Sometimes spotting different wildlife is just luck, being in the right place at the right time, while other times it's because of a growing knowledge of the creatures and their habits. We can't do much about luck, but there are a number of steps that increase your odds of spotting the many birds, animals, and reptiles that live in Eastern Massachusetts.

Thoreau was an expert "wildlife watcher," patient and full of curiosity. He would think nothing of sitting for an hour to watch a bird or animal gather food. "True men of science," he wrote, "will know nature better by his finer organizations; he will smell, taste, see, hear, feel, better than other men. His will be a deeper and finer experience." Nature reveals more of its subtleties when we focus all our senses into the natural surroundings. Try following Thoreau's example and let yourself become absorbed by the forests, fields, and water—even if you don't see wildlife, the walks themselves are more rewarding and refreshing.

Two keys to wildlife watching are knowing where and when to look. The best time to see most wildlife is at dawn and dusk. Many creatures are nocturnal, and there is also some overlap at dawn and dusk with the daytime birds and animals.

Spring and fall are the two best seasons, especially for migratory birds. Animals that hibernate will be active during the spring after a long winter, and in the fall they will eat as much as possible in preparation for the cold months to come. Winter has the least activity but it does offer some advantages, such as easier long-range viewing (no foliage), and the potential to see some animals crossing the ice (such as coyotes); also, animals are often easier to spot against a background of white snow.

Experienced wildlife watchers look everywhere: in the fields; on the forest floor; on the water or ice; along shorelines; in trees; and in the sky. Perhaps the single most productive spot for seeing wildlife is the edge of fields. Hawks and owls often perch here, and many animals make their dens and burrows where the woods meet the meadows. Creatures feel safer around the edges—deer often stay close to these fringe areas before entering a field at nightfall. Red fox and coyotes hunt the edges, and they can sometimes be seen trotting through tall grass on their rounds.

Another productive area for wildlife viewing is along riverbanks and shorelines. Scanning a shoreline with a pair of binoculars can be extremely rewarding— you're likely to see a number of different wildlife species. Minks, weasels, muskrats, and raccoons are among the many animals commonly observed foraging next to water. And of course shorebirds, wading birds, and ducks are found here. Many of the wild areas in this book offer excellent canoeing, and this, too, affords opportunities for nature study at close range.

Obviously, you must walk quietly through the woods if you hope to get near wildlife. But being quiet is not enough. Most creatures would rather hide than run, and they will often remain motionless and let you walk past their hiding spots. You should give the surrounding areas more than a casual glance. For example, when trying to spot deer, look for parts of the animal between the trees rather than for the entire body. Look for the horizontal lines of the deer's back which contrast with the vertical trees. Knowing the size of the animal also helps; most people scan for deer at eye level, yet deer are only about three feet high at the shoulder.

Many animals blend in with their surroundings so well it's almost impossible to see them. The American bittern (a wading bird), for example, sometimes hides by freezing with its head in an upright position to match tall reeds and vegetation around it. A snapping turtle in shallow water looks just like a rock, and ruffed grouse can be indistinguishable from the fallen leaves on the forest floor. Even great blue herons will stop feeding and wait silent and unmoving until perceived danger passes.

Another key factor to consider is wind direction, which can carry your scent to wildlife. If traveling down a trail and the wind is coming from your left, try looking more in that direction since your scent is not being carried there. And if you have a choice when beginning a hike, travel into the wind. The same holds true when approaching a known feeding area.

It is important, by the way, that humans do not approach too closely, or birds like the heron will take wing, thus expending valuable energy to avoid us. Many creatures will allow us to observe them, so long as we do not walk directly at them or linger too long.

Some animals are almost never seen because they are nocturnal and concealed. But you don't have to see them to know that they are present. They will leave clues. You will find the tracks of otter, heron, raccoon, and deer along the soft margin of a river or lake. Hiking after a snowfall can be especially rewarding as fresh tracks can easily be seen. Some astute trackers can also identify creatures by the droppings they leave behind. Owls leave pellets, which can identify their presence and what they have been feeding on. Look for their droppings underneath large pine trees. The burrows and dens of such animals as the fox and groundhog reveal where they live. Deer leave a number of signs, such as the trails they use between feeding and resting grounds, and the scrapes and scars on saplings caused by a buck rubbing its antlers. Peeled bark can indicate the presence of deer, mice, rabbit, or others, depending on the teeth marks, shape, and height of the marking.

The time and patience required to find and identify clues can be significant, but so too are the rewards. It is satisfying to solve the wildlife "puzzle," to not only learn of a specie's presence but to also deduce its activities. Children especially seem to enjoy this detective work.

Besides using your sense of sight, use your hearing to help identify wildlife. Many of us have heard the hooting of an owl at night or the daytime drumming of the male ruffed grouse. It's possible that more and more folks in the outer suburbs will soon be hearing the wild and eerie yapping and howling of coyotes. Some animal sounds are quite surprising. Creatures you wouldn't expect to make a peep can be quite vocal at times. I've heard deer snort, porcupines scream, and woodchucks grunt and click their teeth.

Knowing the behavior of birds and animals can often explain their actions. For example, if a ruffed grouse appears to flutter about with a wounded wing, it is likely its chicks are near and it is trying to draw you away. The mother grouse makes a commotion, dragging its wing in a way sure to get your attention, in an effort to lure you away from the chicks. After watching the mother's act, take a moment to scan the forest floor and you just might see the chicks (look, but don't touch, and be careful where you step). Another example of behavior that's important to understand is the warnings certain creatures give if you get too close. A goshawk guarding its nest will give a warning of "kak, kak, kak"; don't move any closer, it may attack you. (Never get too close to nesting birds, or chase or corner an animal. Often the best way to get a second look at an animal is to remain perfectly still. They may return out of curiosity.)

Nature study is all the more fascinating when you learn the habits of each wild animal: what it eats, where and when it feeds and rests, and whether it is active in the winter or hibernates. Birds can be studied in a similar way, and migration patterns are crucial to understanding when and for how long certain birds are in our region. Cold-blooded reptiles are only active in the warm-weather months. Their temperatures vary with that of the surrounding atmosphere, so they cannot survive freezing temperatures. The relatively few reptiles that live in Massachusetts must hibernate in holes or burrows below the frost line during winter. The best time to see some of them is in the late spring; for example, that's when the snapping turtle comes out of the water to lay its eggs on land.

For wildlife photography, you'll need a zoom lens and a tripod. High-quality shots are extremely difficult to obtain. It's hard enough just locating an animal or uncommon bird, but finding a clear shot for a picture can be quite frustrating. Patience is the key—that's why professional wildlife photographers often spend days in the woods working from a blind.

Consider searching for "small game." Colorful butterflies nectaring on wildflowers, dragonflies hawking for insects along a pond shore, and respotted newts courting at the edge of a pond can be just as fascinating as an encounter with a larger creature. The key is to look closely.

Finally, you'll increase your odds of seeing wildlife by repeat visits to favorite locations.

## Walking With Children

Spending time outdoors with a child is a great way to become closer to one another and teach respect for nature. The key to success is preparation, and even more importantly, the parent's attitude.

Enthusiasm and flexibility can make the difference between a wonderful experience and a potential nightmare! My first outing with my three-year-old son turned into the latter. Brian was fine on the trek to the hilltop, but on the way down he decided he had walked enough, and plopped himself down on the trail, refusing to take another step. Guess who carried him down?

I had ignored one of my own basic rules about walking with children: Don't force your outdoor objective onto the child. In this case it was me who really wanted to get to the hilltop, and I did not fully consider the affect this would have on Brian's little legs. A half-mile walk is about right for a three year old; anything more than a mile and you're asking for trouble.

A little preparation goes a long way. Bringing a snack and a drink is crucial; in fact, it is often the highlight of the trip for a child. A picnic in the woods may be a new experience for a child, and the energy gained from a nutritious snack (such as raisins) refuels the child for more exploration. The same is true of making frequent rest stops. Should the child want to head home, do so—remember, the idea is to have the child learn to enjoy the outdoors, and that means hiking and exploring at his or her pace.

Some of the best walks occur when a parent lets go and shares a sense of wonder and discovery with the child. Sing, skip, and talk to trees. When a child sees a parent enjoy the natural world it creates a positive experience that the child will want to repeat.

Bring a field guide to birds, animals, reptiles, and plants. A guide enables you to work with the child in identifying the natural world. In the springtime, look for lady's slippers or trillium, and admire the beauty of the plant without picking it. Stop and admire the little things: a chipmunk hole, toadstools, and bits of pine cones and acorns where squirrels have been feeding. Binoculars are always a big hit, and if you do spot wildlife binoculars allow the child to see more than a fleeting glimpse of a distant animal. There are some sturdy and inexpensive models on the market. Even a hand lens can open up a whole new world.

Show the child a map of the property you are exploring, and explain how to interpret it. Let them pick a trail to explore. You might want to purchase a small backpack: from the child's viewpoint, this seems to somehow make the trip more of an adventure, as if you are going to explore some far-off place. Pack a whistle in the backpack and explain that it is to be used (blown at regular intervals) only if the child is separated from the parent.

Bringing a playmate along on a hike is a good idea; the two children will enjoy climbing rocks and discovering little caves. Talk to them about the wildlife that lives nearby, and encourage them to tell you about their own outdoor experiences. Praise them for their efforts and teach them responsibility by packing out any trash, even if it's not your own.

In the Eastern Massachusetts area there are a number of fine sanctuaries and reservations that are well suited to children. The ones recommended usually have fairly level terrain and well-maintained trails. Most have water on the property. Children love ponds and streams; it makes a good destination for your walk, and also offers a good chance of glimpsing wildlife.

Spending a day outdoors with a child can enhance your own appreciation of nature. Try to see the world through the child's eyes and enjoy the simple things that feed the child's enthusiasm. When you take a rest, tell stories about nature or browse through a field guide together. Remember to praise and encourage the child each time he or she learns something new or completes a walk.

## Author's Top Ten Walks

1. Ravenswood
2. Coolidge Reservation
3. King Philip Overlook/ Rocky Narrows
4. Whitney and Thayer Woods
5. Ellisville Harbor State Park
6. Fort Hill
7. Atlantic White Cedar Swamp
8. Waseeka Wildlife Sanctuary
9. Ipswich River Wildlife Sanctuary
10. Halibut Point State Park

## Author's Best Walks With Children

1. Ipswich River Wildlife Sanctuary (The Rockery)
2. Parker River National Wildlife Refuge (Hellcat Swamp Nature Trail)
3. John Wing Trail
4. Blue Hills/Trailside Museum
5. North River Wildlife Sanctuary
6. Wellfleet Bay Wildlife Sanctuary
7. Caratunk Wildlife Refuge

# Locator Map

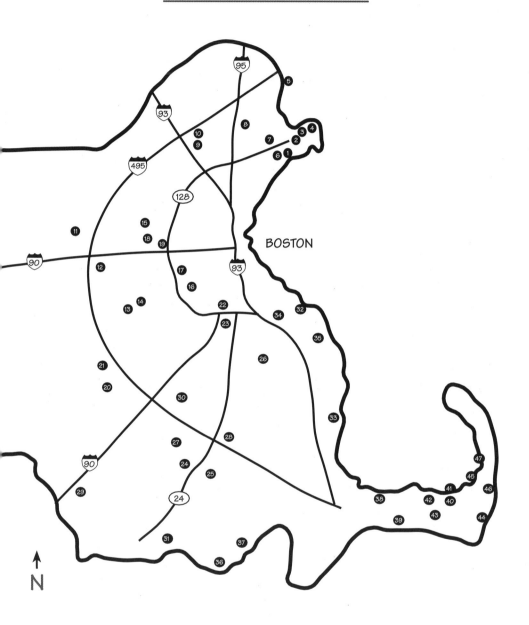

BOSTON

N

1. Coolidge Reservation—Manchester-By-The-Sea

2. Goose Reservoir—Gloucester

3. Goose Cove Reservation—Gloucester

4. Halibut Point State Park—Rockport

5. Parker River National Wildlife Refuge—Newburyport

6. Ravenswood Park—Gloucester

7. Long Hill Reservation—Beverly

8. Ipswich River Wildlife Sanctuary—Topsfield

9. Phillips Academy–Cochran Wildlife Sanctuary—Andover

10. Ward Reservation—Andover

11. Mount Pisgah Conservation Area—Northborough

12. Waseeka Wildlife Sanctuary—Hopkinton

13. Oak Grove Farm—Millis

14. King Philip Overlook & Rocky Narrows—Sherborn

15. Sandy Pond & Lincoln Conservation Land—Lincoln

16. Wilson Mountain Reservation—Dedham

17. Hemlock Gorge—Needham/Newton

18. Weston Reservoir—Weston

19. Case Estates—Weston

20. Joe's Rock & Birchwold Farm—Wrentham

21. Franklin State Forest—Franklin

22. Blue Hills Reservation—Quincy/Milton/Randolph

23. Ponkapoag Pond—Canton

24. Dighton Rock State Park—Berkley

25. Freetown/Fall River State Forest—Assonet

26. Ames Nowell State Park—Abington

27. Boyden Wildlife/Nature Refuge—Taunton

28. Camp Titicut Reservation—Bridgewater

29. Caratunk Wildlife Refuge—Seekonk

30. Wheaton Farm Conservation Area—Easton

31. Tattapanum Trail at Watuppa Reservation—Fall River

32. Whitney and Thayer Woods—Cohasset/Hingham

33. Ellisville Harbor State Park—Plymouth

34. Great Esker Park—Weymouth

35. North River Wildlife Sanctuary—Marshfield

36. Allen's Pond Wildlife Refuge—Dartmouth

37. Demarest Lloyd State Park—South Dartmouth

38. Sandwich Boardwalk/Town Beach—Sandwich

39. Mashpee River Woodlands—Mashpee

40. Punkhorn Parklands—Brewster

41. John Wing Trail—Brewster

42. Yarmouth Historical Society Nature Trail—Yarmouth

43. Hathaway's Pond—Barnstable

44. Fort Hill—Eastham

45. Wellfleet Bay Wildlife Sanctuary—Wellfleet

46. Atlantic White Cedar Swamp Trail—Wellfleet

47. Great Island—Wellfleet

# Walks and Highlights

| Ocean, Lake or Pond | Scenic Vista | Rocky Ledges | Wooden Bridge or Boardwalk | Special Geology | Ownership |
|:---:|:---:|:---:|:---:|:---:|:---|
| ✔ | ✔ | ✔ | | | Trustees |
| ✔ | | | | | Local |
| ✔ | | | | | Essex/Greenbelt |
| ✔ | ✔ | ✔ | | ✔ | Trustees & State |
| ✔ | ✔ | | ✔ | ✔ | National |
| | | ✔ | ✔ | | Trustees |
| | | | | | Trustees |
| ✔ | | ✔ | ✔ | ✔ | Audubon |
| ✔ | | | | | Local |
| ✔ | ✔ | | ✔ | ✔ | Trustees |
| | ✔ | ✔ | | | Local |
| ✔ | | | | | Audubon |
| | | | | | Local |
| | ✔ | ✔ | | ✔ | Trustees & Local |
| ✔ | | | | | Local |
| | ✔ | ✔ | | | MDC |
| | ✔ | ✔ | | ✔ | MDC |
| ✔ | | | | | Local |
| | | | | | Local |

| Ocean, Lake or Pond | Scenic Vista | Rocky Ledges | Wooden Bridge or Boardwalk | Special Geology | Ownership |
|:---:|:---:|:---:|:---:|:---:|---|
| ✔ | ✔ | ✔ | | | Local |
| | | | | | State |
| ✔ | ✔ | ✔ | | | MDC |
| ✔ | | | ✔ | ✔ | MDC |
| | ✔ | | | | State |
| ✔ | ✔ | ✔ | | ✔ | State |
| ✔ | | | ✔ | | State |
| | | | ✔ | | Local |
| | | | | | Local |
| ✔ | | | | ✔ | Audubon |
| ✔ | | | | | Local |
| ✔ | ✔ | ✔ | | | Local |
| | | | | ✔ | Trustees |
| ✔ | ✔ | | | | State |
| | ✔ | ✔ | | ✔ | Local |
| | ✔ | | ✔ | | Audubon |
| ✔ | | | | | Audubon |
| ✔ | ✔ | ✔ | | | State |

| Ocean, Lake or Pond | Scenic Vista | Rocky Ledges | Wooden Bridge or Boardwalk | Special Geology | Ownership |
|:---:|:---:|:---:|:---:|:---:|:---|
| ✔ | ✔ |  | ✔ |  | Local |
| ✔ | ✔ |  | ✔ |  | Local & State |
| ✔ | ✔ |  |  |  | Local |
| ✔ | ✔ |  | ✔ |  | Local |
| ✔ |  |  |  |  | Local |
| ✔ |  |  |  | ✔ | Local |
| ✔ | ✔ |  | ✔ |  | National |
| ✔ | ✔ |  | ✔ |  | Audubon |
| ✔ |  |  | ✔ | ✔ | National |
| ✔ |  |  |  |  | National |

# North of Boston

 # Coolidge Reservation

## Manchester-By-The-Sea

---

* 3 miles

* 2 hours

* Easy

* Great for children

* Best to come on a Saturday when "The Great Lawn" is open.

---

## Highlights

- Magnolia Harbor
- Pond and Hilltop
- "The Great Lawn" overlooking the Atlantic

Coolidge Reservation, one of The Trustee of Reservations' newer reservations (established in 1992), has two very different parcels of land connected by a right-of-way for walkers. The northern portion closest to the parking lot features hilly woodlands and a pond, while the southern section (open only on Saturdays) is comprised of the Great Lawn, an awe-inspiring open space above the ocean. The walking is easy on well-maintained trails and, except for the path to the summit of Bungalow Hill, the trails are flat and appropriate for young children.

Start your walk by entering the woods at the trail adjacent to the signboard at the back of the parking lot. By following the trail to the right you can quickly climb Bungalow Hill. The trail is shaded by the forest and passes an exposed granite ledge and small boulders. Pass a faint trail on the left that is a shortcut to the hilltop and continue on the wider trail which soon curls around the crest of the hill and leads to a small overlook. (Total time to reach the overlook is about eight

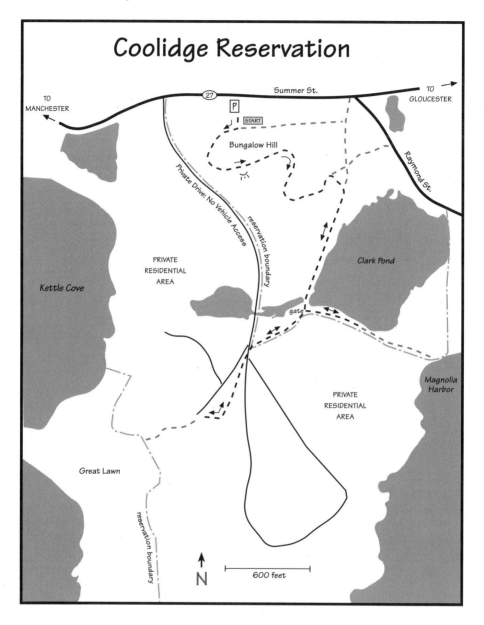

# Coolidge Reservation

minutes.) The view is to the southeast where you can see a portion of Clark Pond in the foreground and Magnolia Harbor beyond.

Oak and white pine are the dominant trees in the vista. Massachusetts has two primary oak trees: the red oak, which tends to have a straight trunk that is clear of branches for some distance from the ground, and the white oak which branches out lower to the ground. The easiest way to distinguish the two trees is by their leaves. Red oak leaves have many lobes that are bristle-tipped while the white oak's leaves have lobes that are bluntly rounded and sometimes remain on the tree through the winter. There are a total of about fifteen native oaks in New England and botanists often group them into two divisions: the white oaks and the black oaks (which includes the red oak tree).

Listen and scan the woods for sounds or sightings of red squirrels, ruffed grouse, or perhaps even a flock of wild turkeys. The wild turkey population has grown throughout Massachusetts. They are much more agile than their farm-raised cousins, able to fly and run through the woods with great speed. Acorns are a primary source of food, and lately there have been wild turkeys on roadsides, eating acorns that cars have crushed open.

To descend the hill and connect with the reservation's main trail, simply follow the path off the hill to the east (in the direction of Clark Pond). The trail snakes downhill, first passing by a closed trail on the right then arriving at a fork where you should bear right. This will bring you to the main trail and by following it to the right you will soon be walking along the edge of Clark Pond passing through a tunnel-like canopy of small trees and bushes. Clark Pond will usually have gulls and ducks floating near its center, and along its edge you might spot wading birds such as great blue herons or green herons.

It's only a five-minute walk along the pond's edge and over a small stone bridge to reach the end of the pond where there is an intersection in the trail at a metal gate. By turning left you will walk east for another five minutes and then arrive at Grey Beach on Magnolia Harbor. During the fall look for sea ducks bobbing in the harbor. This is a fine place to rest, soak up the sun, and listen to the surf before pushing on toward the Great Lawn, if you are fortunate enough to be here on a Saturday.

Retrace your steps back to the metal gate and go left. In about 300 feet the path crosses a road onto private property so please stay on the designated trail. Follow the trail for roughly five minutes and it will lead to a breathtaking view above the ocean. Before you are acres of rolling lawn and magnificent trees. This is the Great Lawn, with Kettle Cove to the northwest and the Atlantic Ocean to the south.

Thomas Jefferson Coolidge, the great-grandson of President Thomas Jefferson, purchased the land in 1871 for $12,000. He built a large white clapboard country home in 1873 and also sold several lots to relatives, friends, and business associates. In 1902 Coolidge had a grand cottage, known as the "Marble Palace," built on the Great Lawn. It featured Roman columns favored by Thomas Jefferson; the entire brick and white-marble house measured 230 feet in length. (It was razed in the 1950s.) Numerous dignitaries stayed at the Marble Palace, including President and Mrs. Woodrow Wilson, who were given the house for a week in 1918.

The Coolidge family donated 41.6 acres to The Trustees of Reservations in 1990 and 1991. In 1992 Essex County Greenbelt Association donated an additional 16.2 acres that had been given to them earlier. With these gifts, most of the

*A seawall runs along the edge of the Great Lawn.*

original land purchased by Thomas Jefferson Coolidge is now protected by The Trustees of Reservations for conservation and historic preservation.

Be sure to bring your camera when visiting the Great Lawn; the vista is unparalleled. The lawn slopes gently down to the ocean, and at the water's edge is a flat-topped cement breakwater that makes an excellent walkway. The Great Lawn is open for picnicking and there are a few large trees, one of which is an enormous beech tree with spreading branches providing a shady spot to spread a blanket. If you walk to the tree's trunk and look up you will see that the main branches of the tree are wired together to prevent splitting. The composition of the tree, the adjacent fence, and the sparkling water of the ocean are enough to keep you going through a whole roll of film.

Another especially scenic spot is the very southern tip of the Great Lawn, where there is a granite bluff offering sweeping views of the offshore islands. Bring your binoculars. Scan the water for harbor seals and such birds as eiders, scoters, and cormorants. There are two primary types of cormorants you will see, the double-crested cormorant and the great cormorant. Both are fish eaters that swim with their bill tilted upward and dive from the water's surface and swim swiftly underwater. You can often identify them from a distance because they perch with wings half-spread to dry. The great cormorant is the only cormorant with a white throat patch, and its bill is yellower and heavier than the double-crested cormorant, which has an orange throat pouch. The great cormorant is a common winter resident off Cape Ann and while it's increasing as a summer straggler, most of the summer cormorants you will see here are the double-crested variety. The double-crested cormorant also visits inland lakes and rivers while the great cormorant hugs the coastline.

My final suggestion for enjoying the Great Lawn is to lie back, soak up the sun, inhale the salt air, and drift off into sleep. There are few places as peaceful and scenic as this!

When you are ready to return to your car, simply retrace your steps.

## Getting There

From Route 128 take Exit 15 and follow signs to Manchester. In 0.5 mile, at the small white sign for Magnolia and Gloucester, take a left onto Lincoln Street. Go about a half mile to its end. At the stop sign, take a left onto Route 127 North. Proceed 2 miles to parking area on the right.

No admission fee but donation recommended; no rest rooms; dogs allowed. Open dawn to dusk.

# Goose Reservoir

## *Gloucester*

---

* 2 miles
* 1 hour
* Easy
* Great for children

---

### *Highlights*

- Circular walk around reservoir on paved service road
- Colorful fall foliage
- Side trail into Dogtown

Goose Reservoir is a popular walking spot for locals because the mostly level service road allows easy walking with water views as you circle the reservoir in a two-mile loop. Young children will enjoy the hike because there are no big hills, plenty of spots to stop and inspect the water, and a few boulders for climbing. It's also almost impossible to get lost if you circle the reservoir. The views across the water and the variety of deciduous trees make this an especially scenic walk during autumn. More ambitious walkers can take a side trail into an area known as Dogtown.

From the parking lot follow the road behind the barrier straight ahead for 100 feet to a point where it intersects with the road that circles the reservoir. The walk goes in a clockwise direction so turn left and in a couple of minutes approach an earthen dike and a spot with wildflowers such as goldenrod and aster. Staghorn sumac, pitch pines, and red cedar line the road. In the autumn the sumac leaves are vivid red. This small tree usually reaches heights between 10 and 20 feet, and tends to grow in clumps in sunny openings, never deep in the woods. It is easily identified by its twigs which are covered with fine hair (as in the velvet stage of a stag's antlers) and its maroon clusters of fruit that grow in a cone-like shape. The staghorn sumac is not poisonous. One way to differentiate between staghorn sumac and poison sumac is by the places where they grow. The poison sumac tends to grow in moist swampy areas, often in the shade of large leaves, while the staghorn prefers dry sunny spots. Leaves of the poison sumac have red veins with smooth margins while the staghorn's leaves have toothed edges.

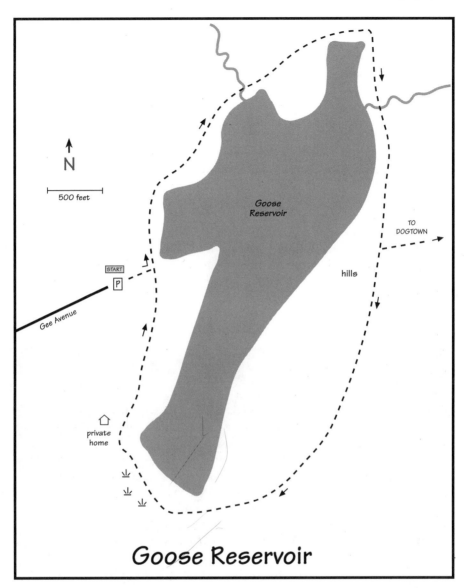

**Goose Reservoir**

After leaving the first dike you enter woods of oak, white pine, maple, ash, and cedar. Gray squirrels forage on the forest floor and cedar waxwings, cardinals, and mockingbirds are just some of the birds you will see in the understory. There are several dead trees standing with woodpecker holes that also serve as nesting locations for a large number of birds. Numerous side trails lead down to the reservoir. Glacial erratics begin to appear in the woods. These large boulders were dropped from the retreating ice sheets approximately 15,000 years ago.

After fifteen minutes of walking you pass over another dike with great views of the water, and more glacial erratics. The northernmost dike is reached about twenty-five minutes into your walk; the road then begins to head south along the eastern side of the reservoir. Sweet birch or cherry birch, which has a wintergreen smell in its stems, grow along the road. The sap of the cherry birch is used to make birch beer. You can pick a sprig and use it as a flavored toothpick.

You pass over a tiny stream that feeds the reservoir. Much of the watershed is protected from development and if you look at a map of the area you will see that a good portion of the northern section of Gloucester and the central part of Rockport have been set aside as conservation land to protect the watershed and water supply, forming a mini accidental wilderness. Some of the birds sighted here include common species such as warblers, flycatchers, scarlet tanager, wood thrush, and veery.

Look for beech trees with their smooth, light gray trunks along the road. It was on a beech tree that the famous legend "D. Boone Cilled a Bar on Tree In Year 1760" was inscribed. Its 3- to 5-inch leaves are toothed, and are luminous in their spring green; and in the fall they are light gold. The beechnut is consumed by

*The great egret is a summertime visitor to coastal Massachusetts.*

many animals including wild turkeys, raccoons, mice, grouse, squirrels, and bears, which often leave their claw marks in the trees. Native Americans roasted the nuts or pressed them to extract their oil for cooking.

As you continue walking south you will pass a side trail on the right that leads into Dogtown, a large patch of woodlands that was once a settlement. About thirty-five minutes from the start of the walk the road climbs two hills in an area where low-bush blueberries and white oaks grow. The trail swings away from the reservoir but continues in a southerly direction. Once you descend the hills, you arrive at the final dike on your right and a small marsh on the left.

The trail curls to the north, past a private residence on the left and through an area of juniper and highbush blueberries growing beneath the oak and pine trees. In fifteen more minutes you are back to the starting point. If you have time, it's always great fun to combine this inland walk with a coastal walk. Besides Halibut Point which is reviewed in this book, the Bass Rocks section of East Gloucester on Atlantic Avenue is a great road for a walk or bicycle ride. And the wonderful Beauport Mansion is located near the southern tip of East Gloucester.

## Getting There

From the Grant Circle Rotary where Route 128 and Route 127 meet, follow Route 127 north for 1.3 miles. Turn right on Gee Avenue and follow 0.4 mile to the end and park in small lot.

No admission fee; no facilities; dogs allowed. Open year-round, dawn to dusk.

# Goose Cove Reservation

## *Gloucester*

---

✳ 26 acres (reservation)

✳ 0.75 mile

✳ 45 minutes

✳ Easy

---

### Highlights

- Great birding
- Salt marsh cove

Goose Cove Reservation is a small property that affords a pleasant woodland walk to the shore of a saltwater cove where there is good birding. The property is owned by Essex County Greenbelt and is open to all. Because it is a short walk you may want to combine a walk here with an exploration of nearby Goose Reservoir (previous chapter).

From the parking area at the south side of the cove follow the main path at the rear of the lot into woods of pitch pine. (Beware of the poison ivy near the edge of the trail. Poison ivy is identified by its groupings of three shiny green leaves, sometimes growing as a vine up the side of trees.) The trail heads in a northeasterly direction and the pine soon give way to a mixture of trees that include popple, maple, birch, oak, and white pine. Look for warblers, vireos, and flycatchers in the early part of the season as they hunt the thickets for insects.

Within five minutes the trail splits. You should bear left. Another two minutes brings you to a tiny point of land jutting into the cove. Cedar trees fringe the point and large boulders lay scattered about the cove, making great climbing for older children. The rocks make a nice place to rest or snack while watching the many birds. The Essex County Greenbelt captures the essence of this little gem—"there is tranquillity where forest meets the sea."

You can watch cormorants sunning themselves on rocks with wings outstretched to catch the sun. Snowy egrets stalk the shallows at the northern end of the pond. Black-crowned night herons, ring-billed gulls, and black ducks are also commonly seen here. The snowy egret is a relative newcomer to Massachusetts: Prior to 1947 only a few of these herons were ever seen here.

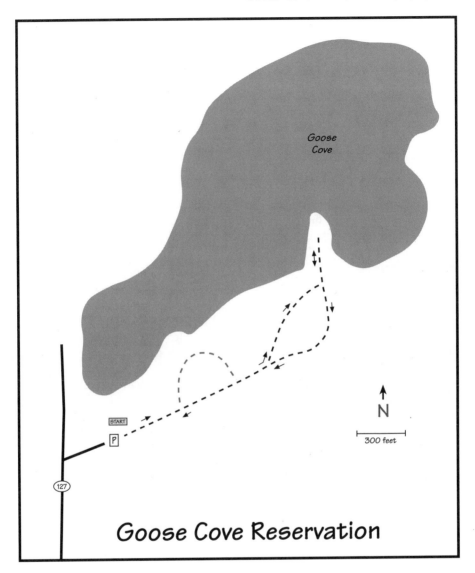

## Goose Cove Reservation

Another heron that frequents Goose Cove is the great blue heron. Unlike the snowy egret, this bird is often seen in inland locations. Its preferred nesting area is usually the dead timber of beaver ponds where it is more difficult for predators to climb the trees. However, great blue herons can also nest in trees near rivers. You might even see a great blue heron at Goose Cove in the winter. It seems they will stay north as long as the winter is not too severe and they can find open water for catching fish.

At low tide you can explore the shoreline, looking at the shells and the many raccoon prints, or just soak up the sun. When it's time to return to your car, simply retrace your steps. If you wish to vary your walk a bit, you can do so by bearing left at the fork in the trail when you leave the point of land. This will take you a little farther into the woods where you might see squirrels, chipmunks, or common woodland birds such as chickadees, flickers, and blue jays. Although raccoon prints are evident both on the trail and along the cove, raccoons are rarely seen in the woods. They are nocturnal animals, so the best chance of spotting a raccoon is at dawn or dusk—the same time mosquitoes are out!

When you reach your car you may want to explore more of Cape Ann. By driving a short distance north on Route 127 you will see the Lobster Cove Footbridge, which spans Lobster Cove and leads to the village of Annisquam. This makes for a nice walk, and just on the other side of the bridge is the Annisquam Historic Society, and an interesting graveyard.

## Getting There

From the Grant Circle rotary where Route 128 and Route 127 meet in Gloucester, follow Route 127 north (toward the village of Annisquam and Lanesville). Go about 1 mile on Route 127 past a combined neighborhood store and gas station called the Willow Rest. Goose Cove is located on the right as you descend the hill. There will be a small green Essex County Greenbelt sign on the right that welcomes you to the small dirt parking lot.

Another nearby reservation owned by Essex County Greenbelt is the Stoney Cove, Presson Reservation in Gloucester. It lies adjacent to a bend in the Little River and has both a freshwater and saltwater marsh. There is a bench overlooking the river affording a good spot to birdwatch or watch clammers work the tidal flats as they have done for centuries.

The reservation is located on the south side of Route 128 between Exit 13 (Concord Street) and the bridge over the Annisquam River. As you drive north on Route 128 be sure to slow down after passing the Concord Street exit as the turnoff is only 3/10 mile further. Be sure to alert other drivers that you will be turning by using your car's blinkers, as this can be a dangerous pull-over.

# Halibut Point State Park

## Rockport

* 1.5 miles
* 1 hour
* Easy
* Great for children

### Highlights

* Spectacular rocky coast
* Sea birds
* Former quarry operations

On the Cape Ann coastline, more reminiscent of Maine than Massachusetts, Halibut Point offers walkers, beachcombers, birders, and history buffs a wonderful network of trails to explore. The State Park (56 acres) and the adjacent shoreline owned by The Trustees of Reservations (12 acres) combine for a unique area of open space on this rocky headland known as Halibut Point. Originally called "haul about" by sailors (because they had to tack around this mass of rock) Halibut Point was the site of numerous quarry operations that began in 1840 when the 450 million-year-old granite was cut for the next 100 years.

The trail begins just across the street from the parking lot and rest rooms. Dense foliage crowds the path, forming a tunnel of green, as you walk in a northerly direction heading toward the open Atlantic. The trail is wide and flat, with a covering of woodchips. Red cedars, wild apples, dogwoods, oaks, mountain ash, wild cherry, and the draping vines of grapes line the path. At the end of the trail, after a five-minute walk, you will reach a T-intersection overlooking the Babson Farm Quarry, now filled with water. While the quarry was being worked, keeping it dry was a major task. Initially, men simply lifted out bucket after bucket of water; later, wind-powered pumps and steam engines, running night and day, were used.

Turn right at the quarry and follow the path around the edge of the quarry, stopping to read the interpretive signs along the way. On your left is marker number 3 at a piece of granite with groves along the edge that were the side of holes drilled to split the rock. Giant blocks of granite were hoisted from the quarry floor by massive derricks, the early ones operated by a series of block and tackle pulleys powered by teams of oxen. Once lifted, the blocks were transported to a shed where cutters

13

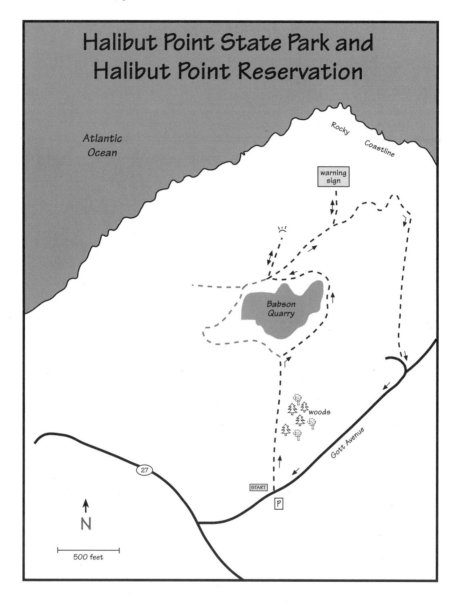

# Halibut Point State Park and Halibut Point Reservation

Atlantic
Ocean

Rocky
Coastline

warning
sign

Babson
Quarry

woods

Gott Avenue

27

START

P

N

500 feet

made a hole in the granite, then split it with a wedge or shaped it into paving, curb-
ing, and building stones. Some of the Halibut quarry now resides in such structures
as the Holland Tunnel, the Brooklyn Bridge, and Boston's Custom House Tower.

Follow the quarry path halfway around the quarry just past marker number
5 to a fork in the trail where you should turn right and follow a sign to an overlook. The jumble of rocks you are standing on is called the Grout Pile, which are
discarded pieces of granite dumped over the years, now forming the perfect van-

tage point to view the coastline and ocean. On clear days you can see the New Hampshire coast and even Mount Agamenticus in Maine. With binoculars you can watch the lobstermen in small boats check their traps or scan the shoreline for seals. Should you see a seal on the rocks below do not walk down and get too close. Young harbor seal pups often rest on the rocks while their mothers continue to feed offshore. The pups will nap then later return to the sea and join their mothers. Disturbing the seals may cause them to return to the ocean when they are still fatigued and they can drown.

Once you have enjoyed the overlook, retrace your steps a couple hundred feet to the intersection near the quarry and this time follow the path and sign that reads "To Ocean." The path slopes downward, first through an area of small scrub oaks and shadbush then to a more open area of large rocks. There is a warning sign that reads "This ocean shoreline is hazardous," due to the pounding surf that can sweep over the rocks. Look for wildflowers such as trout lily, violet, asters, and goldenrod growing in the rocky soil.

Visiting Halibut Point in the fall is highly recommended: the air is clear; the seaside heather, bayberry, and low-lying vegetation takes on tones of russet and gold; and the bracing salt air puts a spring in your step. On sunny days the ocean near the rocks has a mottled color of aqua blue, deep blue, and green, caused by the play of shadows on the seaweed and rocks below.

The boulders along the shore are of various sizes. Between Cape Cod and Cape Elizabeth in Maine, Cape Ann is the largest outcrop of rocky headland, resistant to wave erosion unlike the sand spits and dunes comprising the rest of the Bay State's coastline. The slablike granite rocks and toppled ledges at Halibut Point are a testament to the ice sheet that moved through the land 15,000 years ago. The

*An autumn walk on the rocky coast offers great birding.*

bedrock tended to break along parallel cracks which is why the granite slabs look layered in appearance. Just a few hundred feet farther inland evidence of the glaciers is seen in the huge round boulders that litter the landscape. The boulders, called glacial erratics, were deposited haphazardly by the retreating glaciers, and Cape Ann has an abundance of these boulders.

Birding enthusiasts have long known that Cape Ann is one of the premier birding spots. A sampling of birds include the northern gannet, loons, scoters, red-breasted mergansers, red-necked and horned grebes, and eiders. The fall migration of seabirds along the coast is exceptional with mid-October to early December as a favorite time to see strings of scoters and common eiders migrating southward. Watching birds is especially productive along the shore during the first three hours after dawn when birds are closest to the shore. The common loon winters off Halibut Point, although it does not make its haunting cry in the winter and its distinctive black and white patterned plumage is replaced by a dull brown color on the back with the throat and chest white. Loons migrate in small flocks and continue to dive beneath the water surface hunting for fish. Other wintering ducks seen here include the buffleheads, red-breasted mergansers, white-winged scoters, and common eiders.

During low tide you will be able to observe the marine organisms that survive in this harsh, open space by clinging to rocks. Starfish, barnacles, and algae can sometimes be seen in the tidal pools. The exposed tidal area is also harsh on humans; in the summer the sun can be fierce (no swimming allowed) and in the winter the winds can penetrate right through you. Some nature lovers make it a point to visit when a storm is lashing the shoreline, making for hostile conditions but spectacular viewing of the surf smashing the rocks. Should you venture out in such conditions be sure to dress appropriately.

Once you have enjoyed picking your way through the rocks near the ocean, return to the warning sign and follow the path back up to the intersection and head east (to your left). The trail is difficult to follow because it often crosses exposed rock, but if you continue heading eastward, paralleling the ocean toward a lone house that you can see farther down the coast, you will reach another sign in about five minutes. The sign marks the border of the reservation's boundary and points to the "Sea Rocks," a right-of-way path owned by the town of Rockport along the water. Our walk goes to the right to make a loop back to the parking lot. Follow the path through the vegetation of small trees for about five minutes until it intersects with a dirt road. The first right turn leads to a private home. You should walk straight ahead for about 20 feet and then bear right on the roadway. Follow this road for five minutes and you will arrive back at the parking lot.

## Getting There

From the intersections of Routes 128 and 127, take Route 127 north (Eastern Avenue) toward Rockport. Follow Route 127 for 6.1 miles and then go left on Gott Avenue a couple hundred feet where you will see a large parking lot for the State Park.

If you are coming from Rockport Center take Route 127 north for half a mile to Gott Avenue on the right.

Admission fee; portable rest rooms; no bicycling; pets must be leashed. Park headquarters: 978-546-2997.

# Parker River National Wildlife Refuge

## *Plum Island at Newburyport*

---

* 4,662 acres

* Hellcat Swamp Nature Trail: 2 miles/
  1 hour (easy) (great for children)

* Sandy Point: 3 miles/1.5 hours (moderate)

---

## Highlights

- Boardwalk
- River walk
- Dunes
- Observation blind
- Beachcombing
- Great birding

The Parker River National Wildlife Refuge on Plum Island, a natural barrier beach, is a place nature lovers should try and visit in all seasons. It is one of the premier birding spots in the Northeast. More than 270 species of migratory and local birds have been spotted at the refuge. Spring and fall are the preferred birding months because of the many migrants that fly low over the dunes, but a winter walk is recommended when white snow, golden-brown salt grass, and beach sand mix together in subtle beauty. A winter walk here is a sure cure for cabin fever and may just give you the inspiration to take a walk every weekend.

The Hellcat Swamp Nature Trail is a great place for a first-time visitor to become acquainted with Plum Island and is especially recommended for those traveling with children. The trail begins at Lot 4, which is 3.8 miles down the entrance road from the main gate. There is also an observation blind near the parking, and it's a good idea to stop here first to see the lay of the land and birds in the freshwater marsh. (The freshwater pools by the tower are man-made, constructed so that birds needing fresh water have a supply. You will often see more birds in the freshwater pools than the salt marsh beyond, because the fresh water has a diverse plant life.)

The short path to the observation tower is at the rear of the parking lot. From the top of the tower you can see the dunes, marshes, ocean, and the mainland. Look for black ducks, green-winged teal, pintails, great blue herons, and

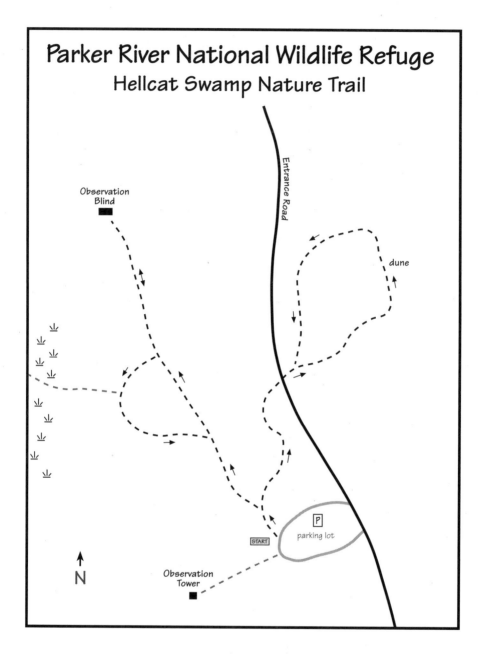

# Parker River National Wildlife Refuge
## Hellcat Swamp Nature Trail

Observation Blind

Entrance Road

dune

Observation Tower

START

P parking lot

N

green-backed herons in the warmer-weather months. Autumn is a good time to see rough-legged hawks and harriers hunting for small mammals, and falcons wheeling in the sky as they migrate south. Lucky birders in the winter are sometimes rewarded with the sight of a snowy owl, a visitor from the Arctic. Although the snowy owl breeds in the tundra, they move south at irregular intervals to winter in New England. Plum Island and the Boston Harbor Islands are the two best locations to see a snowy owl, particularly from December to the end of February. Some years they are fairly common at Plum Island where they hunt in the open salt marshes. They will feed on meadow voles and smaller birds.

The Hellcat Swamp Nature Trail, most of which is a boardwalk, begins at the north side of the parking lot and forks only a couple minutes down the trail. Take the right fork through scrub oaks and freshwater marsh, and follow this for five minutes until you reach the entrance road. Cross the road and continue on the trail where it soon climbs stairs to a panoramic view of the dunes. Scattered vegetation, such as pine, dune grass, false heather, and beach plums grow in the sandy soil. If you are here in September you may be rewarded with the sight of dozens of monarch butterflies migrating through the refuge. The open Atlantic is just a quarter mile to the east from the top of the dune. Surf fishing for striped bass and bluefish is often productive here in spring, summer, and fall.

Plum Island was formed by glaciers and additional sculpturing occurred as the Merrimack River brought silt to the Atlantic, which was swept onto Plum Island. When the first Europeans arrived in the region, the island was covered with mature forest. But the land was cleared for the coveted white pine for ship masts and lumber and then the grazing of sheep wiped out the rest of the vegetation. Today, Plum Island has trees again but only a few that approach 50 feet tall. The trees have gained a foothold in the hollows, where they are sheltered from the wind and closer to the groundwater.

As the steps and boardwalk carry you through the dunes, woodlands, and along the small pockets of freshwater swamp, the trail forms a loop. A twenty-five-minute walk from the beginning of the boardwalk completes the loop on the east side of the entrance road. Turn right here to recross the road and retrace your steps back to the intersection by the parking lot. Now turn right at this intersection, heading north, northwestward. Proceed on this trail, and stay to the right past two forks in the trail, and you will soon reach the observation blind.

Here you can observe birdlife at a freshwater marsh without being seen by the birds. Canada geese, redwing blackbirds, various warblers, and ducks are just some of the birds you will see here. Look for muskrat and even beaver. No one knows for sure how beaver got here, because they cannot tolerate salt water so swimming across from the mainland seems unlikely. Could they have traveled at night along the roadway that leads to the island?

From the observation blind, retrace your steps to the south, then at the first intersection turn right onto the marsh trail. A boardwalk will lead you through wetlands where tall reedgrass and cattails line the path. A side boardwalk leads farther out into the marsh for more exploration. The purple-flowering plant that blooms in August is the purple loosestrife, a nonindigenous plant that is taking over the wetlands.

Once you have circled the marsh the boardwalk intersects with the main trail where you should turn right to return to the parking lot.

For those who want to continue walking, many more trails and possibilities await. A walk along the beach is always a good bet. You can examine the various flotsam that has washed ashore, and listen to the surf—pounding and angry one day, gently lapping in rhythmic wavelets the next. Plants closest to the beach are those that can tolerate the salt spray: beach grass, seaside goldenrod, dusty miller, beach pea, and seabeach sandwort. Be on the lookout as well for the piping plover, an endangered bird that is successfully reproducing on Plum Island. Piping plovers are small sand-colored birds that nest right on the beach and are therefore susceptible to being crushed by beach vehicles and disturbed by beachgoers. At nesting times in the early part of the spring and summer, sections of the beach may be closed for their protection. Harbor seals can also be seen bobbing in the surf beyond the breakers. Shorebirds, such as greater yellowlegs and willets, work the shoreline looking for invertebrates to feed on.

If you go in the summer be sure to wear a hat, bring sunscreen and plenty of water. There are no lifeguards on the beach, and caution should be taken when swimming due to undertow.

## Getting There

From I-95 take Exit 57 and follow Route 113 east. Head into Newburyport for 2.5 miles and then Route 113 feeds into High Street which becomes Route 1A. Proceed south for 1.2 miles. Turn left onto Water Street (there will be a sign for Plum Island) and follow this road to its end. Then turn right on Plum Island Turnpike and proceed for about 2 miles (crossing the Parker River) and turn right on Sunset Road to the entrance gate.

If you miss the left turn from Route 1A onto Water Street, you can take a left on Rolfe's Lane to Plum Island Turnpike and proceed to the refuge.

Open year-round, dawn to dusk. Rest rooms at Lot 4. Admission fee or annual pass. No pets. The refuge parking lots can fill up on summer weekends, so arrive early. Hunting is allowed so always wear blaze orange in the fall and winter. Beach is often closed from April 1 into July due to nesting piping plovers. Ticks are common year-round, so avoid walking through tall grass, and tuck pant legs inside socks when walking in woods. Greenhead flies are present from mid-July to mid-August. Refuge headquarters: 978-465-5753.

# Ravenswood Park

## *Gloucester*

---

* 500 acres
* 2.5 miles
* 2.25 hours
* Easy to Moderate
* Great for children

---

## *Highlights*

* Enormous hemlock trees
* Good cross-country skiing
* Excellent wildlife habitat
* Extensive trail system
* Swamp boardwalk

One of my most memorable outdoors adventures happened in Ravenswood Park one November morning. Beneath a stand of giant hemlocks along the wetlands of Magnolia Swamp, a fisher crossed my path. I was able to observe this large member of the weasel family for a lengthy period as it hunted along the wetlands, probing old stumps and sniffing around trees. When it saw me it climbed about five feet up a tree then turned back to glare at me before moving back to the woods where it continued to hunt. In all my years of hiking it was the first fisher I'd seen, truly an elusive and wild creature.

Ravenswood is a pocket of wilderness within the suburbs of the North Shore. The large hemlock trees, the miles of winding trails, and the magnolias in the swamp are reasons to visit this 500-acre property owned by The Trustees of Reservations. And history lovers will enjoy the story of Mason A. Walton, the "Hermit of Gloucester" who lived in Ravenswood Park for thirty-three years.

When you arrive at the parking lot pause for a moment to read the signboard. It has a series of maps of the property, each one showing the mileage for a different walk. Our walk is a 2.5-mile walk that first goes through Magnolia Swamp then leads to the hermit marker before looping back to the parking area through an area of old trees and rocky terrain. From the parking lot follow the

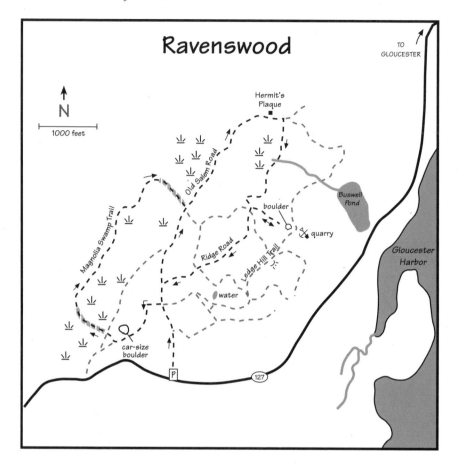

wide gravel road, called Old Salem Road, that leads into woods of beech, red oak, white pine, hemlock, maple, and a few white birches. Boulders of all shapes and sizes litter the floor where they rolled off retreating glaciers roughly 15,000 years ago.

Within five minutes you will pass the Ledge Hill Trail on the right then a couple minutes farther is a sign for the Magnolia Swamp on the left. Take this left and follow the narrow Magnolia Swamp Trail beneath large hemlocks as it winds its way up and down small hills heading in a southwesterly direction. Just three minutes down the trail a narrow trail comes in on the left but you should continue straight. In three or four more minutes you arrive at an exposed ledge of rock where a car-sized glacial boulder is perched on the bedrock. Such boulders are known as glacial erratics because of the haphazard way they were deposited by the glaciers.

Follow the trail to the right of the boulder as the path curls to the right heading toward the swamp passing through an understory of mountain laurel and blueberries. Both the highbush blueberry and mountain laurel are indicators of acidic soil, and both prefer partial shade. The highbush blueberry prefers areas in or near swamps but is also found in upland woods. It is a multi-stemmed shrub with terminal clusters of small urn-shaped white flowers that bloom in May and June. It can get quite large, often reaching heights of ten to fifteen feet. All sorts of wildlife from songbirds to bears feed on the berries and the twigs and foliage are eaten by deer and rabbits.

You soon reach an intersection. Going straight will bring you to a new boardwalk that traverses through ferns and thick foliage in the wet area of the swamp. The last time I hiked through here, Greg Chanis and three other employees of The Trustees of Reservations were installing the boardwalk. Sometimes hikers walk over boardwalks and well-maintained trails, never giving a thought to the work that is involved in keeping them in good shape. Building the two-plank boardwalk through wetlands looked like tough work; the builders should be thanked for their effort. Important work, benefiting all who hike the property—just one more reason to support conservation organizations.

Red maples and sweet pepper grow along the boardwalk, and the low-lying swamp has a decidedly different feel than the upland trail. When the flowers of the sweet pepperbush are blooming, usually in August, the white flowers give off a wonderful fragrance. The plant ranges from three to ten feet in height and has many branches with spikelike clusters of flowers. Even long after the flowers are gone the dry fruiting capsules cling to the plant. Another plant that grows here are magnolia trees (the nearby village of Magnolia gets its name from these trees). This is the northernmost stand of magnolias and even Thoreau visited the swamp to see the trees. During the 1800s and early 1900s magnolia plants were taken from the swamp and the population was on the verge of extinction before protective measures and replanting insured the survival of a limited number of magnolias (they are on the state's endangered species list). In this northern climate the magnolias are not very tall, and difficult to distinguish among the other trees. Perhaps the best time to spot one is in June when they have creamy white flowers and give off a delicate scent. The species growing here is the sweet bay magnolia (*Magnolia virginiana*), which is native to lowlands and prefers rich, moist soil. Please be sure not to bend the trees to see the flowers up close as this can damage growth.

The boardwalk is a short one so you reach dry ground in four or five minutes. The trail forks and you should bear right, following along the edge of the swamp in a northerly direction. More large hemlocks and exposed rock are along the trail and it takes about ten minutes to reach the next boardwalk that recrosses the swamp. The hemlocks and the hilly terrain give this area of the reservation a wild, north country flavor.

It was here that I saw the fisher. Also known as a fisher cat, the fisher is a large member of the weasel family. Its muzzle is pointed, its ears broad and rounded, and its legs and feet are stout. Its glossy coat is brownish-black, with small

*A boardwalk leads into the Magnolia swamp.*

white patches on the neck. Males can measure as much as forty inches long, with a foot-long tail, although the maximum weight is only about 20 pounds. Chances are if there are fisher in the reservation there are also porcupine. Fisher are one of the few animals that kills and eats porcupine. They do so by circling the porcupine, biting its exposed face, and tiring it before moving in for the kill. The hemlocks along the trail are a chief food source for the porcupine and the exposed ledges offer good denning areas. Look for porcupine tracks in the snow, when you can see the pigeon-toed paw prints, the tail drag, and even the marks left by their quills.

After you cross the second boardwalk and wind your way uphill, past more hemlocks with winterberry growing beneath, you reach the carriage road called Old Salem Road where you should turn left. In about five minutes the road forks and you should stay to the left. Look for a few yellow birch off to your left followed by another wet area where red maple grow and a few white pines grow. While the red maple tree likes having "wet feet," white pine usually prefer a little dryer soil. Stone walls lace the woods, indicating this was pasture or farm land at one time. By the looks of the number of stones and boulders scattered on the ground, chances are the soil was too bony for growing crops and was used for sheep or cattle pasture.

Ten minutes after leaving the Magnolia Trail you will arrive at a boulder with a plaque dedicated to the Hermit of Gloucester, Mason. A. Walton. Like Thoreau, Walton recorded his experiences in a book titled *A Hermit's Wild Friends*. This scholarly man initially came to Gloucester to cure himself of tuberculosis; as his health improved he built a cabin on the north side of Ravenswood and spent his days writing and studying wildlife. People came to his cabin to listen to him discuss the flora and fauna of Ravenswood.

Near the cabin you may encounter wildlife such as the somewhat uncommon and elusive pileated woodpecker, identified by its conspicuous red crest. Its call is always in a series, and its drumming on the trees is very loud at first then softer at the end. Other birds here include great horned owls, partridges, downy woodpeckers, and red-tailed hawks.

From the plaque, continue on the wide road passing by a narrow trail that leads straight ahead where the wide road curls to the right. This wide trail is called Ridge Road. About five minutes farther down the road it passes over a tiny stream where a nice stand of mountain laurel grows beneath the canopy of tall hemlocks. About five more minutes of walking brings you to a road on the left. Turn left here, then about a minute later the road splits and you should bear right, continuing on the Ridge Trail. (On future trips you may want to walk even longer by turning left here to visit a small former quarry and return to the parking area via the Ledge Hill Trail, a narrow, snaking path through very rocky terrain.) Our walk stays on the well-maintained Ridge Road for about ten more minutes, passing beneath more impressive-sized pines and hemlocks, until it intersects Old Salem Road. To reach the parking lot turn left and follow the road for five minutes.

## Getting There

From Route 128 take Exit 14/Route 133. Follow Route 133 east for 3 miles to Route 127. Turn right on Route 127 and proceed south for 2 miles. Look for sign and parking area on the right.

Admission donation suggested; no facilities; dogs allowed. Open dawn to dusk year-round.

# Long Hill
# Reservation

## *Beverly*

* 114 acres
* Easy
* 2 miles
* 1 hour

## Highlights

• Formal gardens and woodland trails

Long Hill is the headquarters of The Trustees of Reservations, an organization founded more than one hundred years ago to preserve, "for the benefit of the public, beautiful and historic places in Massachusetts." Seventy-seven extraordinary properties have been protected since then. Surprisingly, Long Hill is often overlooked by nature walkers, but it offers quiet strolls through handsome gardens and a loop trail through surrounding woodlands.

The first part of our walk visits the gardens. From the parking lot walk up the road to the left for a hundred feet to the southern-styled house where the offices of The Trustees of Reservations are located. The mountain laurel and rhododendron along the road are quite large, and their evergreen leaves add color to a winter's outing. The easiest way to differentiate between these two plants when they are not blooming is by the leaves. The mountain laurel leaves are from 3 to 4 inches in length and are dark green and glossy on top and yellow-green underneath. The leaves of the rhododendron are much larger: up to ten inches in length and are thick and leathery. Although the mountain laurel tends to bloom a few days earlier than the rhododendron, in June you have a chance of seeing both in bloom. Blueberry, dogwood trees, and sassafras (identified by its mitten-shaped leaves) also grow along the road.

The antebellum house at the end of the road was the summer home of Ellery Sedgwick, a noted author and editor of *Atlantic Monthly* magazine from 1909 to 1938. Construction of the house, a reproduction of the Isaac Ball House in Charleston, South Carolina, began in 1921. All of the ornate wood carvings and woodwork at the Long Hill House were purchased from the Ball House. The house and the surrounding 114 acres were given to The Trustees of Reservations by Ellery Sedgwick's children in 1979.

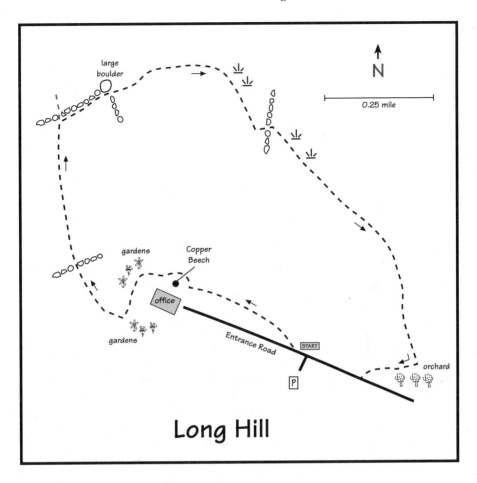

Long Hill

As spectacular as the house is, the enormous copper beech tree that grows by its side is also eye-catching. The expansive limbs of this grand old tree shade a large area, and hold a great canopy of foliage, as you'll see when you look up. (The tree was planted in 1917, before the house was built.)

From the beech tree head around to the back of the house where a porch on the second story will make you feel like you're in Dixie. There are 5 acres of gardens with Indian lotus, which blooms in small ponds; golden rain trees; Chinese tree peonies; dogwoods; azaleas; magnolias; and weeping cherries. Daffodils, foam flowers, and lilies are just some of the flowers that cover the ground. (The foam flower is a delicate looking plant that grows between 6 to 12 inches in height and has small white flowers that bloom in the early spring.) More than 400 species of plants grow in the gardens!

As you stand in the garden and face the side of the house with the porches, walk to your right, through a small white gate, and then turn right again and follow the path that leads into woods of cedar, oak, birch, and maple. This is a good area to see woodland birds such as the hermit thrush, which has a spotted breast, rusty colored tail, and olive-brown back. They are usually seen on the forest floor scratching up the leaves while searching for insects. Although there are several types of thrushes with spotted breast, the hermit thrush is the only one that winters here.

As you follow the path, large pines and oaks appear, and after about ten minutes of walking, pass through an opening in a stone wall. In another ten minutes you'll reach a second stone wall and a property boundary sign. Turn right here, walking parallel to the stone wall. You'll come to yet another stone wall with a large boulder on the left. Pass through the opening in the wall and continue to follow the trail. Look for the delicate lady's slipper (also called the moccasin-flower) which blooms in May and June. Its pouch-like pink flower is heavily veined and stands atop a stem of 6 to 12 inches that grows above two oval basal leaves.

The walk is mostly shaded by a mix of trees which will be welcomed on hot summer days. Mosquitoes also favor these shady places, so bring bug repellent if you are here in the warm-weather months. About thirty minutes into the walk the trail traverses through some low-lying spots that are wet in the spring, and filled with an assortment of ferns. Trail bridges have recently been erected over the wettest area. Hemlock trees now are mixed with the oaks, pines, and maples.

Some of the wildlife seen here include red fox, raccoon, white-tailed deer, and wild turkey. The wild turkey is an elusive bird that travels in flocks and can quickly scatter either by running (up to 25 MPH) or taking flight (reaching bursts of 55 MPH). The few times that I've seen the wild turkey they seemed to melt into the woods by running into thick cover. There are about 15,000 wild turkeys in Massachusetts, all the successful offspring of a reintroduction program that began in 1971 when wild turkeys trapped in New York were released in the Berkshires. Prior to that the birds had been absent from the state after they were extirpated in the 1800s.

After walking through the low woodlands for about fifteen minutes the trail rises up a small ridge and leads to a grassy opening at the back end of an orchard. Turn right here, walk through the orchard and you will be at the entrance road. Walk to the right on the entrance road and in three or four minutes you will be back at the parking lot. (There are more gardens to explore just beyond the parking lot on the left side of the entrance road near the southeast corner of the house. Here you can enjoy rose arbors with unusual specimens, a Chinese pagoda, a small woodland pool with waterlilies, and the cherry garden with dramatic weeping cherries. The Trustees of Reservations also have plans to add new trails, which will allow visitors to take shorter or longer walks and have access to different areas of the reservation.)

## Getting There

From Route 128, Exit 18, take Route 22 Essex Street left (north) for 1.3 miles (bear left at the fork) to a brick gate post and sign on the left. Follow the driveway to the parking lot on the left.

No admission fee (donations accepted); no facilities; dogs allowed on leash. Open dawn to dusk. Garden and house tours arranged by appointment: 978-921-1944.

# Ipswich River Wildlife Sanctuary

## *Topsfield*

---

* More than 2,800 acres
* 4 miles
* 2 hours
* Easy to Moderate
* Great for children

---

### Highlights

- Fields and woods
- Ponds and the Ipswich River
- Great birding and wildlife
- The Rockery

The best nature walks for children are locations where there is water and rock formations. Ipswich River Wildlife Sanctuary has both. The area called The Rockery is a man-made maze of rocks and boulders formed into paths, bridges, and tunnels adjacent to a picture-perfect pond, surrounded by azaleas, rhododendrons, and mountain laurel. Ten miles of trails wind through meadows, ponds, marsh, forest, and the Ipswich River. (Maps with labeled trails are available at the office. Numbers on the maps correspond with numbers placed on posts at all trail intersections.)

The outing described here is a solid two-hour walk. If you are exploring with young children, you may want to shorten the walk, yet still visit the features most appreciated by children. This can be done by walking to Waterfowl Pond and then going on to The Rockery, bypassing the loop of Averill's Island (see map).

The parking lot and nature center rest atop Bradstreet Hill, a glacial drumlin, formed during the last ice age when the glacier deposited its debris and shaped it into a smooth elongated mound. Also on the property are eskers, long ridges of sand and gravel. Eskers formed when meltwater streams within the glaciers deposited their load of debris within the ice, leaving raised streambeds after all the ice melted.

From the parking lot follow the path toward the office and turn left on the driveway that goes by the red buildings. There is a wooden post with the number "2" on it. Turn right and in ten feet you will see a post with the letter "I" on it sig-

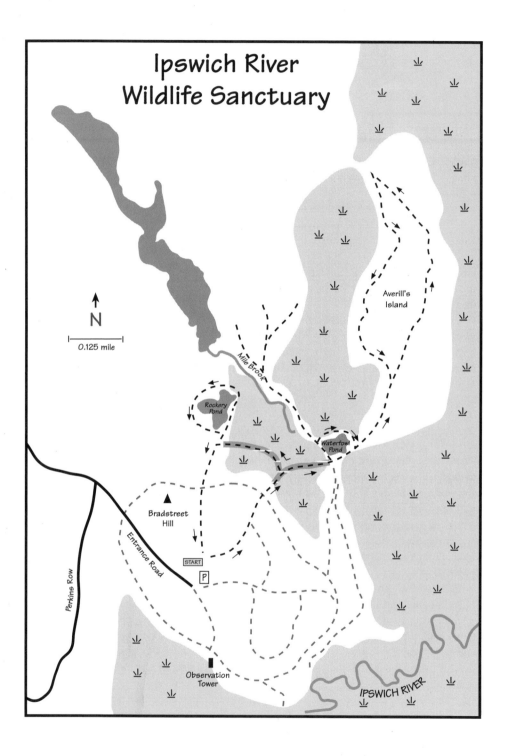

# Ipswich River
# Wildlife Sanctuary

N

0.125 mile

Mile Brook

Averill's
Island

Rockery
Pond

Waterfowl
Pond

Bradstreet
Hill

Entrance Road

Perkins Row

START

P

Observation
Tower

IPSWICH RIVER

nifying the Innermost Trail. Follow this wide grassy trail to the northeast, passing through goldenrod, Queen Anne's lace, and milkweed. Be careful of poison ivy (shiny green leaves in groups of three).

After walking roughly fifty feet you will be at marker #3. Bear left here, following a trail that leads downhill through foliage that has formed a tunnel. Here's where you can let your imagination (and your child's) conjure up images of entering a long winding cave! From within the foliage of crab apple and cedars you may hear the calls of mockingbirds, blue jays, and catbirds. In three minutes you will arrive at marker #18, where you should continue straight on the trail, passing beneath white pines and maples. Within a couple minutes you will reach marker #19; continue walking straight ahead. A beech tree brightens the woods with its light gray trunks, contrasting beautifully with the darker hemlocks that begin to appear.

The trail crosses a boardwalk through a swamp of cattails, purple loosestrife, and swamp maples, soon reaching marker #27. Turn right, passing by more wetlands where dead timber rises from the lowlands. Standing dead timber is particularly important to birds, as it provides nesting spots. Woodpeckers will drill into the wood to get at the insects, and the holes they create are used by other birds as nesting cavities.

In three or four minutes you will arrive at marker #28. Turn left to get a good view of Waterfowl Pond from a small handsome stone bridge. Look for wading birds such as great blue herons and night herons. Scan the water for frogs and painted turtles. Just a few feet past the bridge at markers #30 and #31 take a right on a small trail that circles the pond. If you are walking here in May inspect the edges of the path for recent signs of digging. Snapping turtles lay their eggs in the dry ground adjacent to the pond where the digging is easy. Snappers can be found in just about every body of water from dark mud-holes to clear lakes. Once her eggs are laid into the shallow depression the female covers it with dirt, but skunks and raccoons still manage to find many nests. Snappers play an important role in the health of ponds by eating dead fish, so teach your children not to harm them. Much of the reptile population in Massachusetts is at risk, and they need all the help we can give them.

At the back end of the pond the trail intersects with another trail and you should go left, heading toward Averill's Island. (If you are with young children, you may wish to bypass Averill's Island and head to The Rockery.) This is the Averill's Island Trail, one of the less frequented pathways at the sanctuary. Passing beneath white pine, hemlocks, and an occasional beech tree, the trail swings to the north. Look and listen for red squirrels, which prefer the evergreen habitat. About five minutes down the trail is marker #32, where the loop of Averill's Island begins. Bear right, passing towering white pines, which give the forest an enchanting quality. In about ten minutes you can see an open marsh on the right and just beyond that the Ipswich River. Winding for 35 miles, from marshlands in Wilmington to Ipswich Bay, the river has some great flatwater canoeing. The portion of the river that runs through the sanctuary is particularly scenic, with 8 miles protected from development. But like other rivers in Eastern Massachusetts, the Ipswich is being threatened by water withdrawals, with fourteen communities drawing water from the Ipswich River Basin. The need for water conservation programs is immediate if we are to protect the river and its aquatic life from the stresses of reduced flow.

The trail now angles to the northwest through mixed woodland. It is flat and well maintained, excellent for cross-country skiing in the winter. Averill's Island was not always this wild. In the seventeenth century the Averill family ran a carpentry business and printed a local newspaper here, and a small community was situated on the island. In five more minutes of walking you will reach the northern end of Averill's Island at marker #34, and you should turn left to complete your loop. (If you were to go straight you'd head into the northernmost end of the sanctuary, but sometimes the trails are flooded from beaver activity.) By heading south, you will arrive back at marker #32 in fifteen minutes, completing your loop of the island.

*Children love the boardwalks through the wetlands.*

For the second part of the walk to The Rockery, bear right, and retrace your steps past Waterfowl Pond, all the way to marker #27. Bear right, and the trail will take you through the heart of a marsh. Look for tree swallows and red-wing blackbirds in the wetlands, and see if you can spot nesting cavities of the swallows in the dead timber. In five minutes you'll arrive at marker #24. Turn right here onto a boardwalk that brings you to Rockery Pond at marker #25. Circle the pond in a counterclockwise direction by bearing right. Mountain laurel and rhododendrons make this an especially appealing walk in the late spring. There are openings to look across the pond at the rock formations, which give the pond its name. At the back end of the pond cross a small bridge, walk through cedars and spruce, and arrive at the boulders of The Rockery. This spot offers a peaceful view of the pond's tranquil waters, but if you are here with children they will run into The Rockery, exploring the nooks and crannies. In one section slabs of rock have been placed over the path making you walk through a dark tunnel. It's a magical place, made more so by the many evergreens.

The Rockery was cleverly designed in 1902 by Shintare Anamete, a Japanese landscape architect. It was commissioned by Thomas E. Proctor, the former owner of the area, as a setting for his collection of exotic shrubs, trees, and flowers. Constructed by immigrant Italian laborers, it took seven years to build. Rocks were bought by Proctor from surrounding farms because there were no boulders or glacial erratics on this property. Some of the boulders were transported here by horse and cart from more than 10 miles away. The beauty of The Rockery is its appearance of having been created by nature. But if you look closely you will see stone steps, and sitting stones angled perfectly to offer unencumbered views of the pond, which is also man-made. Massachusetts Audubon bought the sanctuary from the Proctor family in 1951.

To return to the parking lot walk from the rock tunnel and marker #26 to a small wooden bridge and cross the bridge to marker #25. Then turn right, retracing your steps over the boardwalk to marker #24 and go straight, continuing on the boardwalk to marker #20. At this intersection go straight on the trail that mostly goes uphill through woods and then brings you to the field by the parking lot. It's about a fifteen-minute walk from The Rockery to your car.

There are many more miles of trails to explore on future trips, including a walk to the southern end of the property where there is an observation tower overlooking Bunker Meadows, and a trail that brings you to the banks of the Ipswich River.

## Getting There

From Route 95 take Exit 50 (Route 1-Topsfield) and go north about 3 miles on Route 1 to its intersection with Route 97. Turn right (south) on Route 97 and proceed 0.6 mile then turn left on Perkins Row. Go 1 mile to the entrance on the right.

Open dawn to dusk, Tuesday through Sunday. Closed Mondays (open Monday holidays). Admission fee for nonmembers, rest rooms, and nature center programs. Canoe and cabin rental for member. Telephone: 978-887-9264.

# Phillips Academy— Cochran Wildlife Sanctuary

*Andover*

* 65 acres
* 2 miles
* 1 hour
* Easy
* Great for children

## Highlights

- Ponds
- Rhododendrons and mountain laurel
- Good cross-country skiing
- Gently rolling trails with benches

The wide, well maintained network of trails at the Cochran Wildlife Sanctuary make these woodlands a favorite for local walkers, cross-country skiers, and joggers. Located on the grounds of Phillips Academy, the oldest boarding school in the nation, the sanctuary offers a two-mile loop walk that is particularly impressive in June when the rhododendrons, azaleas, and mountain laurel are blooming. It's not a particularly big property, and certainly not the wildest place described in this book, but the sanctuary makes for an easy, pleasant walk that children as well as adults will enjoy.

Enter the sanctuary by passing through an ornate wooden gate and stone arches and walk down the wide dirt road in a northerly direction. Large mountain laurel and rhododendron beneath oak and pine line the trail. The rhododendron's flowers can vary in color from white to lavender and they are larger than the mountain laurel, which has clusters of white and pink blooms. Both plants have dark green leaves that do not fall off in winter. A few azaleas (which lose their leaves in winter) are mixed in with the larger bushes. Their fragrant blossoms are between one to two inches long and are tubular and vase-shaped. All three of these flowering bushes can tolerate acidic soil and shade. The mountain laurel is the most shade-loving of the three, and does poorly in sunny, wind-swept locations.

# Cochran Wildlife Sanctuary

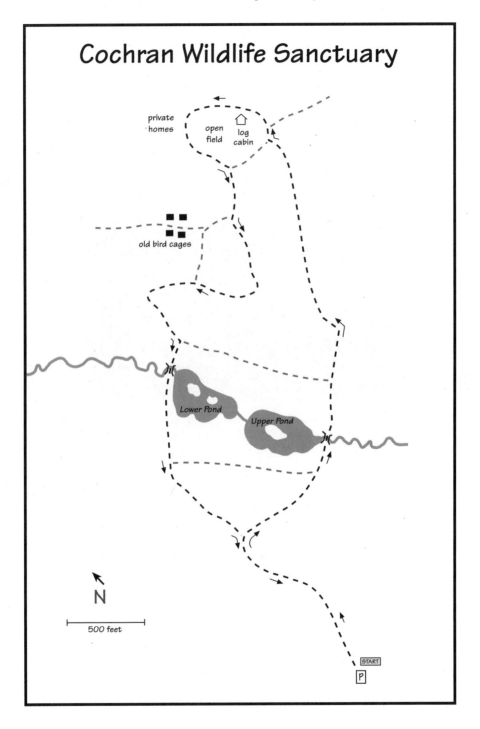

*A great blue heron patiently waits in the stream for prey.*
*Rather than stabbing fish, the heron grabs them in a light-*
*ing-swift move and swallows them whole.*

In about five-hundred feet bear right where the road forks and follow it
down a slight incline, passing some stately hemlock trees. Red squirrels prefer
evergreen trees like the hemlock. They build nests in tree cavities, old crows nest,
and sometimes in stone walls, but most often construct a nest of leaves and twigs
near the very top of a tree. Seeds of trees comprise the bulk of their diet, which
they supplement with berries, buds, tender leaves, inner bark, the flowering part
of trees, snails, insects, and maple syrup (often stripping the bark to get it).

In another five-hundred feet a wide trail goes to the left, but continue
straight ahead, quickly reaching Upper Pond on the left. Just before the little stone
bridge ahead there is a path to the shore where a bench overlooks the pond. Red
squirrels, chipmunks, and a variety of birds (including, chickadees, titmice, cardinals, and blue jays) grace the woods here. These birds are here year-round, adding
color and song to the winter woods. Both the male and female cardinal have point-

ed crests and thick red beaks. The male has the unmistakable bright red feathers with black throat, while the female's feathers are light brown.

Continue your walk, passing by the pond and over a small stone bridge that spans a stream that feeds the pond. (Children will enjoy exploring the pond's shoreline looking for ducks on the water and frogs and minnows near the shoreline.) About five-hundred feet beyond the pond another trail goes off to the left but you should continue straight ahead. Red pine, white pine, and spruce line the trail. Ten minutes of walking will bring you to a couple of log cabins. There is an open area behind the larger log cabin which provides a nice sunny spot for a rest. Built in 1931, the larger cabin is used for Phillips Academy alumni and faculty functions. Follow the road that curls around the north side of the larger cabin and then heads southwest through the open area and then into the woods. You will pass a paved road on the right and some residential homes. Stay on the woodland trail which goes beneath some large hemlocks and white pines.

After a couple minutes of walking you will be south of the cabin and you should bear right, passing by a dirt road on the left that leads back toward the cabin. You will soon pass some bird cages and a garage on your right. Stay left. Swans, ducks, and geese once lived in the sanctuary and the bird cages were used in the 1930s when Thomas Cochran, who donated this land to the academy, kept the birds within the sanctuary behind a seven-foot-high fence that ringed the entire property.

Your walk now passes through woodlands dominated by white oaks and mountain laurel, as you head toward Lower Pond. (Ignore the trail to the left just before the pond.) There is a small waterfall where the stream exits the man-made pond. Cinnamon ferns, bracken ferns, and sensitive ferns are scattered in the woods near the pond. Stop for a moment to scan the pond, looking for tree swallows and kingbirds. Tree swallows always live near water, catching insects and nesting in tree cavities. Their backs are black with a green-blue sheen, and they have white throats and flanks. The eastern kingbird, also an insect eater, can be identified by its dark back, white belly, and white terminal band across the end of its tail.

It's just a ten-minute walk to reach the parking lot from Lower Pond, just continue on the trail and stay to the right, passing trails on the left.

After your walk you want wish to visit the Peabody Museum of Archaeology on Route 28 on the opposite side of the street from the campus entrance. For museum hours call 978-749-4490.

## Getting There

From Route 495 take Exit 41A (Route 28 South) and follow Route 28 for 2.4 miles to Chapel Avenue on the left (there will be a large brick church on the left). Follow Chapel Avenue to its end (0.3 mile) and park at the cul de sac. The trail enters the woods through a big wooden gate.

No admission; no facilities; dogs must be leashed. Open year-round dawn to dusk.

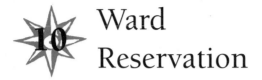

# Ward Reservation

## Andover and North Andover

---

* 686 acres

* Bog Nature Trail: 3/4 mile/30 minutes, easy, great for children

* Holt Hill & Northern Section: 4 miles/ 2 hours, moderate

---

## Highlights

• Quaking bog with unusual plants

• Vistas from Holt Hill and the Solstice Stones

• Extensive woodland trails

• Good cross-country skiing

Featuring both a quaking bog, fantastic vista, and miles of woodland trails, the Ward Reservation requires a full day to explore all its trails. The two walks in this chapter will include the bog, Holt Hill, and the northern section of woodlands.

A quaking bog is a fascinating natural place where rare and unusual plant life can be observed. The walk to the bog is a short one. From the parking area, cross the grassy area to the south past a private residence that will be on your left. After walking 150 feet through the field with the woods on your right, you will come to the beginning of the trail that leads into the woods. Follow this woodland trail and be on the lookout for low-growing club mosses, poison ivy (three shiny green leaves), and Indian pipe, a flowering plant that lacks the green pigment chlorophyll and is unable to manufacture its own food by photosynthesis. With the aid of a fungus that connects it to the roots of nearby trees, the Indian pipe collects its food from the host tree. The Indian pipe is four to ten inches tall and its nodding flowers are white or pink, similar in shape to a pipe. The woodland trail goes only a short distance and after a couple minutes you will soon pass a wet area on the right. Shortly afterward you will reach a T-intersection where you should turn right onto a boardwalk.

As soon as you begin walking on the boardwalk you will smell the dank earth and spruce and hemlock. The boardwalk rests on a mat of vegetation and below that is at least 19 feet of muck (as measured during the creation of the

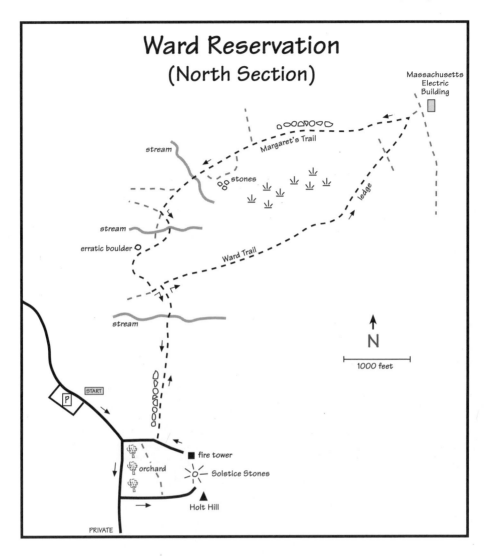

# Ward Reservation
## (North Section)

Massachusetts
Electric
Building

Margaret's Trail

stream

stones

stream

erratic boulder

Ward Trail

ledge

stream

N

1000 feet

START

P

fire tower

orchard

Solstice Stones

Holt Hill

PRIVATE

boardwalk). Look for cattail, cotton grass (a member of the sedge family that has a cottony tuft in late summer), and highbush blueberries which prefer the acidic soil of the bog.

It is only a five-minute walk on the boardwalk to the bog pond where the boardwalk ends. Ringed by dark cedars, the bog is particularly appealing in the fall when the golden grasses along its edge frame the black water. Both black spruce and tamarack, which are usually only found in northern New England, grow in the bog. And although the trees are small they are actually quite old. Sphagnum moss rings the bog, and it is this decayed moss that becomes peat. It is very spongy and absorbent. First used by the Native Americans to line their babies' diapers, it was later used as dressing for wounds.

Some of the rare plants here include rose begonia, bog orchids, and two insect-eating plants—the sundew and the pitcher plant. The pitcher plant attracts insects with the fluids that collect in its hollow leaves. The tiny hairs on the leaves allow the insect to enter but the same hairs block their escape. Then the plant's enzymes digest the insect, absorbing its nutrients. You can spot the pitcher plant by looking for a plant roughly eight to twenty-four inches tall with a red flower hanging from the center of green or purplish pitcher-shaped leaves.

The sundew is a much smaller plant, with round leaves and white or pink flowers. It too traps insects in the sticky fluid, only this plant's leaves actually close around the insect, trapping it in the fluid. The insects provide the plants with some of the nutrients, like nitrogen, that are lacking in the bog.

The bog formed twelve- to-fourteen thousand years ago when the last glacier retreated. It rests on a glacial kettle hole, a depression made when a huge block of ice from the glacier was left buried in the ground. Unlike other bodies of water, decay

*A boardwalk leads past rare plants in the quaking bog.*

in a bog is extremely slow, and as the plants die they accumulate at the bottom of the bog forming thick organic matter known as peat. In time, the open water in the bog will disappear as plants such as leather leaf and sphagnum moss take over.

To return to your car or begin the second walk, simply retrace your steps. (The Bog Nature Trail has interpretive numbers at various intervals. For those who seek an in-depth review of the bog, an interpretive booklet can be purchased from the property owners, The Trustees of Reservations, by calling 508-921-1944.)

## Holt Hill & Northern Section Walk

If you are hiking with young children, I recommend the first part of this walk to the summit of Holt Hill, returning to the parking area via the paved road that begins by the radio and fire tower. The walk through the woods and wetlands at the northern end of the property may be too long for children.

From the parking lot go up the paved road 200 feet to where a road comes in on the left. Continue straight, climbing uphill, passing an apple orchard on the left. If you are here in the early morning, scan the orchard for deer, particularly when there is fruit on the trees. Approach a large birch tree on the right where there are partial views looking back down toward the bog. On your left is a path with a chain across it. Turn left here. Climb the hill through the orchard, then through an open field, and finally into woods. Stay straight, passing a trail on the left, and within a couple minutes you will enter a field again. Look for birds that prefer open meadows such as bluebirds, bobolinks, and kestrels (a small hawk that primarily hunts insects).

To your left you will see a radio tower. Take the path through the meadow that leads that way and you will quickly arrive at the Solstice Stones and the summit of Holt Hill. The Solstice Stones were assembled at the direction of the property's former owner, Mrs. Charles Ward. They are laid out like a compass, with the largest stones indicating the four primary points. (The north stone is marked.) The narrow stone in the NE quadrant points in the direction of the sun rise on the summer solstice, the longest day of the year, which usually is on June 21. The view is breathtaking from Holt Hill. At 420 feet it is the highest hill in Essex County. Looking southward you can see the Boston skyline and the great Blue Hill in Milton. During the Revolutionary War the townspeople from Andover watched the burning of Charlestown from Holt Hill.

After enjoying the view, walk toward the radio tower and follow the paved road downhill about four minutes to a trail on the right with white blazes. Take this trail, which runs northward along a stone wall, indicating that this was once pasture. Large white pines have now grown here, and farther along the trail more oaks and maples appear. The trail gradually goes downhill, and after about eight minutes of walking you will cross a tiny stream on wooden boards.

On the other side of the stream approach a three-way intersection. Turn right onto Ward Trail. After about five minutes of walking you will pass wetlands on the left. Look for tree swallows (dark on the top, white on the bottom) flying here. Tree swallows have a greenish-black sheen on their backs and are about 5 inches long. In the spring they prefer to nest in cavities in standing timber and are easily attracted to backyard birdhouses if you live anywhere near water. Tree swallows are very social birds and can provide hours of viewing pleasure as they dip and wheel in the sky, chasing each other or catching insects.

After five more minutes of walking, approach a ledge of granite rock on the right, which older children may enjoy investigating. Next pass through an area of small white pines that crowd the trail, making for a tunnel effect. Deer use the same trail as they make their nocturnal rounds—see if you can spot their heart-shaped hoofprints in the ground. You will soon pass an intersection with a narrow trail. Continue straight until you see a Massachusetts Electrical building. Turn left at an intersection just before the building (and before a trail map) to loop back toward the parking area. The trail, called Margaret's Trail, heads in a westerly direction alongside lowlands and a stone wall.

A side trail enters on the right about ten minutes down, but you should continue straight, stepping up on exposed bedrock. In another couple hundred feet the trail forks. Stay straight (bearing right), following the trail to a tiny stream that drains the marsh on your left. Before crossing, you might want to go upstream to listen to the stream making four-inch drops over rocks. You can also explore the little side trail that loops back to a partial view of the wetlands by some stones that have been arranged in a semicircle around a fire pit. In the winter sun filters into this spot making it a good place to snack before tackling the final leg of the walk.

Look along the edge of the stream for animal tracks such as those made by the raccoons or minks that forage along wet areas. Mink can grow as long as 35 inches, including tail, yet the weight of a mink that size would be only about 2.5 pounds. They are crafty hunters that prey primarily on small rodents, but will also eat birds, snakes, frogs, crayfish, and even muskrat.

Back on the main trail, just beyond the stream, approach a fork and follow the trail to the left, where it is crowded by pines. In three more minutes you'll arrive at a four-way intersection. Turn left and cross another small stream and then walk a couple minutes toward a trail on the right. Bear left here and pass the exposed ledge. A small glacial erratic boulder will be resting on the ledge. In about five minutes you'll reach an intersection where you should turn left, then go right after ten feet. You are now back on one of the original trails from the paved road. About fifteen or twenty minutes of walking will bring you back to the parking lot.

In the spring or after heavy rains these northern trails by the wetlands can be quite muddy.

## Getting There

From Route 93 take Route 125 north 5 miles and then go right on Prospect Road. Follow Prospect Road 0.3 mile to the parking area on the right.

From Route 495 take Route 114 east about 2 miles and then go right on Route 125 south 1.6 miles. Go left on Prospect Road and travel 0.3 miles to the parking lot on the right.

Open dawn to dusk, seven days a week, year-round. No admission but donations accepted; no facilities; dogs allowed.

# West of Boston

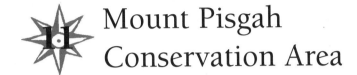 ## Mount Pisgah Conservation Area

## *Northborough*

* 190 acres
* 2 miles
* 1.5 hours
* Easy

### *Highlights*

* Hilltop view
* Seldom used trails
* Old stone walls

Mount Pisgah is located in the hilly northwest section of Northborough, adjacent to the Berlin town line. A mix of narrow footpaths and old dirt roads traverses a forest of red oak, white pine, maple, and beech. Stone walls, small streams, and a scenic overlook await your discovery. The Mount Pisgah property abuts other conservation land, so it's a fairly large patch of second or third growth forest. Northborough Conservation Commissioner Sue Bracket stated that an assortment of owls such as great horned and barred owls have been seen here, in addition to hawks, deer, and fox. Massachusetts has both gray fox and red fox, but the northern limit of the gray fox is approximately in the southeastern section of the state, so chances are Mount Pisgah is home only to the red fox.

From the parking area, follow the wide trail heading east, passing beneath tall white pines. A couple minutes down the trail on your left will be a small forest area with young trees, where forest is springing up from what was once a field. Such opportunistic trees as gray birch, popple, pin cherry, and white pines are the first to become established here, later to be followed by oaks and maples. Look for rabbits in the tangle of undergrowth and in the thick grasses.

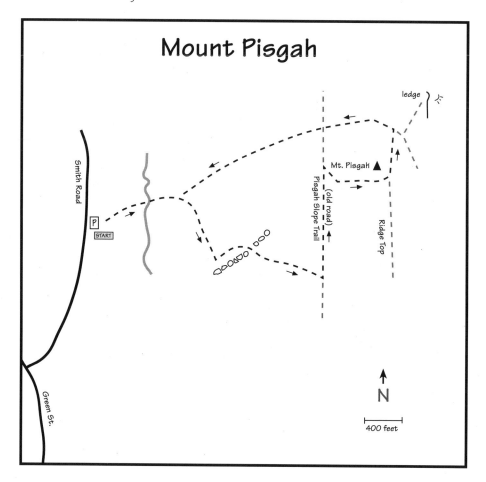

Within five minutes step your way over a tiny stream to where the trail splits. Go to the right. (The walk takes the longer route to the top, but descends on the shorter, more direct trail.) Red maple, oaks, and pines line the path, which is quite rocky in places. On the forest floor are blueberry bushes, sheep laurel, and such herbaceous plants as partridge berry, mosses, and princess pine. In about five more minutes the path hits a stone wall and curls to the left, following the stone wall. By examining stone walls you can often tell what the land was used for. If many small rocks are used in the wall it's likely the land was farmed and almost every rock was removed from the field. The same holds true if it's a double wall with small rocks in the center. If the wall is comprised primarily of large rocks with few small ones, it suggests that the land was used for grazing and only the biggest rocks were removed.

After following the stone wall for a couple minutes there is a break; follow the path through the break to the right. The path now heads primarily eastward again. In five minutes it intersects with an old logging road called the Pisgah Slope Trail. Turn left on the logging road and follow for about ten minutes until you come to a trail on the right. Take this right (marked by orange tape on trees) and go about five minutes to a T-intersection and turn left. You are now on the spine of a ridge. A few feet off the trail imbedded in a rock to the left is the US Geological survey marker indicating the summit of Mount Pisgah. The vista from the ridge, however, requires about five more minutes of walking to the next T-intersection, where you should turn right and go twenty feet to where the trail forks. Bear left, proceeding about 200 feet to the exposed rock ridge with a view overlooking Hudson and Marlborough to the east. On a clear day you can even make out a Boston skyscraper or two.

The remains of stone walls, some with large impressive flat boulders, criss-cross the ridge top. The woods here are most likely third growth, but this hilltop, like most of Massachusetts, had been cleared for pasture in the late 1700s and early 1800s. Then the stone-free soil of the western plains lured the farmers away, and

*A climb to the summit of Mount Pisgah gives you the feeling of being in northern New England.*

the fields reverted to woodlands, leaving stone walls as the only reminders of agriculture's dominance in Massachusetts.

The walk down from the hilltop only takes about twenty to twenty-five minutes. To return, make a more direct route down the mountain. From the overlook, return to the last intersection described earlier and instead of going left on the Ridge Top trail, go straight, and follow the yellow disc markers on the trees. Five minutes down this path will take you to an intersection with the old logging road known as the Pisgah Slope Trail. Stay on the narrow path you have descended the hill on, leading directly across the Pisgah Slope Trail. The path will lead through a stand of hardwoods where white birch soon become more numerous. It is not uncommon to come across deer and raccoon tracks here. A friend of mine who lives nearby once saw a fisher, a large member of the weasel family that is expanding its range into more suburban areas of Massachusetts. Fisher are deadly hunters, preying on squirrels, porcupines, rabbits, mice, and birds. They will also kill housecats, if given the opportunity.

The trail you are on soon enters into the shade of a pine grove, then merges with the main trail by the stream you crossed on your way up. Turn right here, cross the stream, and you will be back at the parking lot.

## Getting There

From Route 290 take the Church Street Boylston/Northborough exit (Exit 24). At the end of the exit go toward Boylston. After about a hundred feet turn right onto Ball Street. (There will be a sign pointing to Tougas Farm.) Follow Ball Street 1.6 miles to its end. Go left on Green Street for 0.5 mile to where road forks, then bear right onto Smith Road. Travel 0.3 mile to parking area on the right.

No admission fee; no facilities; dogs allowed. Open year-round dawn to dusk.

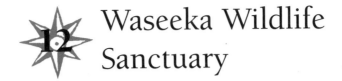

# Waseeka Wildlife Sanctuary

## *Hopkinton*

---

* 219 acres
* 1.5 miles
* 1 hour
* Easy
* Great for children

---

### Highlights

* Pond
* Great birding
* Large white pines

Waseeka Wildlife Sanctuary in Hopkinton is one of the lesser known properties of the Massachusetts Audubon Society. Featuring a shallow pond and 219 wooded acres, it is an excellent habitat for a variety of wildlife. Large mammals such as deer to raccoon live in the forest, birds such as wood ducks and great blue heron feed at the pond, and reptiles and amphibians live in the pond and along the shoreline. A walk at Waseeka during the week is highly recommended; you may be the only person to visit the property, and your odds of seeing wildlife will be greatly increased.

The walk begins by following the trail from the parking area to the northeast through woods of small oak, white pine, and gray birch. (In the early twentieth century this was open pasture, once part of the former Waseeka Farm.) Stay on the main path as it crosses an intersection with another trail, and you will reach the pond in approximately fifteen minutes. The pond is man-made, and the trail follows an earthen dam along its eastern end. Many of the ponds in New England that appear to be natural were actually made by early settlers. They were used as holding ponds for mills, which were powered by the water released from the ponds. In later years some ponds were created on farms to provide a water source for irrigating fields. Usually the man-made ponds can be identified by a square side where an earthen dike was built, even though the dike might be covered with trees today. If you look closely, you might also find the sluiceway (where water ran from the pond into the mill), a millstone, or stone slabs used in the construction of the mill.

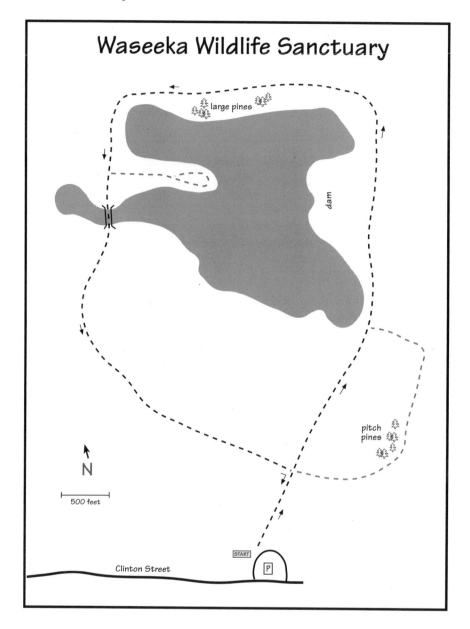

Waseeka Wildlife Sanctuary

large pines

dam

pitch
pines

N

500 feet

START

P

Clinton Street

In the past, there was a great blue heron nest in one of the dead trees out toward the center of the pond. Ponds with standing dead timber are the preferred nesting spots of great blue herons, perhaps because a predator trying to get at the nest would first have to swim out to the tree. One of the reasons that we are seeing more great blue herons, besides cleaner water, is that there are more beaver in the state, and the standing timber in the beaver ponds are perfect nesting platforms

*The earthen dike at the end of the pond makes a great trail.*

for the herons. A wide variety of birds such as wood ducks, green herons, kingfishers, and mergansers are also attracted to the water. Water snakes, painted turtles, and snapping turtles are also at home in these quiet waters. In the woods, goshawk, great horned owl, turkey, and grouse are sometimes seen.

After you walk to the end of the earthen dam, the trail circles the pond to the left, hugging the northern shore where large white pines shade your walk. Look for the tracks of raccoon and mink which frequent the shoreline. Coyote, otter, fox, and deer have also been spotted. If you visit in late spring, you might even see a snapping turtle on or near the shore at egg-laying time. Snappers emerge from the water and dig holes about six inches deep in sandy areas, lay their eggs, and then cover them. The eggs are sometimes found and eaten by skunks and raccoons. Snapping turtles are vulnerable on land and if approached will defend themselves by biting, as they are unable to retreat fully into their shells. They play an important role in the health of a pond by eating dead fish. Reptiles in general are particularly threatened by man's development and many species that were once common are now endangered.

Walk along the northern end of the pond for about ten minutes and the trail curls to the left. Along the shoreline is a short trail that leads out to a point of land jutting into the water. With the aid of binoculars this is a good place to watch for wading birds, as well as warblers, ring-necked ducks, and flycatchers. The flycatcher family of birds are medium to small birds. Their feet are adapted to perching with three toes in the front and one long one behind. They have broad flat bills that make a loud snap when they swoop over the pond and catch insects. Flycatchers that might be seen at Waseeka include the eastern kingbird, eastern wood-pewee, and eastern phoebe. The kingbird is often seen chasing crows away from its territory and can easily be identified by the white terminal band at the end of dark gray-black feathers.

The final leg of the walk after crossing a wet area through an oak woodland laced with old stone walls leads away from the pond. A twenty-minute walk brings you back to the main trail, not far from the parking area. If you turn right you will soon be back at your car. If you cross the main trail, on a narrow footpath, this will lead past pitch pines (uncommon in this area) and ultimately reconnect with the main trail by the pond.

## Getting There

Take Route 495 to Exit 21A (West Main St., Hopkinton) then follow to Hopkinton Center. Merge with Route 135. Take first right after Weston Nurseries onto Clinton Street. Sanctuary is 2.1 miles on the left.

No admission fee but donations encouraged; no facilities; no dogs. Open year-round dawn to dusk.

# Oak Grove Farm

## *Millis*

- ✳ 108 acres
- ✳ Easy
- ✳ 1.5 miles
- ✳ 1 hour
- ✳ Great for children

## *Highlights*

- Open meadows and farmland reverting to woods
- Great cross-country skiing

Oak Grove Farm has a combination of open fields and woodlands spread over level terrain that make for a pleasant and easy walk. A large playground and ball fields are also on the property and children will enjoy capping there walk off with a romp in the playground.

To begin your walk, look for the Trail Map sign at the back end of the playground next to the parking area. Walk beyond the Trail Map sign about 50 feet and you will see a wooden post with arrows. Turn right here and follow the North Trail. On the right of the trail is an open field and on the left are young woodlands that have recently sprung up in an area that was once pasture or agricultural land. Notice the species of trees that have established themselves among the low-lying vegetation. Cedars and white pines are just two of the trees that are the first to populate abandoned fields.

Open areas with nearby woods are attractive hunting spots for hawks such as red-tailed hawks and kestrels. The red-tailed hawk is a large bird with a dark brown back and beige belly. Unlike most other hawks the red-tailed hawk stays in New England throughout the winter, hunting small rodents. They can often be seen resting on branches near open areas, including the side of highways where the grass is kept mowed. Winter is the best time to see red-tailed hawks as they are most conspicuous. They typically select white pines for nesting in the early spring. Often, people see the hawk flying above and assume it is not a red-tailed hawk because the tail is a tan to pinkish color beneath. But the top side of the tail, seen when the hawk is perched, is the side that has a rusty red color. These soaring hawks hunt

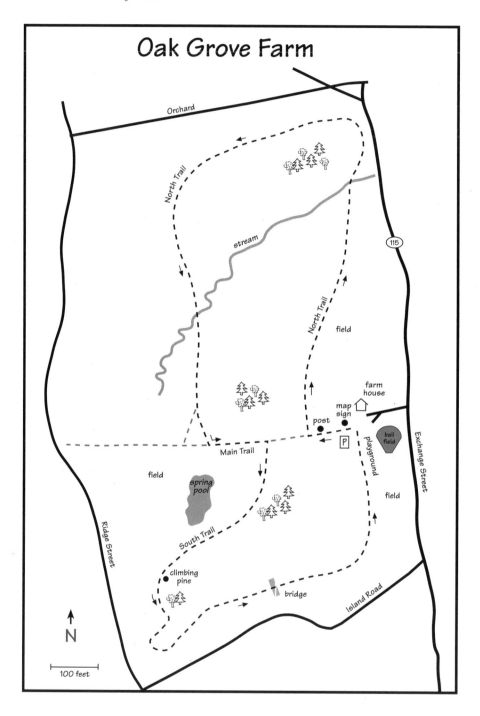

# Oak Grove Farm

alone and drop upon their prey in a steep dive. They measure about 18 inches in length with a large wingspan up to 48 inches.

About six or seven minutes into the walk the trail enters the woods and crosses a wooden bridge spanning a small stream. Beyond this point the trail gets muddy in the springtime, so be sure to wear boots. Scan the woods, or if it's winter look for the tracks of rabbit, fox, and even coyote. Coyotes have moved into New England over the last 30 years, perhaps coming from the west or through Canada, and they are now found throughout Massachusetts, including Cape Cod.

Next, the trail heads west then south before intersecting with the Main Trail about twenty minutes from the start of the walk. At the intersection turn left. Then about 50 feet down the Main Trail turn right onto the South Trail. It leads by woodlands on the left side and on the right skirts the edge of a low-lying area that collects water in the spring. Here you might spot a ruffed grouse, a non-migrating bird about 14 inches long, with rust and gray feathers and a black terminal band on its tail. When flushed it can burst into full flight (which can really startle you) usually traveling a short distance before touching down again. The drumbeat you may hear in the woods is actually the male grouse rapidly beating its wings, trying to attract a female. And should you come across a grouse doing a wounded wing act, stop and look carefully about—there may be several chicks hiding near your feet in the grass or the leaves. Take care not to disturb the chicks. Never touch or otherwise harass wildlife.

About five minutes down this trail there is a large white pine tree on the left with low branches, making it a great climbing tree for children. During colonial times, large pines (over 24 inches in diameter) that were within three miles of the water were claimed by the king, and were reserved for use by the Royal Navy. Pines often grow taller than 100 feet, and the older trees have broad, horizontal branches with irregular-shaped tops. The easiest way to identify white pines is to look at the needles. They are in clusters of five and are from 3 to 5 inches long and are soft and flexible. At the end of the second growing season they turn brownish and fall off in the autumn. The cones are nodding and curved, about 4 to 8 inches long. They drop their seeds at the end of the second growing season.

The other tree that quickly takes over old fields is the cedar, and there are plenty scattered around Oak Grove Farm. The red cedar is a small evergreen, usually growing to a height of 15 feet, and seems to flourish in the sterile soils of abandon fields as long as it gets plenty of sunlight. A wide assortment of birds feed on the bluish-white berries, which are globular in shape and about a quarter inch in size. The soft, fragrant wood is used for posts sills, lead pencils, and the interior finish of buildings, particularly in cedar closets and chests, as a protection against the house moth. New England also has a southern white cedar that grows in bogs and swamps in southern New England, reaching 60 feet in height. In northern New England the northern white cedar is a similar tree that prefers wet areas and has a very dense conical crown. Similar to the cedar is the juniper, which is more of a shrub than a tree, growing along the ground with sharp pointed needles that

*This large white pine makes a great climbing tree for children.*

are prickly to the touch. It needs sunlight to grow and when larger trees take over abandoned fields it soon disappears.

Further along the trail is a row of impressive oak trees with one large maple at the end of the row. The trees were spared the farmer's ax because they grow along the remains of a stone wall.

At the back end of the field the trail enters the woods. Stop for a moment at the large oak tree that is laying next to the path. Where a chain saw cut through it you can count the rings in the wood to estimate its age. The trail then passes through pine woodlands, over a wooden bridge, and heads eastward for a quarter mile before ending near the playground. Because the trails are wide and flat at Oak Grove Farm, you may want to check it out in the winter for cross-country skiing.

Visitors to Oak Grove Farm may want to combine their walk with some nearby canoeing. The Charles River winds its way through greater Millis and there are a number of access points. Just north of Oak Grove Farm off Route 115 is South End Pond, which has a stream connecting it to the Charles. You can launch at the pond and paddle across it, then a few feet down the stream into the Charles. This area of the Charles is known as the Great Marsh with many small islands scattered about the wetlands. This is a good birding spot, especially for wading birds and ducks. Largemouth bass and pickerel are found throughout the river so bring your fishing rod. You can also canoe up Bogastow Brook, which enters South End Pond just to the right of the launch area.

There are other access points on the Charles such as at the Route 27 bridge. From this launch site you can paddle upstream into the Great Marsh and South End Pond, or downstream into Rocky Narrows (see Rocky Narrows in *Nature Walks in Eastern Massachusetts*). The stretch of river that passes through Rocky Narrows is quite a contrast from the openness of the Great Marsh. Hemlock trees and granite ledge abut the river through Rocky Narrows; and as the name suggests, the river narrows considerably. This is one of the best outings on the entire Charles River. (Detailed paddles on the Charles River can be found in *Exploring the Hidden Charles*, also published by AMC Books.)

## Getting There

From the intersection of Route 109 and Route 115 go north on Route 115. Follow Route 115 for 1.1 miles and look for the Oak Grove Farm sign and parking lot on the right.

Open dawn to dusk year-round, seven days a week. No admission fee; no facilities; dogs allowed on leash.

# King Philip Overlook
# & Rocky Narrows

## *Sherborn*

* 300+ acres
* 3 miles (approx.)
* 1.5 hours
* Moderate

## *Highlights*

* commanding view of Charles River from high on a bluff
* hemlock forest and rugged, rocky terrain.

Rocky Narrows (owned by The Trustees of Reservations) and King Philip Overlook (part of the Sherborn Town Forest) lie adjacent to one another and offer hikers a relatively wild section of woodlands to explore. Until recently access was difficult either by canoe from the river or from a small lot on Forest Street. Now, however, there is a parking lot on Route 27 in Sherborn large enough to accommodate several cars. The highlight of the walk is the King Philip Overlook, which offers a fantastic view of the Charles River. (Some walkers may want to continue farther down the trail for the partial view offered at the Rocky Narrows Overlook.) Hemlock trees cover much of the hills in the reservations, and a walk here feels more reminiscent of northern New England than suburban Boston. This reservation has many unmarked trails. You may get lost, so start your walk well before dark!

From the parking lot follow the trail into woodlands of oak, maple, and white pine. The trail will be marked by white discs and white slashes on trees. Remain on this white-marked trail for the entire walk. Side trails will intersect with the white trail at various intervals so be sure to follow the white marking. There is a healthy population of white-tailed deer here, and during springtime you might see their tracks in the damp earth of the trail. The tracks are heart-shaped, with the narrow part of the track indicating the front of the deer's hoof, which shows the way it was traveling. Another large mammal that lives here is the coyote. It is estimated there are more than three thousand coyotes in Massachusetts. They are very adaptable animals, using whatever food source is available (including house cats) and they are secretive as well, doing most of their hunting at night. A coyote howl in the wee hours of the morning is a sound you won't soon forget.

The first natural landmark you will reach is a small stream with an earthen bridge across it, located about fifteen minutes from the parking lot. Five minutes

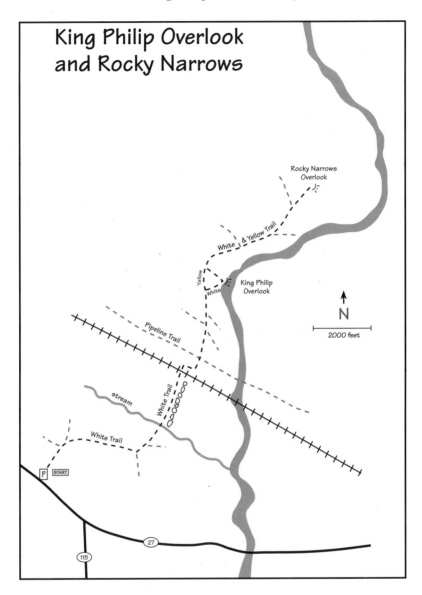

later you will reach a set of railroad tracks. (Caution: The tracks are active.) Cross the tracks and turn right. Walk about 20 yards and you will see the white-paint markers on your left. Follow this trail uphill into the woods and it will soon cross a wide trail that follows a pipeline.

About five or ten minutes after crossing the railroad tracks the white trail will make a sharp right turn (the trail directly ahead will be the yellow trail). Turn right here. This will lead you to the King Philip Overlook in a couple minutes.

The view from the overlook (a granite ledge with an open face) is to the south and the southwest. You can see upstream on the Charles where it passes beneath the railroad tracks (the same tracks you crossed earlier). The ledge is not always as quiet as you might like because model airplanes are sometimes flown from a field on the other side of the river. But even the planes can be fun to watch as they swoop and glide overhead and in front of the ledge.

Like so many hilltops in Massachusetts, King Philip Overlook is named for the Native American leader Metacom whose English-given name was Philip. Beginning in 1675, Philip led an uprising of Wampanoags, Nipmucks, and Narragansetts to try and regain tribal lands from European settlers. One of the towns especially hard hit by the warriors was Medfield, which lies in front of you as you look off across the river from the overlook. Many homes were burned and several settlers were killed, but the Indians could not overpower the garrison.

After the Indians withdrew from Medfield, a warrior who had learned English left a note by a burned bridge at the Charles that read: "Know by this paper, that the Indians that thou hast provoked to wrath and anger, will war this twenty-one years if you will: there are many Indians yet, we come three hundred this time. You must consider the Indians lost nothing but their life; you must lose your fair houses and cattle." But the Indians were not strong in number, and there were many more English. The attack on Medfield occurred in February of 1676, and by August of the same year so many natives had been killed, including Philip, that the war was over. Ironically, Philip was the son of Massasoit, the Wampanoag leader that showed kindness to the Pilgrims during their first disastrous year in Plymouth.

The overlook is a good place to look for hawks soaring above the river. Great blue herons also make their way up and down the river. Their population has increased now that our rivers are cleaner, and because the increasing beaver population in Massachusetts has led to the creation of more ponds with standing timber, the heron's preferred nesting spot.

Many walkers prefer to rest on this beautiful bluff before heading back. Others push on into Rocky Narrows proper to see the hemlock trees and the Rocky Narrows Overlook. You can do so by following the white trail directly behind the overlook. After a few feet on this trail it intersects with a trail that has both white and yellow markings; turn right. Soon you will see some of the large hemlocks that make the Rocky Narrows Overlook a special place.

Hemlocks prefer rocky ridges and ravines, growing to a height of 70 feet in cool, moist spots. To distinguish the hemlock from other evergreen examine its needles closely. The needles are flat with blunt tips and there are usually several needles upside down on the branchlet. They are about a quarter to a half inch long, shorter in length than spruce and fir. Although they are dark green on the top, turn them over and you will see a silvery underside. Because the needles are acidic, there is often little undergrowth beneath the tree where needles have fallen year after year. Hemlocks have brown cones, about three-quarters of an inch long, that hang from the tip of the branches. They mature in the fall and stay on the tree until spring. Another way to distinguish the hemlock from fir trees is to look at the crown of the tree: the hemlock will be rounded while the fir comes to a sharp dense point.

*Fantastic views of the Charles await at King Philip Overlook.*

After walking about seven or eight minutes you will see a split in the trail where a tree in the middle of the split has two white marks on it. Bear left here and follow the white markers for about five minutes to the Rocky Narrows Overlook. The view here is not nearly as scenic as the King Philip Overlook, offering only a partial vista of a meadow and small part of the Charles River. The terrain, however, is interesting with rugged hills, granite outcrops, and towering hemlocks.

Below you the Charles River is constricted by the granite ledges, forming a narrow passageway, hence the name Rocky Narrows. This is a prime canoeing spot, with a good launch site just downstream at the Farm Road/Bridge Street bridge, and another launch site (quite steep) at Route 27. For an afternoon canoe ride, put in at Route 27 and follow it downstream to the South Natick Dam, where you could have a second car waiting. Or, if you are partial to exploring wetlands, you could launch at Route 109 on the Millis/Medfield border and head downstream through the Great Marsh then through Rocky Narrows with a take-out on Farm Road/Bridge Street.

To return to your car simply retrace your steps.

## Getting There

From the intersection of Routes 115 and 27, take Route 27 north for 0.3 mile to parking area on the right.

Open dawn to dusk, year-round. No admission fee; no facilities; dogs allowed on leash.

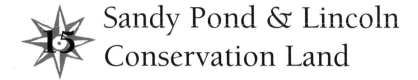

# Sandy Pond & Lincoln Conservation Land

## Lincoln

* 300 acres
* 3.5 miles
* 2.25 hours
* Moderate

### Highlight

• Long walk around beautiful Sandy Pond

The Sandy Pond Loop walk offers a long walk on level terrain through mixed woodlands. About twice the size of Walden Pond, Sandy Pond is a public drinking water reservoir, and its trails are not crowded with tourists. If you walk during mid-week, you will probably have the place to yourself. Much of the walk is at or near the water's edge, allowing you to enjoy the open vistas and scan the pond for ducks and the sky above for hawks. It's a long walk, the kind best done with a good friend rather than young children.

The walk begins at the back end of the main parking lot at the DeCordova Museum. Look for a brown trail sign for Lincoln Conservation Land and follow that trail toward Sandy Pond through woods of oak and maple. (Sandy Pond is also known as Flint's Pond.) In a couple hundred feet, near the pond, the trail you are on intersects with another near an old fireplace with chimney. You should turn right here to begin your loop of the pond. From this point on, almost every turn is to the left as you circle the pond in a counterclockwise direction.

The path takes you past a number of stone walls and through a grove of hemlocks. Like virtually all of Massachusetts, the woods here were pasture over a hundred years ago when agriculture dominated the landscape. A couple minutes later the trail forks and you should stay left. The trail now begins to skirt wetlands. Another trail soon appears on your left, which you should take to cross the marsh. (If it is too muddy take the next left to the other side of the marsh.) The trail then comes to a T-intersection. Bear left again, heading back toward the pond now that you have walked around the marsh.

In about five minutes you'll arrive back at the water's edge where a small opening in the wooded shore offers a view of the pond. This is a good spot to scan the shoreline for wood ducks, especially late in the day during the fall when they

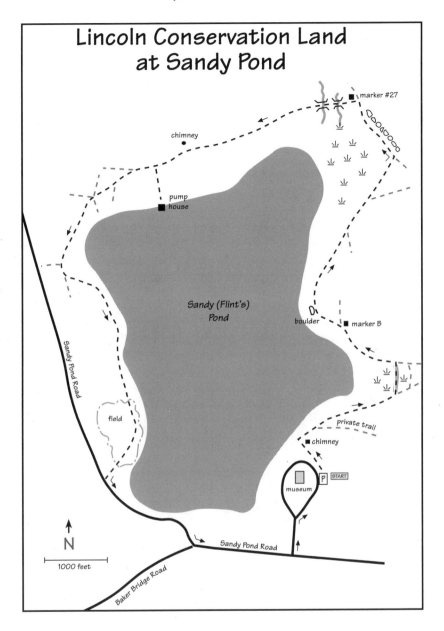

gather in small flocks, preparing for the migration southward. Besides the brilliant coloration of the male, a good method for identifying this species is by the large head, short neck, and long square tail. In the spring they make their nests in hollow trees and the babies leave the nest within twenty-four hours of birth, plummeting to the ground or water. With the ducklings so vulnerable, the parents must be secretive in guarding their young.

Soon you'll come to a fork in the trail, at marker B, and here you should bear left. A handful of white birches add contrast to the brown and gray trunks of oaks, pines, and maples that dominate these woods. A couple minutes down the trail you will see a boulder with a sobering message on a plaque that reads:

Aureet Bar-Yam
1957–1991
Shiver to think of her light, her warmth forever frozen in
this clear cold pond. May its glimmer give you pause . . . .
For ice broke hearts the day she drowned.

The plaque should make all of us consider the dangers of ice in the winter, and to remind children to stay off the ice. After pausing at the boulder, proceed down the trail, passing two trails on the right. You will soon begin to skirt more wetlands (you are now about forty-five minutes into walk from the start). Once past the wetlands, the trail comes to a T-intersection. Go left again toward the pond, passing beneath some large oaks. This section of the trail is open to mountain biking and has a stone wall paralleling it on the right. About seven or eight more minutes down the trail you will come to a trail heading to the left at marker #27. Take this left, again heading closer to the pond. The trail will carry you over two tiny streams on wooden plank bridges heading in a westward direction.

This section of trail is often used by mountain bikers in the warm-weather months and cross-country skiers in the winter, and fortunately the trail is wide enough to accommodate people traveling in both directions. After walking about half a mile notice that beech trees, followed by hemlocks, mix with the pines, oaks, and maples. An old fireplace and chimney will be on your right; shortly thereafter is a trail on your left. This leads to the water's edge near a pumping station. This is a great place to rest, particularly during the cold-weather months, when the

*Red fox kits sunning themselves. To spot a fox den, look for a large mound of sand by a hole in the ground.*

southern sun hits the shore here and you can rest with your back against the building and overlook the pond. Looking across the pond you will see the DeCordova Museum and you can see how far you've walked. You might want to pack a copy of Thoreau's *Walden* and read it here while basking in the sun.

One of the creatures you might glimpse on this back part of Sandy Pond is the red fox, which Thoreau especially enjoyed seeing. "His recent tracks still give variety to a winter's walk. I tread in the steps of the fox that has gone before me by some hours, or which perhaps I have started, with such a tiptoe of expectation as if I were on the trail of the Spirit itself which resides in the wood, and expected soon to catch it in its lair. I am curious to know what has determined its graceful curvatures. . . . When I see a fox run across the pond on the snow, with the carelessness of freedom, or at intervals trace his course in the sunshine along the ridge of a hill, I give up to him sun and earth as to their true proprietor."

From the pump house retrace your steps to the main trail and go left. In a few feet the trail forks. Turn left. Then it will fork again and you should bear right, which will take you to a five-trail intersection. Go straight on a narrow trail that has a sign reading "Closed to Horseback Riders and Biking." You will soon be traveling parallel to Sandy Pond Road and will hear the traffic through the woods. A trail on the right will lead up to the road, and you should continue straight to a fork where you should bear left toward the pond. A warning is in order. This trail gets muddy in the spring and after rains, so you may want to return to your car by walking down Sandy Pond Road. But if the conditions are good, the trail is the better choice because it keeps you in the woods longer. The trail is rocky in places, so your progress will be a bit slower than on the wide trail, but in about fifteen minutes the trail crosses a field. The field is a nice change of scenery from the woods, and you might get lucky and see a deer here, as there are many in this area. Also, be on the lookout for bluebirds—there is a bluebird house nailed to a lone popple tree in the center of the field.

After you cross the field the trail leads to Sandy Pond Road, follow it left to return to the DeCordova entrance and your car. The walk on the road takes about fifteen minutes.

A nearby point of interest is Audubon's Drumlin Farm which is great for the children. It is located on Route 117 in Lincoln, 4.5 miles west of the Route 117 overpass at Route 128. Children will love farm animals and live exhibit of wild animals. The property spans 180 acres and there are trails traversing woods, fields, pastures, and ponds. There is also a gift shop, and nature center where programs are held.

## Getting There

From Route 128 take Exit 28B (Trapelo Road–Lincoln). Follow Trapelo Road 2.6 miles to a stop sign and intersection. Go straight through the intersection onto Sandy Pond Road. Follow 0.4 mile to the entrance to the DeCordova Museum on the right. Follow the entrance road past the sculptures to the signs for the main parking lot and park at the rear.

Open year-round dawn to dusk. No admission; no facilities. Dogs are allowed, but are prohibited from going in or near the water (public water supply). Lincoln Conservation Commission: 781-259-2612.

# Wilson Mountain Reservation

## Dedham

- 207 acres
- 2 miles
- 1.5 hours
- Easy
- Children will enjoy the first part of this walk that goes to summit

## Highlights

- Rocky ledges
- Scenic views
- Hemlock and white pine groves
- Rhododendrons

Thanks are due to all the people that saved Wilson Mountain from development in 1994 and kept it natural. Just ten miles from Boston, these two-hundred wooded acres could have easily become the site of a mall or housing lots, but instead, thanks to funds made available through the Open Space Bond Bill, it is now managed by the Metropolitan District Commission (MDC) and is open to all. Anyone can walk through the pine groves, admire the view from the hilltop, and traverse along the edges of buttonbush swamps and streams.

Let's enjoy a stroll to the hilltop overlook and then explore the trails adjacent to the wetlands at the southern end of the property. The MDC has recently labeled two loop trails: the Red Dot Loop is roughly 3/4 mile long and circles Wilson Mountain at the northeast end of the property, while the Green Dot Trail covers 2 miles heading from north to south. This walk covers a little of both.

But before you start the walk, take a moment to examine the poison ivy at the edges of the parking area—it's a good idea to know what it looks like and you should educate children if they are with you. Identified by its three shiny green leaves with pointed tips, poison ivy can grow as a low plant in sunny edges, or as a vine, wrapping itself around trees. Its yellow-green flowers grow in clusters and the fruit is dry and white. The painful rash can come from any part of the plant

# Wilson Mountain Reservation

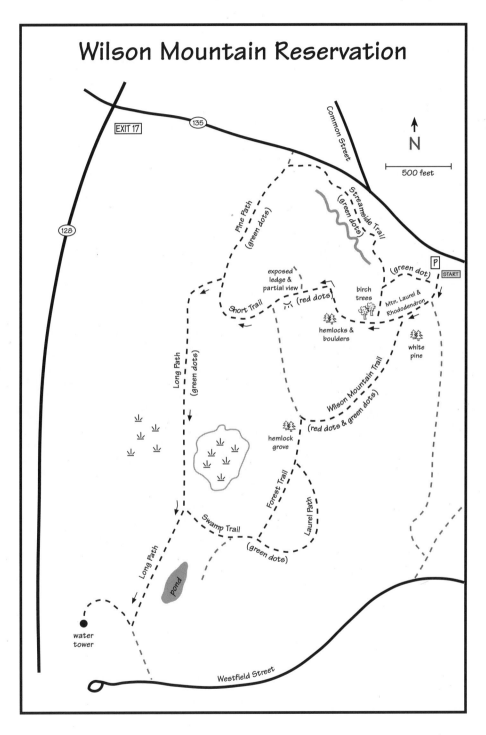

the fruit is dry and white. The painful rash can come from any part of the plant and even the smoke from burning poison ivy is poisonous.

Begin your walk by following the trail that starts behind the iron gate. The first part of the walk follows the red dots along the trail. Just thirty feet down the path is a side trail going off to your right leading into lowlands, but you should stay straight on the main trail. About fifty feet later the main trail splits at a granite marker and you should bear right, following the trail that leads uphill into a white pine grove. Rhododendron bushes grow in the shade on your right on the steep hillside. At the next fork in the trail, after a couple minutes more of walking, bear to the right. The pines are crowded together and consequently they grow tall and thin, with most of the branches near the upper part of the tree where they can receive some sunlight. If a pine is growing in an open field it will have filled out more evenly, with branches even at the lower levels because of unlimited sunshine.

About two minutes farther down the trail a side path comes in on the right by some birch trees. Stay straight, following the red dots uphill. On the right, where the hill slopes downward, a few mountain laurel bushes grow in the understory. Mountain laurel leaves are 3 to 4 inches long, dark green and glossy on the top, and yellow-green underneath. Mature leaves are thick and leathery. The saucer-shaped flowers, which bloom at the end of June, can vary from pink to white or various shades in between. In southern Connecticut, mountain laurel can reach heights of twenty feet, but in northern New England it is rare and much smaller.

Some of the more common birds you are likely to see along the path to Wilson Mountain include tufted titmice (small gray birds with tufted caps at the back of their heads), chickadees (black and white coloring), and nuthatches (usually on tree trunks looking for insects). Another common bird is the flicker. Flickers are about the size of blue jays with a brown back and a black breast crest. They are most easily identified, however, by the white rump seen in flight. While nuthatches usually work their way down a tree, flickers go up the trunk. They make their nests in tree cavities—just one more reason why dead standing timber is so important to birds.

As you continue on the trail, the pines give way to mixed woodlands of ash, maple, oak, hemlock, and birch. These trees, some quite large, provide the walker with almost total shade during periods of summer heat. Huge boulders, called glacial erratics because of the way they were haphazardly deposited by the glaciers, litter the forest floor. This northern face of the mountain will remind people of the forest more typical of northern New England than Massachusetts. Because this section does not receive the summer sun it is cooler and more moist than the other slopes of the mountain. Yellow birch, white birch, and hemlocks thrive here. Look for delicate pink lady's slippers growing beneath the trees, identified by their drooping slipper-shaped flowers. A member of the orchid family, lady's slippers are protected by law and should never be picked.

The trail soon makes a 90-degree turn to the left, roughly fifteen minutes after the start of the walk, and now becomes a more steep ascent up Wilson

*Although not really a mountain, the views from the summit are still worth the climb.*

Mountain. About fifty feet up the trail, it splits; bear left on the path that climbs to the exposed granite ledge. (Children will love climbing on the rocks.) After three minutes of picking your way through rocky terrain, you will arrive at the summit, a nice sunny spot to enjoy the warming rays and a view to the north. There is a partial view of the Boston skyline. The total walk to the summit from the parking lot is an easy twenty minutes. (At this point, if you are hiking with younger children, you may want to retrace your steps back to the parking lot or follow the red dots on the Wilson Mountain Trail back.

To continue the walk, follow the path behind the rocky summit, staying straight where a side trail comes in from the left. (That side trail leads to more exposed ledge, but there are no good views.) The trail you walk on is called the

Short Trail and is not marked by red dots. Oaks and maples dominate this section of woodlands with sassafras growing in the understory. Identified by its mitten-shaped leaves, the sassafras tree rarely grows taller than thirty feet, but there have been individual trees that have reached a height of eighty feet. The branches, leaves, and even the root are all aromatic.

It was on this trail that I once saw a pileated woodpecker, a large wood-pecker with a distinctive red crest at the back of the head. These uncommon birds are about the size of crows, and when they drum into a tree with their beaks in search of insects, it is quite loud at the beginning and softer at the end. Their call is always in a series, never a single call. They are a wary bird, and I've yet to get a great picture of one.

The Short Trail is fairly level for the first five minutes then it starts a gradual descent and in a couple minutes you will approach an intersection. Turn left here, heading into the southern end of the property, following the Long Path, marked by green dots. Although there are no unusual features or vistas, it's a pleasant walk through mixed woodlands with wetlands on either side of the path. Approximately ten minutes down the path is a fork; bear left, no longer following the green dots. After walking another ten minutes you will arrive at an intersection. To the right is a water tower and to the left is Westfield Street. From here retrace your steps back to the parking lot to complete a total walk of about an hour and a half. If you wish to vary your return trip, there are three different ways to do so. One option is to follow the green dots all the way back down the Long Path to the Pine Path and then onto the Streamside Path that brings you back to the parking lot (see map). The second option is to take the Swamp Trail to Laurel Path and then fol-low the Wilson Mountain Trail back to the parking lot. A third option is to retrace your steps back to the Short Trail and just before the Wilson Mountain summit, turn right on the Wilson Mountain Trail and follow the red dots back to the park-ing lot.

If you still have energy at the end of your hike try the Streamside Path that leaves from the parking area and follows two small brooks through the woods. Children will enjoy seeing the water and climbing on the rock ledges in the area.

## Getting There

From Route 128 take Exit 17 onto Route 135 east and go 0.7 mile into Dedham. Park at the second small lot on the right side of Route 135 (just after Common Street and before a ball field) where a sign welcomes you to the reservation.

Open dawn to dusk, seven days a week, year-round. Dogs must be on leash. No mountain biking. No admission fee; no facilities. MDC: 617-727-4573.

# Hemlock Gorge

## Needham/Newton

* 23 acres
* 1 mile
* 40 minutes
* Easy
* Great for children

## Highlights

* Steep gorge along Charles River, Echo Bridge, Mill Falls
* Huge hemlock trees

Situated on a rocky knoll above the Charles River on the Needham-Newton line, Hemlock Gorge is a natural oasis surrounded by development. It may be small, but the reservation has a wide variety of both man-made and natural wonders. Some of the attractions include the Charles River pouring over Mill Falls then passing beneath historic Echo Bridge and some enormous hemlock trees growing on the edge of the gorge.

The variety of trees and plants at the reservation includes mulberries; red pines; white pines; birch; beech; chestnut; witch hazel; rhododendron; mountain laurel; oaks; and of course, the majestic hemlocks. Treat yourself to a late spring-time walk here when the shrubs are blooming.

Enter the reservation from Central Avenue in Needham and follow the trail behind the steel gate. The trail splits in a hundred feet and you should bear right to see the falls. About two hundred feet farther a narrow trail on the left goes uphill, but you should stay straight and within a couple minutes you will reach an overlook above Mill Falls, the highest waterfall on the Charles. Also known as Upper Falls and Silk Mill Dam, it was first dammed in 1688. There have been sawmills, iron mills, and silk mills located here over the years. In the springtime or after heavy rains the water thunders over the dam in a spray of white mist. Perched above the falls, on the opposite side of the river, is the Mill Falls Restaurant. During the warm weather it's a nice place to relax with a drink, listening to and watching the cascade.

If you look to your left from the overlook you can see Echo Bridge. A short side trail leads down to the riverside where there is an even better view of the

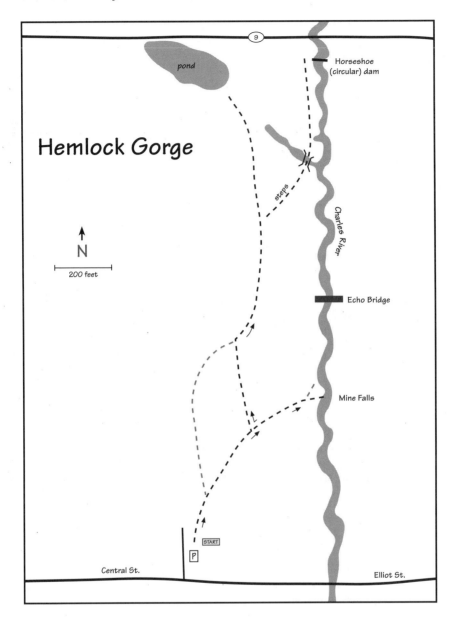

Hemlock Gorge

N

200 feet

pond

Horseshoe
(circular) dam

steps

Charles River

Echo Bridge

Mine Falls

START

P

Central St.

Elliot St.

bridge. This massive arch bridge, spanning the river, makes a great photo. Another interesting view is from the top of the bridge which is where our walk leads. Retrace your steps from the overlook to the narrow trail that leads uphill on your right. Follow this for a hundred feet and arrive at the top of Echo Bridge. The bridge has recently been restored and you can walk along its top to the center of the river for a bird's-eye view of the gorge. (The bridge has safety railings, but small children should be accompanied by an adult.) From this vantage point you get a good look at the mighty hemlock trees for which the gorge is named. It's fun to try and identify the various trees from this view where you can see treetops rather than the trunks. A fir tree come to a point at its top whereas the hemlock's crown is more spread out. This is also a good spot to observe bird life—on my last visit I watched crows harass a red-tailed hawk that was soaring above the gorge.

Echo Bridge was built in 1877 and at that time was the second largest masonry-arch bridge in the United States. This huge granite and brick structure was designated a National Historic Landmark in 1982. Charles Eliot, a famous architect who first proposed the creation of the Metropolitan Parks System at the turn of the century, described the bridge, gorge, and river as follows: "The narrow stream flows swift and dark between quaintly broken rocks, and the great stone arch which bears the Sudbury River aqueduct leaps boldly across from bank to bank." It truly is a handsome bridge, built at a time when engineers produced structures of both function and beauty.

*At the northern end of Hemlock Gorge, the
Charles River cascades over the Horseshoe Dam.*

Retrace your steps and turn right at the first intersection. Towering hemlock, beech, and oak shade the path. The large hemlocks here probably escaped the ax of earlier days because of the steepness of the terrain which made removing the trees by horse difficult. Almost every acre in Massachusetts has been cleared at one time or another for pastures, and there are only a few true old growth forests left in the state, most of which are in the mountains of the Berkshires.

Wildlife in this area includes chipmunks, squirrels, hawks, and a wide variety of smaller birds attracted by the combination of woods and water. Within the squirrel family the park has red squirrels, gray squirrels, and probably flying squirrels. Although flying squirrels don't fly, they can glide for long distances through the air. From a height of 60 feet they can soar for 150 feet by extending their spread legs and extending a membrane that acts like a wing. The membrane is supported by a spur of cartilage at the wrist that allows it to extend beyond the outstretched wrist. Even the tail is designed for soaring as it is both broad and flat. Flying squirrels can be identified by their white undersides, dark brown sides, and light brown backs. Their heads are blunt and round and their eyes wide. Because they are nocturnal few are ever seen as they spend the day sleeping in tree cavities.

At a fork in the trail go right and descend the steps that lead to the water's edge. A footbridge spans a cove, which appears to have been a sluiceway for another mill site. Cross the footbridge and follow the path that now is close to the water. Directly ahead you will see Route 9 and the uniquely shaped Circular Dam near the Wellesley border (also called Horseshoe Dam and Crescent Dam).

After viewing the Circular Dam, retrace your steps back over the footbridge, and up the steps. If you go right, the path follows the crest of the ridge. Notice how little vegetation can grow beneath the hemlocks. Due to the high acidity content of hemlock needles few plants can survive beneath these trees. The trail ends by a pond where two huge pines compete with the hemlocks for prominence.

To return to your car, simply retrace your steps. The entire walk is only about thirty-five or forty minutes but double that if you stop for picture taking, and triple the time if you're with children who will love climbing this hilly terrain.

In the late 1800s Hemlock Gorge was a popular site, with hundreds, and sometimes thousands of people visiting the woods and river on warm weekend days. This stretch of the Charles, with the steep gorge, has attracted people because of its uniqueness. It is unlike the meandering parts of the Charles found in most other places.

## Getting There

From Route 128 take Exit 19 (Highland Avenue/Needham). Follow Highland Avenue about 0.3 mile to first stop light by Muzi Ford, and turn right on Gould Street. Go 0.5 mile to the end of Gould Street. Turn right on Central Avenue and follow for 0.4 mile to sign and parking for Hemlock Gorge on the left.

From Route 9, turn off at the Newton Upper Falls exit and go south on Elliot Street then right onto Chestnut Street. At the next stop light go right onto Elliot Street which turns into Central Avenue on the other side of the river where there is parking.

No admission fee; no facilities; dogs allowed. Open dawn to dusk.

# Weston Reservoir

## Weston

---

* 2 miles
* 45 minutes
* Easy

---

## Highlight

* Circular trail around reservoir—great for a fast walk

The loop trail around Weston Reservoir is a popular spot for local walkers and joggers, offering a quiet pathway to enjoy fresh air, water views, and a chance to see wildlife. The reservoir is about the size of Walden Pond, about 50 acres, but you will encounter far fewer people. The loop trail around the reservoir is flat and wide, and because most of it is shaded by evergreen trees, this is a good choice for a summer walk.

From the parking area, cross Ash Street to the larger section of the reservoir and follow the path on the southeast side. It first passes through an open field, a good habitat to spot bluebirds. Bluebirds feed primarily on insects, scanning the ground from perches on tree branches. Look for the female with wings part blue and tail with gray on the back. The males can be identified by their deeper, more vivid blue feathers. Younger bluebirds are more difficult to distinguish, with more drab gray-brown coloring and spots like a thrush's. Thoreau, who hiked the fields of Concord and surrounding towns, described the bluebirds as carrying the "sky on their backs."

In about five minutes you reach the end of the open space and enter woods of cedar and pine. Look for chipmunks and red squirrels on the forest floor and in the trees gathering seeds and nuts. The reservoir will be on your left. Scan the water for ducks and the occasional great blue heron stalking the shoreline. Sometimes large white mute swans float on the surface, although they typically prefer more shallow areas with lots of vegetation. Introduced to America from Europe, the mute swan is a destructive bird, ripping aquatic plants from the water rather than nibbling on them. From the few birds that escaped from captivity in the 1800s there are now more than 10,000 mute swans on the eastern seaboard, aggressively driving out native ducks and geese. Extremely territorial, mute swans will attack almost anything coming within their territory. In some New England

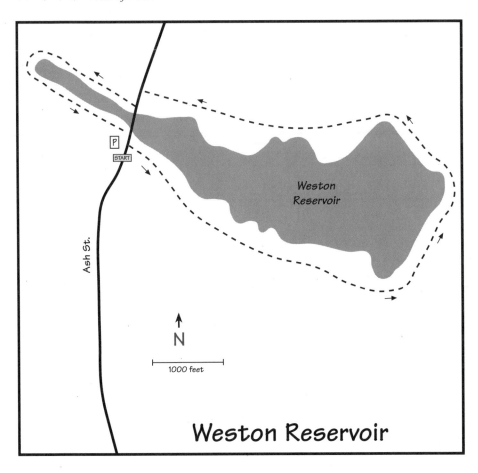

Weston Reservoir

states wildlife biologists shake or puncture swan eggs to keep them from hatching in an effort to control the burgeoning population.

The far end of the pond (about a twenty-minute walk) is the halfway point and the trail swings around the eastern edge of the pond then heads back toward the parking area. You will soon pass a low-lying section with some wetlands, and if mosquitoes are active, this place can be bothersome. At various intervals small streams feed the reservoir and the woods serve as an important buffer of protection from roadside automotive pollutants for the watershed.

Because the trail is popular with local walkers and joggers your best opportunity for seeing wildlife is in the early morning. You might see a deer, fox, cottontail, or even an owl. Great horned owls are deadly hunters at night, descending on rabbits, opossum, and even skunks. They are one of the few predators of skunks, and if you are in the woods and smell a skunk try looking up. You just might see a great horned owl with a skunk gripped in its talons.

When you reach the parking lot after about forty minutes of walking, you can extend your walk by circling the narrow portion of the reservoir on the west side of Ash Street. A plantation of cedar trees extends in a line on either side of the trail. Beyond the cedars, on the right side, are spruce and red pine, with younger white pines mixing in with these planted trees. Look for more common birds here, such as titmice, chickadees, and blue jays—all are hardy species that stay in New England through the winter.

On the loop back toward Ash Street there are three rows of handsome cedars, one on the right and two on the left, with mixed woodlands beyond. Red cedars are small evergreens that seldom grow more than thirty to forty feet tall. Their fruit is globular in shape, whitish to blue to purple, and eaten by many animals. Red cedar wood is soft, light, and fragrant, and frequently used in closets, where it provides protection from the house moth. The walk around this narrow western section of the reservoir adds another fifteen minutes to your outing.

## More Weston Walks

Cat Rock Reservation, located at the end of Drabbington Road in the northeast section of Weston, has an excellent trail system for walking, running, and cross-country skiing. Approximately 80 acres of open space await your discovery. Old stone

*The reservoir is ringed by evergreens and is always a quiet spot for walking.*

walls crisscross the woods. On the northern end of the property is secluded Hobbs Pond, where water tumbles over a dam. As you face the pond from the dam, turn left and follow the trail into the field. Wildflowers grow beneath blue spruce, making this meadow especially colorful in the summer.

Another nice walk is just off Church Street, where the old Weston Train Station still stands. Trails traverse streams and meander through woods of enormous hemlocks.

(The Weston Forest and Trails Association has produced an excellent trail map for all of Weston's open space. It can be purchased at the town hall.)

## Getting There

From Route 128 take the Route 30 exit (Exit 24) and go west. Follow Route 30 1.9 miles to Ash Street. Turn right on Ash Street and proceed 0.7 mile to parking area on the left.

No admission fee; no facilities; dogs allowed.

# Case Estates

## *Weston*

---

* 100 acres (approx.)
* 1 mile
* 1 hour
* Easy
* Great for children

---

## *Highlights*

- Thousands of flowers and plants
- Forest and field trails
- Unique stone wall
- Enormous specimen trees
- Nearby organic farm

For those who love nature's color, a visit to the Case Estates in late spring is a special treat. As a satellite garden and nursery to the Arnold Arboretum, the Case Estates feature a wide variety of flowers, shrubs, and trees scattered throughout acres of fields and woodlands. Although this walk runs a little more than a mile, you could easily stroll for hours, extending your walk into the woods at the west end of the property or into nearby Case Field.

The walk begins at the parking lot by the red barn, where a gravel path first circles a white ash tree and then intersects a rutted road that has grass in the middle. Turn right on this road and follow it in a northwesterly direction into the fields. There is a beautiful white birch growing in the field on the right, and on the left is a beehive-shaped stone incinerator built in 1924. Stumps and brush are now burned in the incinerator and the wood ashes are then used as organic fertilizer in the fields.

During a morning walk I once saw a red fox trot across the field. Foxes hunt rabbits and mice, and often prowl the edge of meadows at dawn or dusk in search of prey. To watch a fox hunt mice is absolutely fascinating, particularly when the fox springs straight up into the air and tries to come down on a mouse or vole. Look in the grass for the one and half inch wide tunnels made by the voles. Notice

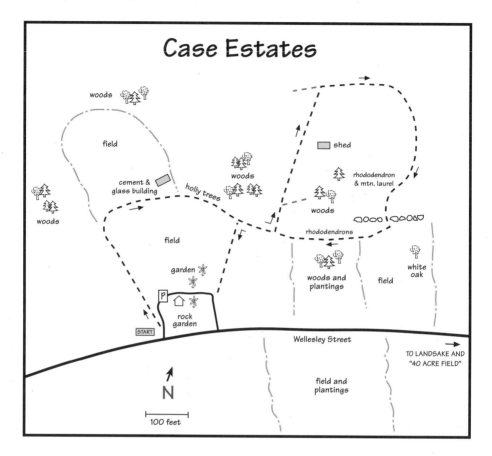

# Case Estates

that instead of pushing the grass aside, voles construct these tunnels by boring through the grass. These one ounce rodents are also hunted by owls, hawks, snakes, and coyotes.

Just past the stone structure, turn right onto a trail that heads into the field and then passes behind a small cement building with glass windows. Next, the trail skirts the edge of the woods, where you will notice a few American holly trees with their shiny green foliage and bright red berries, which are eaten by songbirds, bobwhites, and wild turkey. Distinguishing features of the holly are the prickly leaves which are evergreens; they brighten up the forest even in the snow. Continue to follow this trail for about four minutes, ignoring side trails, until you come to a wooden sign with an arrow and #7 written on it. The arrow points left into the woods and you should go that way. The trail forks in about 15 yards and you should stay left, passing rhododendron bushes and a small shed. The forest is almost exclusively white pine, identified by their long, straight trunks and slender, green needles. Look for the delicate pink flowers of lady's slippers growing beneath the pines in the late spring. Trillium, trout lily, and other wildflowers that grow in woodland shade are scattered about.

After passing the shed, the trail continues in a northerly direction through the woods for another five minutes of walking before you reach an intersection. Turn right here. This trail loops around the northeast end of the property, passing behind a school, then curving into a plantation of rhododendron, azaleas, and mountain laurel. There is a small grassy opening here with benches for resting. This is a quiet, charming spot that explodes with color in the late spring. A few white birch trees contrast beautifully with the dense green foliage of the bushes.

When you are ready to leave this special spot, follow the path to the south, which leads through an enormous wooden gate within an even bigger stone wall. This stone wall, built in 1911, is said to be the longest freestanding dry wall of native stones in New England. The rocks are laid horizontally in the wall, except for the top layer, which has been placed vertically, making for an interesting pattern. Examining the wall you will see the details of the craftsmanship and the

*Try and visit the Case Estates in June when many of the plants are in bloom.*

many fist-sized stones that fill the cracks. Hardy daylilies grow along the base of the wall.

After you pass through the gate and into a field, turn right along the path but take a moment to observe the huge white oak with drooping branches growing out in the field. The path you are on follows the edge of the field then turns back into the woods. Here the path is lined by twenty-foot-tall rhododendron bushes, giving it the look of a tunnel. The trail follows a southwesterly route and soon you will see the barn and parking area.

Before you leave take time to visit the general nursery area. Some of the plants grown here are tested for hardiness, since Weston winters average 13 degrees colder than at the Arnold Arboretum in Jamaica Plain.

Each month ushers in a new bloom: in April, look for magnolias, forsythias, daffodils, cherries; in May, look for crab apples, lady's slippers, azaleas, dogwoods, daffodils; in June, look for rhododendrons, mountain laurel, iris, daylilies, peonies; in July, look for hostas, clematis, perennials; in August, look for perennials; and in September, look for franklinias and asters.

More fields await your discovery on the other side of Wellesley Street. Also nearby is Case Field owned by the town of Weston and farmed by Land's Sake, a private nonprofit organization that grows organic produce. It is located where Wellesley Street intersects School Street, about a quarter mile north of the Case Estates. Case Field was formerly owned by the Arnold Arboretum and still has beautiful specimen trees. Some of the trees you will see include Norway maple, pagoda tree, mountain ash, weeping willow, golden larch, magnolia, honey locust, sugar maple, silver bell, Sargent's Cherry, Scots pine, and linden tree. There is also a spectacular dawn redwood that originated in the prehistoric forest of 50 million years ago.

Case Field is managed by the Weston Conservation Commission and is open to the public. Be sure to check out the fantastic view from the stone wall near Newton Street overlooking the field and trees.

(Many of the programs offered by the Arnold Arboretum are presented at the Case Estates and walking tours are available by reservation. For more information call the Arnold Arboretum at 617-524-1718.)

## Getting There

From Route 128 exit onto Route 20 West and proceed to the stop lights where a sign reads "Regis College/Route 30." Take this left and proceed 0.7 miles to where the road forks. (Land's Sake will be on your left.) Bear right onto Wellesley Street and go 0.3 mile to entrance on the right. There is a small black "Case Estates" sign.

From the Massachusetts Turnpike take the Route 30/Weston exit. Go west on Route 30 for 2.5 miles and then turn right onto Wellesley Street. The Case Estates are 1 mile further on the right.

No admission fee; no facilities; dogs must be leased. Open year-round dawn to dusk.

# Southeastern Massachusetts

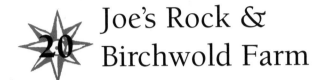

## 20 Joe's Rock & Birchwold Farm

### *Wrentham*

---

* ✴ 140 acres
* ✴ 2 miles
* ✴ 1.5 hours
* ✴ Easy
* ✴ Great for children

---

## Highlights

* Pond
* Hilltop view
* Unusual tree
* Fields
* Climbing rocks for children

Joe's Rock and Birchwold Farm are two lesser known conservation areas situated next to each other along West Street (Route 121) in Wrentham. They are easily accessible from Route 495, and offer something for everyone. The properties, owned by the Wrentham Conservation Commission, feature a hilltop with scenic views, two small ponds, streams, meadows, and woods. Children will love the easy climb to the overlook known as Joe's Rock, as well as the footbridge and boulders at Birchwold Farm.

First we explore Joe's Rock, on the north side of Route 121. From the parking lot follow the main trail that heads in a northerly direction, crossing over a small stream. In a few feet you will see a pond ahead; the trail forks here. Bear right, keeping the pond on your left. You will pass a stone wall and picnic table on

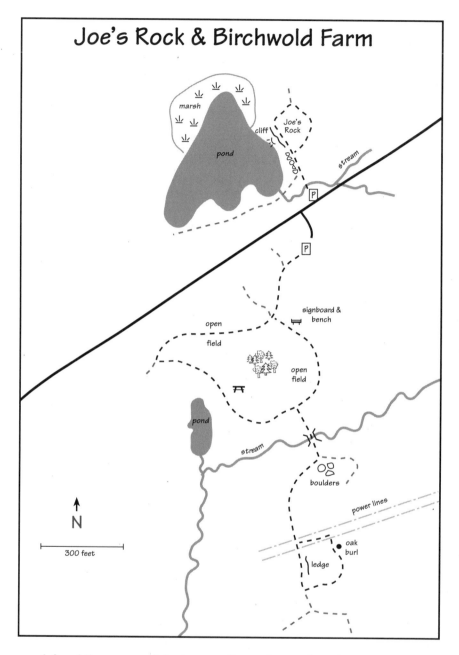

# Joe's Rock & Birchwold Farm

your left, while to your right is a small meadow with cedars and apple trees. (Cedars provide food in the form of berries for birds such as cedar waxwings.)

Within three or four minutes the trail begins to climb Bucks Hill. There will be another fork in the path. The trail to the right makes a gradual climb up the hill and the one to the left makes a direct climb that is steeper, but is still a quicker way to the summit. Our walk goes to the left, and within two or three minutes you will arrive at Joe's Rock, an exposed ledge of granite. The cliff rises 150 feet from the edge of the pond below. The *Wrentham Guide to Open Space* says that the cliff has been called one of the most interesting features in this corner of southeastern Massachusetts from a geologic and aesthetic viewpoint.

Joe's Rock has an elevation of 490 feet and has a great view to the southwest. Surprisingly, only one house is visible. In the foreground is a small pond with a marsh at its northwestern end, and in the distance are low rolling hills that stretch into Rhode Island. You might see a broad-winged hawk or red-tailed hawk floating above the pond. Osprey, identified by the crook in their wings and white underbelly, may circle near the summit, perhaps scanning the pond's surface for signs of fish. The osprey is also known as fish hawk, because it uses its sharp talons and keen eyesight to pluck unsuspecting fish from the water below.

By retracing your steps off the summit and toward the parking lot, you will pass a trail on your right just after the southern end of the pond. This follows the edge of the pond, where you will pass an earthen dike indicating that the pond was man-made. Many years ago cranberries were cultivated here, and there is evidence of a dam at the southern end of the pond. The pond is now a good birding spot in the warm-weather months, and a popular ice-skating site in the winter.

The path along this southern end of the pond was once an old stage coach road. It leads through pine woodlands for an eighth of a mile before ending at private property. There are a couple openings along the path that offer good views of the pond. To return to the parking lot simply retrace your steps to the main trail and turn right.

## Birchwold Farm

To explore Birchwold Farm, cross West Street (be careful of traffic), and walk a few feet west (to your right) to an entrance road and parking area. A wooden marker and arrow indicate the start of a trail that first passes a hundred feet through the woods and then leads to an open field (good for cross-country skiing in the winter). If you are the first person at the field in the morning approach quietly; there is a good chance of seeing rabbit, groundhog, or red fox. During winter months the field is crisscrossed with animal tracks in the snow, so you might want to bring a tracking field guide.

Follow the trail on your left that skirts the edge of the field. In a hundred feet you will come to a bench and signboard which explains the history of the property. (Birchwold Farm was formerly a dairy farm which was purchased by the town of Wrentham in 1985 and is now conservation land.) Aspens, also known as poplar, mix with the cedars, oaks, and small shrubs along the meadow's edge. A wide variety of birds find the habitat to their liking; look for bluebirds, mockingbirds, finches, and tree swallows. American kestrels, members of the falcon family, prefer this open terrain from which to hunt. The kestrel has a rust-colored back with a lighter belly and is about 8 inches long with a 21-inch wingspan. Males are especially handsome with a touch of blue on the wings. Kestrels are often seen

*Kids will enjoy climbing the rock ledges at Birchwold Farm.*

perched on dead tree limbs or telephone wires, surveying the field for insects and small birds to feed on. (The fields are occasionally mowed to improve wildlife habitat.)

After walking five minutes along the edge of the field the trail forks. Turn left and cross the footbridge that spans a small stream. This area is a big hit with young children. They can explore the stream and climb the boulders that form a thirty-foot hill directly across from the bridge. There is a small cluster of beech trees around the rocks. In the fall the beech leaves first turn gold then a rich copper color. Some of the leaves stay on the lower branches during the winter, making for a beautiful contrast against the tree's smooth gray trunk and branches.

To continue the walk, follow the path to the right of the boulders. You'll enter an area of small trees, primarily white pines and cedars. About a hundred feet farther you will reach a set of power lines in an open area. Turn left here and follow the trail paralleling the power lines for another hundred feet until a side trail leads to the right where a wooden post has been placed. Take this right, passing beneath the power lines. As soon as the trail enters the woods be on the lookout for an unusual growth on an oak tree adjacent to the path. The growth or bulge in the tree measures roughly two feet by three feet, and is at eye level. Its proper name is a burl, one of nature's oddities.

Continue on this trail, over a ridge for a couple hundred feet, until the trail ends at a T-intersection where you should turn right. This marks the halfway point in the walk, and from here on you will be looping back to the parking area. On the right is an exposed granite ledge with small patches of quartz mixed. This is another great place for both children and adults to explore. The ledge rises above the trail roughly forty feet, but there are footholds so that it can be climbed. About halfway up notice the white pine that seems to be growing out of the rock. At the summit of the cliff children will enjoy pushing on the four-foot boulder that seems to be positioned to roll off the hill. It is probably a glacial erratic, deposited here as the glaciers retreated roughly ten thousand years ago. While the boulder may look like it can be rolled, it has probably not moved an inch since the ice age.

Continue the walk by following the trail beneath the power lines where it will intersect with the original trail that first left the field and crossed the brook. Retrace your steps, and when you reach the field, go left to complete a loop of this open area. Two picnic tables are in the middle of the field—the perfect place to rest and snack. Another good spot for resting is just up ahead on the left, at a bench overlooking a small pond fringed with cattails at its northern end.

To return simply continue on the trail and bear right at the next fork. This will lead you across the field and back toward the parking area.

## Getting There

From Route 495, take the King Street/Franklin exit. Head toward Pawtucket (southwest) and just a hundred feet from the highway exit, turn left onto Upper Union Street. Follow Upper Union Street (it will turn into Arnold Street) 2.9 miles to its end at West Street/Route 121. Turn right onto West Street/Route 121 and proceed 0.8 mile to the parking lot on the right. (Joe's Rock is on the north side of West Street and Birchwold Farm is across the street.)

No admission fee; no facilities; dogs allowed. Open dawn to dusk.

# Franklin
# State Forest

## *Franklin*

---

* 1.5 mile
* 45 minutes
* Easy

---

## Highlights

- Loop Trail through forest
- Beech and white pine trees
- Stone walls

Franklin is one of the fastest growing towns in Massachusetts, and the increased development has made the Franklin State Forest an oasis of green in this suburban town. The walk described here is not as scenic as most of the other outings in this book, but it does offer a convenient place to exercise in a wooded setting. The mile and a half trail offers a brisk walk in woodlands that receive few visitors.

From the State Forest sign on Grove Street you will see the trail leading uphill behind the sign. It is marked by small metal blue triangles nailed to trees. White pines and oaks line the trail, keeping it mostly shaded during warm weather. Before the Europeans arrived in America, enormous old-growth white pines stretched across the east and it was said a squirrel could hop from the crown of one white pine to another all the way from the Atlantic to the Mississippi without ever touching the ground. But by the end of the 1800s, almost every single acre of virgin pine had been cut for lumber and to make pastureland for sheep and cattle. The trees before you, although tall, are probably no more than 50 to 60 years old.

During the month of May, look for the delicate pink flowers of lady's slippers growing beneath the pines. The lady's slippers flower is a veined pouch, with two oval leaves at its base. The pink lady's slipper, also called the moccasin-flower, grows on a stem about a foot tall. This member of the orchid family prefers acidic soil like the areas where acidic pine needles have dropped. Trillium, another acid-loving wildflower, often grows alongside lady's slippers; it has a smaller flower with three leaves below.

About ten minutes into the walk you will pass a few houses on the right; then the trail passes through an opening in a stone wall. Take a moment to exam-

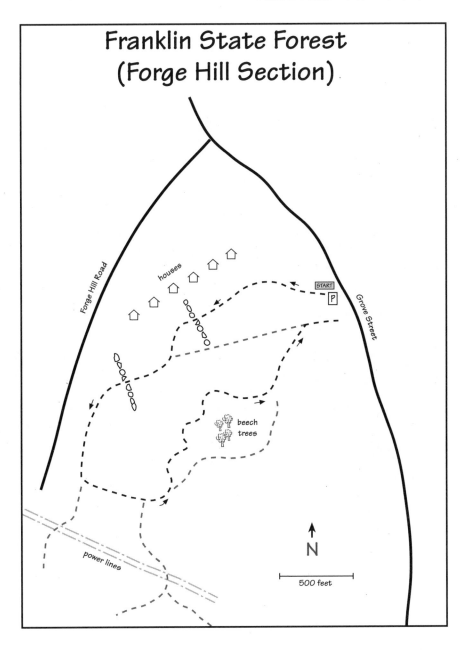

# Franklin State Forest
# (Forge Hill Section)

ine the size of the stones used to construct the wall. Farmers used "stone boats," simple flat wooden sleds on which rocks were piled and slid on the grass, to clear the land.

Stone walls were used as depositories for rocks cleared from the bony New England soil. The walls served as both boundary markers and as fencing to keep

*Oak and pine woodlands await exploration at Franklin State Forest.*

sheep and cattle from wandering. Some farmers used tree stumps, set upside down with roots stretching out, as fencing.

Twenty feet after passing through the stone wall a trail goes off to the left but continue ahead, bearing right. The trail passes by a few more houses on the right before curving deeper into the woods then through another stone wall. The woods here are almost exclusively comprised of white pine, and a bench for resting is located in the pine grove along the side of the trail. Be on the lookout for white-tailed deer, fox, coyote, and partridge. The eastern coyote is a relative newcomer in Massachusetts, having migrated into the state in the 1950s. Coyote have been steadily expanding their range, and have even been seen on Cape Cod. They are intelligent animals, and very adaptable, learning to live and even prosper alongside human development. Coyote's normal diet includes small mammals, birds, fruits and berries, and just about anything else it stumbles upon. They often hunt and travel in packs, with a distinct pecking order among members. A coyote den is often located near rocky ledges and may have more than one entrance. Like foxes, coyotes will use the abandoned dens of other animals. A mother coyote will often move newborn pups from one den to another for extra protection.

Soon you will see the power lines through the trees directly ahead. Our walk continues to follow the blue triangles which line the path to your left; you may want to check out the area beneath the power lines for any signs of wildlife. Birds feed in the open area, and hawks, such as kestrels, often survey the ground from the power line poles. You could extend your walk by following the dirt road beneath the power lines toward the southeast and then turning right on a path that reenters pine woods laced with more stone walls. (Avoid this area during hunting season.)

Back on the blue triangle trail, follow it parallel to the high-tension lines in a southeasterly direction then stay on the path as it curves to the left away from the power lines. The trail begins to zigzag through the woods and soon enters a stand of young beech trees. When they grow on rocky slopes such as this they tend to form pure stands. The bark of the beech is very smooth and is a light gray color with the occasional dark patch. Leaves are oval-shaped with sharp-toothed margins. The small nuts that fall from the beech trees are a valuable food for wildlife from birds to bears.

This is a beautiful spot in the winter with the gray trunks of the beeches rising from the white snow, and paper-thin brown leaves clinging to lower branches. Even on dark, dreary days these beech trees seem to brighten up the woods with their silvery bark.

After leaving the beech grove the trail begins to wind downhill, then merges with another trail just a couple minutes before reaching the pull-off to the parking area. The total walk is about forty-five minutes.

## Getting There

If coming from the south on Route 495 take the King Street/Franklin exit. Go west on King Street (away from the center of Franklin) and travel 1.6 miles. Turn right onto Grove Street and proceed 1.8 miles to the State Forest sign on the left side of the road. Park on the side of the road.

If coming from the north on Route 495 take the Franklin/Route 140 exit. Go toward Bellingham (northwest on Route 140) about 100 feet from exit and turn left on Grove Street. Follow Grove Street 0.7 mile to pull-off and State Forest sign on the right.

No admission fee; no facilities; dogs allowed. Open dawn to dusk.

# Blue Hills Reservation

## Quincy/Milton/Randolph

---

* More than 7,000 acres
* 2 miles
* 1.5 hours
* Moderate
* Great for children

---

### Highlights

* Hilltop views
* Rigorous climbs
* Forest
* Excellent nature center
* More than 125 miles of trails

Blue Hills has so many trails it was difficult to choose a single walk. The walk selected here is to the summit and observation tower, chosen because of the tremendous view and the variety of woodlands passed along the way. Best of all, the parking area for this hike is adjacent to the Trailside Museum, which is popular with children. The trails in this chapter are popular on the weekends, so visit early on a Sunday morning to have the summit of Blue Hill to yourself. If you are hiking with young children you might want to go only part way up the hill or reverse the walk and go up the gentler incline first. Another option is to walk up the Summit Road, which is closed to traffic (see map). Children age six and up should have no trouble with the climb. Just bring water, snacks, and take rests whenever the child shows signs of fatigue. Remember, you don't want to carry your child all the way down.

Begin your walk from the trailhead that starts at the parking lot just to the right of the Trailside Museum (as you face it from the street). There is a signboard, and red dots on trees mark the trail. This is the most direct route to the summit and it rises steeply in some places. In some sections logs are imbedded in the ground to serve as stairs. White pine, maple, beech, oak, and hickory shade the path. On your right is the open slopes of the Blue Hill Ski Area.

# Blue Hills
## (Western Section by Trailside Museum)

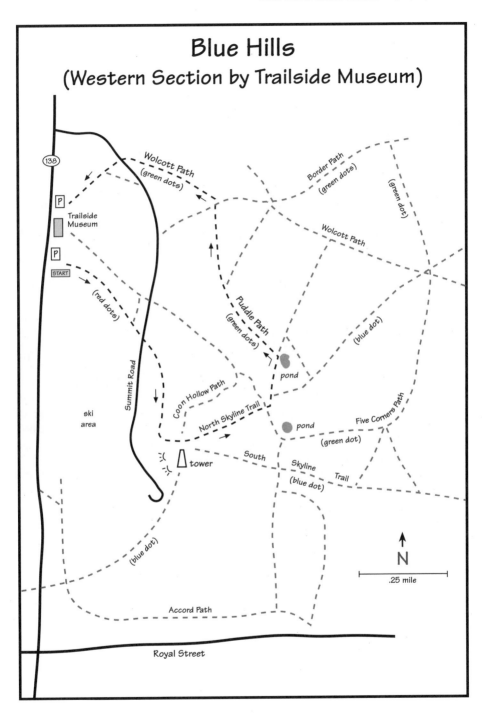

There are exposed ledges of granite to pick your way over and children love the challenge of "mountain climbing." This is a great place to introduce children to mountainous hikes, without taxing their endurance. Be sure to stop every now and then after the first ten minutes of climbing both to catch your breath and to admire the view of the Boston skyline over your shoulder. The birch trees growing in this rocky soil are mostly gray birch which are among the first trees to colonize an area of poor soil or a section of land where a fire has destroyed a more mature forest.

Red paint dots mark the climb. About fifteen minutes into the hike you will cross a narrow trail and then cross the paved Summit Road. Then proceed through an area of red pine. They can be distinguished from the more common white pine because their needles are thicker and a bit longer, and the bark of the red pine is lighter with a rusty hue.

Keep following the red dots and at about the 25- to-30 minute mark you will arrive at the stone observation tower. The tower is called the Eliot Tower after famed landscape architect and lover of open spaces, Charles Eliot. (There are two picnic benches beneath the shelter of the tower structure.) Low-bush blueberries grow in sunny spots, and in autumn their scarlet leaves contrast nicely with the gray bedrock. During the spring and fall migration of hawks, the summit of Blue Hill provides a good vantage point to watch them wing their way. Early September is usually the best time for a successful hawk watch. Go on days when the wind is out of the north or west, this helps propel the hawks (mostly broadwings) on their southerly journey.

The summit of Blue Hill is 635 feet and provides for sweeping vistas of Boston and the ocean beyond. But it is the trees and hilltops in the foreground that will capture your attention. From this vantage point it's interesting to see the patterns of tree species, particularly in the fall when the rusty-colored oaks dominate with patches of hemlock and white pine scattered about the hills.

The Massachusetts tribe of Native Americans lived by the Blue Hills and the word Massachusetts means "people of the great hill." The area was ideally situated for Native Americans because of its close proximity to the ocean and the Neponset River, its high vantage points, and the quarry materials (brown volcanic rock or hornfels) used to make tools and weapons. Later, the granite hills at the east end of the reservation were quarried for their granite. In 1825, a large-scale quarry produced granite for buildings, monuments, and fortifications across the nation. The top of Blue Hill also was the scene of one of the first weather observatories in the country, when in 1885 meteorologist Abbott Lawrence Rotch established his wind-swept outpost to conduct weather-related experiments.

Although the most direct route back to the parking area is on another section of the red dot trail called the Corn Hollow Path, you may want a more gradual descent in a northwesterly direction. Follow the North Skyline Trail (so marked on a granite post), which begins near the back of the tower. The trail is marked by blue dots, but be aware that the South Skyline Trail is also marked by blue dots. As you descend on the North Skyline Trail you will have partial views of the surrounding hills, which will give you an appreciation for just how large the reservation is. The footing on the trail can be a bit tricky because of the many small rocks and steepness.

After ten minutes of walking you will reach an intersection. Take the second left onto a trail called the Puddle Path, which is marked by both blue and green dots. (Do not take the first hard left on the unmarked trail going uphill.) In thirty feet the blue dot trail goes to the right but you should stay straight on the Puddle Path, following the green dots. In a couple minutes you will come to a fork in the trail. Go left, continuing to follow the green dots. The reservation has both large wildlife, such as deer, fox, coyote, and raccoon, and the smaller wildlife that we sometime overlook: insects, salamanders, and common birds.

The Puddle Path is a wide trail passing through an area of handsome beech trees. Even in the dead of winter the lower branches of the beech trees still are cov-

*The otters at the Trailside Museum are a big hit with children and adults.*

ered with paper-thin tan leaves, which do not fall off until new growth begins in the spring. In ten minutes you will pass an unmarked trail on the right, and in five more minutes you will begin to notice hemlock seedlings followed by a large hemlock with sweeping branches on the right. The hemlock needles are only about a quarter inch long and have rounded edges. More hemlocks shade the path ahead before the trail comes to a T-intersection. Turn left here on the wide Wolcott Path, ignoring the narrow trail also on the left just before the T-intersection. In five minutes the trail crosses the Summit Road and in another three or four minutes you will arrive back at the parking lot and the museum.

Outside the Trailside Museum is a water-filled pool and pen, which is the home to two otters. Spend some time here, as the otters put on quite a show, sliding down the chute, diving beneath the water, and rolling on the surface. (I once had the rare experience of coming upon three otters on a river, and was able to watch them play what appeared to be a game of tag by a large boulder.) Next to the otter pen are other pens for injured wildlife, such as deer, turkey, hawks, and owls. Inside the Trailside Museum there are interpretive exhibits such as a wigwam and live animals including a timber rattlesnake, a copperhead, and snapping turtle. (The museum's phone number is 617-333-0690.)

Be sure to make repeat visits to the reservation to travel the trails to the east of the Great Blue Hill. You might want to consider making an all-day hike with a friend, leaving one car at the opposite end of the reservation. The Skyline Trail is approximately 14 miles long, and some hikers use this as a training ground to get in shape before they climb the White Mountains of New Hampshire. Several great views can be seen from the Skyline Trail. (The entrance off Chickatabet Street was recommended by park rangers as a less traveled section of the reservation.)

A complete map of the reservation can be purchased for $1.00 in the museum.

## Getting There

From Route 128 take Exit 2B (Route 138 North) and go 1 mile to parking lot on the right adjacent to the Trailside Museum.

Museum hours: Tuesday–Sunday, 10 A.M. to 5 P.M. Closed Mondays.

Reservation open dawn to dusk, seven days a week. No admission fee. Hiking boots rather than sneakers are recommended. Dogs allowed on leash. MDC/Blue Hills: 617-698-1802.

# 23 Ponkapoag Pond

## (Part of the Blue Hills Reservation)
## Canton

---

* 4 miles (around pond)
* 2 hours
* Easy
* Boardwalk is good for children (This can be reached in a 1 mile round-trip walk.)

---

## Highlights

* Pond
* Loop trail
* Atlantic white cedar bog

Due to its location near Route 128, Ponkapoag Pond is a popular hiking, cross-country skiing, and mountain biking destination. If you come here on a weekday, however, the reservation is usually free of people, even after work. Ponkapoag has wide, well-maintained trails through primarily level terrain. The main trail makes a loop of 200-acre Ponkapoag Pond and a unique Atlantic white cedar bog, located on the property's northwest side. The pond attracts all sorts of wildlife, including ospreys and great blue herons.

There are three different entrances to this section of the Blue Hills Reservation, which is run by the Metropolitan District Commission. One entrance is on Randolph Street in Canton (which has good parking); another entrance is off Exit 3 from Route 128, which has limited parking; and the most popular entrance is through the MDC/Ponkapoag Golf Course. The loop trail around the pond is about a four-mile walk. This is a good deal of walking, and it's easy to get lost at the back end of the pond; so bring a bottle of water and begin your hike well before evening. It is possible to view the pond and tour the bog without doing the entire loop.

From the parking lot of the golf course, look for a paved road on the right side of the buildings, which passes through the fairways (no cars allowed). It is easy to spot the entrance to this road; just look for the row of stately sugar maples

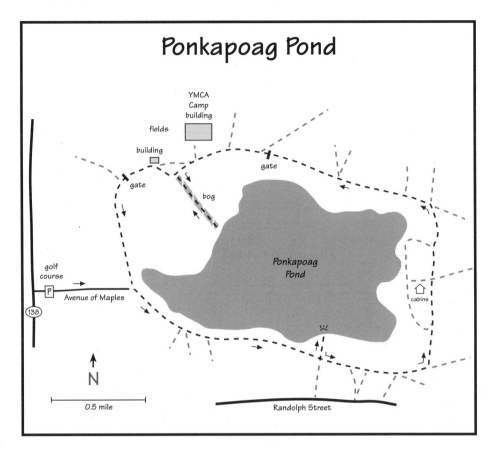

that line it. Appropriately enough, the road is called the Avenue of the Maples. Walk down this road, through the golf course, and to the edge of Ponkapoag Pond. The paved road ends here and a wide, well-maintained dirt road circles the pond. If you go left you can reach the quaking bog, after a short walk of about half a mile. This would be a good ramble with young children. The boardwalk leading into the bog begins opposite a ballfield and some cabins operated by the YMCA. (More information about the bog later.)

The following directions take you completely around the pond. At the end of the Avenue of the Maples go right on the dirt road. The terrain at Ponkapoag is fairly level and most trails are wide, making this a good spot for mountain biking and cross-country skiing as well as hiking. The trail hugs the edge of the pond, offering plenty of spots to get to the shoreline. Great blue heron frequent the pond, which is not surprising, due to the abundance of warm-water fish. Both the heron and anglers try their skill for largemouth bass and pickerel, but the heron tend to fish for those under five inches! Shore-bound anglers have the best chance of catching fish in the spring when the fish look for warm, shallow water to either spawn or feed. A quiet approach is needed so you do not alert the fish. Sometimes bass are near the shore if there are weeds or fallen weeds to provide cover. You can also fish on the pond. All kinds of lures are effective, but rubber worms are a favorite choice of many anglers. Children can use a simple garden worm on a hook—the fish tend to hook themselves. If you bring a canoe down to the pond (via Randolph Street) try the section of the pond farthest from the golf course. And please remember to practice catch and release to preserve the fishing for future generations.

Back on the trail look for skunk cabbage, one of the first harbingers of spring. It has large, cabbage-like leaves, and sometimes grows right through late-season snow, melting it with its energy. It has an odor quite similar to a skunk. During the summer months the odor of the skunk cabbage along the trail is replaced by the pleasant fragrance of the sweet pepperbush. You can identify the plant by the tiny clusters of white flowers at the end of the branches growing in a dense, slender spike. The plant reaches heights of ten feet and has narrow green leaves.

Osprey occasionally stop at the Ponkapoag, so be sure to bring binoculars. They are migrating birds, and spring and fall offer the best opportunities for sighting one. The sight of an osprey diving from the sky to snatch a fish is a scene you will never forget. The osprey skims low over the water and grabs the fish with its talons. (I once saw a bald eagle harass an osprey into dropping its catch and the eagle caught the fish in mid-air, claiming it for its own.) Migrating black red-winged blackbirds also descend upon the pond, and in the springtime you can see the red-shouldered males arrive first in huge flocks. They explore the entire shoreline as they wait for female birds. Mosquitoes also inhabit the reservation—so come prepared.

The first mile of the pond trail has rich, moist soil. Trees normally associated with more northern forests can be found here. Yellow birch, hemlock, maples, and beech grow above the ferns below. The trees are quite large, but most of them are probably under a hundred years old. As with most of Massachusetts, early settlers cleared the forests to make pastures and farmland, and used the wood for lumber and fuel. Sadly, there are no significant tracks of virgin forests left in the state and many areas have been harvested more than once. As farming moved westward toward the Mississippi and fossil fuel replaced wood as a heating source, the forests of New England were allowed to make a comeback. Still, we don't have the huge trees that the first explorers had seen. They described the woods as "park-like" because the trees were so massive they blocked out all sunlight from reaching the understory—barely any brush or saplings grew beneath them. In small areas, Native Americans would also burn undergrowth to improve hunting.

A little more than a half mile down the trail circling the pond is an open beach area. There is a nice view of the Blue Hill across the water. The road opposite the beach leads to Randolph Street. This entrance is also known as Fisherman's Landing, because cartop boats can be carried down the path and launched. (The entrance off Randolph Street is right next to Temple Beth David, across the street

*Woodland trails circle Ponkapoag Pond.*

from Westdale Road. This is a good place to park if you want to bypass the golf course, but it also bypasses the beautiful Avenue of the Maples.)

As the trail passes around the back of the pond, blue diamond markers attached to trees help keep you on the main path. Cottages managed by the Appalachian Mountain Club are located here, and the side roads can get a bit confusing. The trails going to the left lead to the cabins, so stay to the right. At the third trail juncture you will go down a steep hill where a map is posted. The path is noticeably rougher in this area. Soon the trail intersects with another and you should go left, following the blue markers. Finally you will come to a gate where you turn left again.

You are now at the north side of the pond. The YMCA Outdoor Center is located a little farther down the trail. The boardwalk to the bog is opposite the ballfield. Because of the bog's unique ecosystem, it has been designated a National Environmental Study Area. A beautiful stand of Atlantic white cedars grows here, along with such carnivorous plants as the unusual pitcher plant. Because the nutrients in the bog soil are relatively sterile, pitcher plants and other carnivorous plants, like the sundew, obtain their nourishment from insects. While many people are familiar with the Venus flytrap (indigenous to the southeastern U.S.), which captures its prey by snapping shut over them, the bog plants of the northeast use a different method of entrapment. The pitcher plant attracts insects into its pitcher-shaped leaves with scent and colorful veins. Once the insect enters, it has a hard time escaping because tiny hairs in the plant point downward trapping it and drowning it in the liquid at the bottom of the pitcher. Then the plant's enzymes digest the insect. To identify the plant, look for the pitcher-shaped, reddish-green leaves. It is between one to two feet tall. In the summer it will have a large, solitary, purplish-red flower on a leafless stalk.

The boardwalk is quite narrow and starts out through a dense jungle of swamp maples and other trees before it reaches the white cedars, and finally penetrates the more open area of the bog, dominated by leather leaf. In the summer you will see the pink flowers (about a half inch wide) of sheep laurel. The sheep laurel grows between one to three feet tall and looks similar to the more common mountain laurel plants. It thrives in bog areas, and is expanding its range here at Ponkapoag as the size of the bog area expands. Each year the pond becomes shallower, as vegetation closes its ring around the pond. There are no underground streams and few springs to replenish and oxygenate the water. Sphagnum moss flourish in the stagnant water of the bog, and as it dies it fills the pond.

Retrace your steps back along the boardwalk to the main path by the YMCA Outdoor Center and go left. It's only a short walk (about half a mile) down the main trail to reach the golf course and then the Avenue of the Maples which will lead to the parking area.

## Getting There

Ponkapoag can be reached by exiting Route 128 at Exit 2 onto Washington Street in Canton. Turn left just before the first set of lights into the golf course parking lot. Signs lead you directly to the reservation.

No admission fee; no facilities; dogs allowed.

# Dighton Rock State Park

## Berkley

---

* 108 acres
* 1.5 miles
* 1 hour
* Easy

---

## Highlights

* Taunton River
* Mysterious inscriptions on Dighton Rock
* Woodland trail
* Great picnic sites

Situated on the banks of the Taunton River, Dighton Rock State Park offers a unique combination of history and natural history. The park is best known for mysterious Dighton Rock, a large boulder with markings thought to date back before the arrival of the Pilgrims. Also featured is a large picnic area along the river and nature trails that crisscross woods and meadow. It is the perfect place for both nature lovers and history buffs.

To begin this one-hour walk, leave the parking lot and head toward the river, passing through the open picnic area. As you face the river, follow the shoreline to your left (south), away from the white building that houses Dighton Rock. Where the open lawn of the picnic area meets the woods, you will see a trail that parallels the river. Follow this into the woods. Oak and white pine are the dominant trees, with cedars and swamp maples scattered about.

Just three or four minutes ahead is a stone wall on the right that abuts the river at a small opening, making a great spot to soak up the beauty of the marsh grass and sparkling waters of the Taunton. This vantage point offers a more quiet setting than the picnic area to enjoy the river, and you may want to return here at the end of your walk for rest or snack.

The Taunton River is a 50-mile long river that originates in Bridgewater and flows southwestward into Mount Hope Bay. The stretch of river before you is tidal, so you might smell salt air. In the eighteenth and nineteenth centuries the Taunton

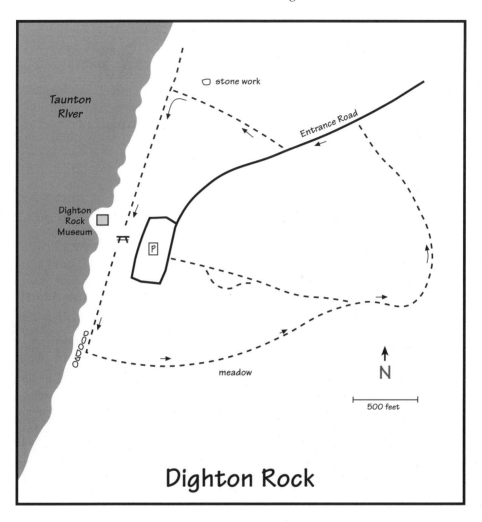

# Dighton Rock

River was a major shipping route, with schooners of all sizes passing Dighton Rock on their way to the inland port of Taunton.

Striped bass and bluefish often enter the Taunton from Mount Hope Bay and cruise past the park while searching for prey. A wide variety of bird life also hunts in the river, including cormorants, great blue herons, osprey, and even an occasional bald eagle. Considered a "dead river" just twenty-five years ago, the Taunton is much cleaner now, thanks to the Clean Water Act and the efforts of the Taunton River Watershed Association.

The trail turns away from the river here and heads to the east, passing through a stand of swamp maples. Also known as red maple, the swamp maple likes wet feet, and is the first deciduous tree to turn color in the fall. It usually shows its scarlet foliage as early as the beginning of September. Farther up the path cedar trees begin to appear, indicating that this area is in transition from pasture or meadow to woodland. The cedar is an opportunistic tree that is among the first to grow in old fields and dry soil. A variety of birds, such as cedar waxwings and bobwhite, feed on the fruit of the cedar (small blue berries) that grow on the tree each autumn. The wood is strong and durable, making it a good choice for fence posts.

There is a small meadow with a few scattered cedars roughly five minutes up the path from the river. Then the trail reenters woods and within a couple more minutes another trail joins the one you are walking. Go straight. New species of trees appear such as oak, white pine, and birch. The trail is flat, and during periods of snow coverage is good for cross-country skiing.

Be on the lookout for ruffed grouse, which often stay perfectly still until you approach too closely, and then explode into the air in rapid flight. Another bird you might see is the pheasant. Ring-necked pheasants were first introduced in the U.S. from Asia in 1881. They have a distinctive white ring around their necks, and their feathers have hues of green, purple, and red. There are few purebred pheasants left as the ring-necked and the English pheasant have been bred together. In the fall and winter, pheasants congregate together, but in the spring the males go off to establish their harems, crowing regularly to attract the hens. The hens lay an average of twelve to thirteen eggs and the male goes on its way, leaving all the parenting to the hen.

Just a couple more minutes of walking and the trail swings to the north, passing over a tiny wetland. Notice the standing maple on the left that is rotted out. Raccoons and other wildlife often make the hollow trunk their home. Hawks use the tops of such trees for perches because the dead branches are void of foliage, allowing the hawk to scan the forest floor for prey. If you see a large hawk here in winter, chances are its a red-tailed hawk, one of the few hawks that winters in Massachusetts.

The path continues in a northerly direction for another quarter mile then joins the park's entrance road. Turn left here. Notice the scotch pines, which have been planted along the road, and compare their needles to those of the white pines. Scotch pine needles are thick, while the white pine needles are slender and more flexible. About 50 feet down the road is a gate on your right; turn here and follow this old road in a northwesterly direction. Beneath your feet you can see and feel that this was a paved road, but the forest is reclaiming it. Moss, grass, and bush are growing from cracks in the road and in places where leaf mold has accumulated. About 200 yards down the old road look on the right for some handsome stone retaining walls, also being reclaimed by the woods.

Soon the path ends where it meets another trail that runs parallel to the Taunton River. You may see cottontails hiding beneath the low vegetation. Their brown coloring makes them difficult to distinguish against the forest floor and in the marsh, but with snow on the ground its much easier to spot them. Turn left on

*Situated along the Taunton River, Dighton Rock State Park is a great place for a picnic.*

the trail passing beneath some large maples. You'll get a glimpse of marsh grass and the river through the trees to your right. The trail next passes through a small wetland then narrows considerably before it ends at the open picnic area adjacent to the parking lot.

The white building at the water's edge is a small museum featuring Dighton Rock. The origin of the inscriptions on this sandstone rock has remained a mystery. Various theories have attributed the writings to Vikings, Native Americans, Phoenicians, or Portuguese. The theory that has gained the most attention is that the rock was inscribed by Portuguese explorer Miguel Cortereal in 1511. Cortereal set sail for the new world in 1502, to look for his brother, who disappeared on an earlier exploratory mission. But Miguel met the same fate, and was never heard from again. Dighton Rock may provide a clue to Miguel's fate. It is thought that his ship may have wrecked near Mount Hope Bay, and he subsequently lived with the Indians. Whether this theory is correct will probably never be known. Although the inscription is hard to read, some experts believe that it is written in Latin and translates to "M. Cortereal, 1511, by the grace of God, Leader of the Indians."

The Taunton River is a great canoeing river, but this particular stretch is recommended only for experienced canoeists because the tides create some strong currents and the open expanse of water receives some strong gusts of winds. Better canoeing on the river can be found upstream in the Middleborough/Raynham area, where there is no tidal influence and the river is narrower. (If you are interested in learning more about the Taunton River check out the author's book *A Taunton River Journey*.)

## Getting There

From Route 24 take Exit 10. Go west on North Street toward Berkley for 0.6 mile. Turn left on Friends Street and follow 0.7 mile to its end. Turn left on Bayview Avenue and go 0.2 mile to the park entrance. Turn left into the park and follow the entrance road 0.7 mile to its end where there is a large parking lot.

Open dawn to dusk, seven days a week, except in winter when park closes at 3:30 P.M. No admission fee; portable rest rooms available; dogs allowed.

The museum housing Dighton Rock is open from Memorial Day to Labor Day, 10 A.M. to 6 P.M., or by appointment (508-644-5522).

Hunting is not allowed at this state park.

Entrance road is sometimes closed after significant snow.

# Freetown/Fall River State Forest

## Assonet

---

* 5,441 acres

* Profile Rock Area: easy, great for children, 0.5 mile/20 minutes

* Rattlesnake Brook Area: moderate, 3.5 miles/2 hours

---

### Highlights

* Good vistas

* Good cross-country skiing

* Trout fishing in Rattlesnake Brook

Freetown/Fall River State Forest is one of the larger parks in Massachusetts (5,441 acres), and offers a wide variety of activities beyond hiking. Snowmobiling, horseback riding, mountain biking, and hunting are all allowed here. This walk focuses on the quieter trails best suited for nature study.

### Profile Rock Area

Profile Rock is located at the northernmost end of the park, and it is a "must see." It's only a five-minute walk from the parking lot. To reach Profile Rock take the trail from the parking lot that is lined with stones and begins by two large beech trees. Follow the trail through woodlands of oak, beech, and pine for about 500 yards and you will see Profile Rock ahead to your left. The rock is a 50-foot geological formation that offers 360-degree views of the surrounding countryside.

Children will enjoy Profile Rock with all its nooks, crannies, and boulders. Although there is no real path to the top, it can be scaled with care. Because the surrounding terrain is relatively flat, the views from the summit are excellent. To the west you see a church steeple rising from what seems like an endless expanse of forest.

To return to your car from the summit, simply retrace your steps. There are many trails on the other side of Slab Bridge Road, but the most interesting terrain is just to the south, at the Rattlesnake Brook area of Freetown/Fall River State Forest. The entrance to Rattlesnake Brook area is off Bell Rock Road (see directions at the end of this chapter).

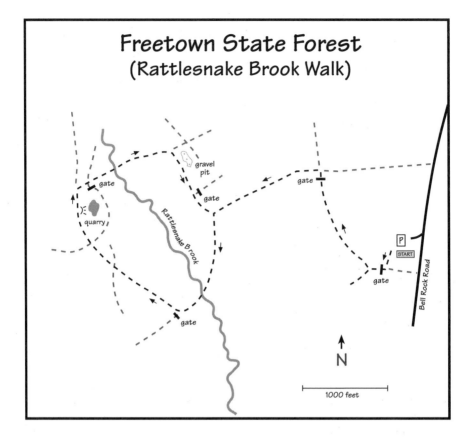

## Rattlesnake Brook Area (southwest area of State Forest)

Of the many miles of trails crisscrossing Freetown/Fall River State Forest, this southwest corner may be the best for long walks because of Rattlesnake Brook and an old quarry pond. There is also an overlook above the quarry that provides good views to the east.

Begin the walk by heading to far left end of the parking area (as you face the woods) where a signboard and trail sign are located. Follow the path by the trail sign for about forty feet until it intersects with a dirt road at a metal gate. On the forest side of the gate, the dirt road forks, and you should bear to the right. The woods are a typical southeastern Massachusetts mixture of oak, white pine, and pitch pine. The pitch pine has shorter, thicker needles than the white pine, and can grow in poor soils. It is very fire-resistant and sometimes is the only tree to survive a forest fire. Although it may reach heights up to seventy-five feet, it is usually smaller. Pitch pine cones are from one to three inches long with sharp points at the end and often come in small clusters. Pitch pine bark is deeply furrowed and is a dark reddish-brown color.

Continue walking on the dirt road (ignoring smaller side trails) until you reach another gate at a four-way intersection, about ten minutes from the start of your walk. Turn left here. As you walk along, glance down at the road for deer prints. They can be identified by their heart shape, with the pointed part of the track indicating the front of the deer hoof. This allows you to determine which direction the deer was traveling. White-tailed deer are primarily nocturnal, avoiding man by keeping to the thick woods during the daytime, and venturing out to feed at night. They have learned that it is safe to use the trails at night, and it's not uncommon to see tracks going right down the center of the trail for a considerable distance. The population of white-tailed deer is roughly as high as it was when Europeans first settled in America. Their numbers, however, were quite low in the mid nineteenth century when much of Massachusetts' forest was cleared for agriculture and the deer were hunted year-round for food. Thoreau lamented this in his essay *Natural History of Massachusetts,* writing; "The bear, wolf, lynx, wildcat, deer, beaver and marten have disappeared..."

The road you are now on will soon fork (about six or seven minutes from the four-way intersection) and you should bear left. During the winter months, when the leaves have fallen from the oaks, you can see a few beech trees in the forest to the right. Beech trees usually retain some of their golden-brown leaves on the lower branches through most of the winter. They are handsome trees, with smooth gray bark, and add color and contrast to the surrounding forest of dark brown oak limbs and green pine boughs.

When you cross the brook, take a moment to follow the path on the right that parallels the water. The little culvert under the road you were on has a stone facade and makes for a nice picture when taken from the streamside path.

Rattlesnake Brook is part of the Taunton River Watershed. It flows into the Assonet River, which in turn flows into the Taunton River before mingling its waters with Mount Hope Bay. The brook is named for the rattlesnakes that once lived here and throughout Massachusetts. Today there are only a handful of timber rattlers left in the state, making them an endangered species protected by law. Rattlers are identified by their triangular head and a rattle at the end of their tails that makes a buzzing sound when vibrated. The body color ranges from yellow-brown to almost black, with dark V-shaped crossbands across the back. They bask during the daytime and hunt at night for rabbits, shrews, mice, chipmunks, and other small animals and birds.

While people almost never encounter rattlesnakes in Massachusetts, there are a number of other snakes that can be seen in our woodlands. Garter snake, milk snake, ribbon snake, and black racer are all found in terrain such as that of the Freetown/Fall River State Forest. The black racer is an especially interesting snake, as it is the only black snake in New England with smooth scales.

As you continue on the dirt road on the south side of the bridge you have left Freetown and entered Fall River. Ignore the trail on the left with the gate and stay on the dirt road, which now curves to the right in a northwest direction. The trail will follow a gentle incline, passing an intersection with another dirt road that

*The rocky crag called Profile Rock is a favorite with kids.*

has large wooden posts on either side. Stay straight on the road you are on, passing an exposed ledge and boulder on the left. If it is winter, look carefully for the tracks of animals, such as fox. Massachusetts has both red fox and gray fox. The gray fox is smaller than the red fox and is a skillful tree climber. Hunting in both the woods and fields, grey foxes eat a wide variety of small mammals, supplemented by insects, fruit, snakes, turtles, and frogs. It is said that they establish regular routes, following waterways and valleys on their hunting forays.

About ten or fifteen minutes after crossing Rattlesnake Brook you will see an opening on your right with exposed bedrock. If you are walking with young children, hold their hands, as the overlook to your right has a 100-foot drop to a water-filled quarry below. The ledge affords a good view to the east, and it makes a nice resting spot.

As you face the view, there will be a trail to your left that descends the over-look and heads down to the quarry. The trail is rough in spots, but is also short, so it should not present too many problems. At the bottom of the trail, children might want to stop at the quarry and throw stones into the water.

There is a metal gate directly ahead near the quarry. You should follow the dirt road that goes to the left of the gate. A two-minute walk down this road will carry you over Rattlesnake Brook and then to a fork in the road where you should bear right. Next you will pass a small gravel pit and gate on your left. About ten minutes from the quarry the trail ends at a T-intersection where you should turn left and follow the road up a slight incline. This is one of the original trails you came in on, and in six or seven minutes you will be back at the four-way intersection with the gate on your right. Turn right here, and you will be back at the parking area in ten minutes.

## Getting There

### Profile Rock Area

From Route 24 take Exit 10 and go toward Freetown. Travel 0.9 mile on Main Street, then left on Elm Street (following signs for state forest). At 0.2 mile the road forks, bear right onto Slab Bridge Road and follow 0.6 mile to Profile Rock entrance road on the left. Follow entrance road to parking area.

### Rattlesnake Brook Area

From Route 24 take Exit 9 and go south on South Main Street in the opposite direction as Assonet/Route 79 North. (For those coming from the north the prop-er turn off the exit will be to the right, and if you are coming from the south, turn left.) Follow South Main Street 0.5 mile to Copicut Road on the left. Take a left on . Copicut and follow 1.2 miles to its end, then turn right on Bell Rock Road/High Street and follow 0.6 mile to the large parking lot on the right.

If you go to Profile Rock first and then want to go to the Rattlesnake Brook area, you can either get back on Route 24 and follow the directions or return to intersection of Slab Bridge Road and Elm Street and look for Route 79. Follow Route 79 south until it turns into South Main Street, then follow the directions for Rattlesnake Brook Area.

Open seven days a week, dawn to dusk. No admission fee; rest rooms; dogs allowed. Profile Rock gate usually closes at 6 P.M. from Memorial Day to Labor Day.

Hunting is allowed at this state park so wear blaze orange in season. 508-644-5522

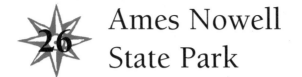

# Ames Nowell State Park

## Abington

* 600 acres
* 2 miles (can be extended to 4 miles if you walk the east side of the pond)
* 1.5 hours
* Easy
* Great for children

## Highlights

- Pond
- Fishing
- Boardwalk through swamp
- Great fall foliage

Ames Nowell State Park is one of Massachusetts' more scenic parks. It features an 88-acre pond, a waterfall, brooks, boardwalk, and approximately 7 miles of hiking trails. Because of its proximity to Brockton and other densely populated towns, you might want to arrive early in the morning so you can have the trails to yourself and improve your chances of seeing wildlife.

After parking your car in the large lot go to the front of the contact station (park rangers are often on duty here and offer a wealth of knowledge about the property's flora and fauna). Standing at the front of the contact station, take the road before you that leads slightly downhill. It is located about fifty feet in front of the contact station and leads directly toward the pond.

Follow this road about 200 feet and bear left toward the water ignoring paths on your right. You will soon be at the dam at the southern end of Cleveland Pond, also known as Ames Pond. The pond is man-made, formed in 1920 when Beaver Brook was dammed. At the time the Holmes family owned the land, and on a cement marker near where the water flows over the dam you will see the date the pond was built and the words "Semloh Pond"—Holmes spelled backward—yet another name for the pond.

No matter what the name, it's a scenic body of water that supports a wide range of warm-water fish such as largemouth bass, pickerel, crappie, and sunfish.

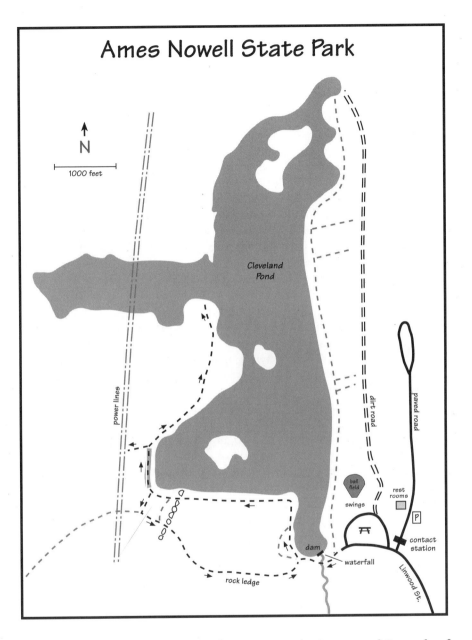

# Ames Nowell State Park

(Access to the boat launch is open during June, July, August, and September for canoes and boats with motors of 10 horsepower or less.) To catch bass and pickerel, try bouncing a rubber worm off the bottom or using an imitation minnow lure, such as a Rapala.

White and yellow flowers of the waterlilies and purple flowers of pickerel weed grace the pond with color in the warm-weather months. The elegant flowers of the pickerel weed are funnel-shaped and bloom from June into the autumn. Its leaves are heart-shaped and taper to a point. It is typically found in quiet water, the same type of habitat where pickerel live. (If you arrive at the pond in the early morning you just might see a deer feeding on the pickerel weed.) Along the edge of the pond you will find blueberries, huckleberries, raspberries, and sweet pepper bush with its pleasant summertime scent. In the winter, ice skating is allowed.

A footbridge spans the brook that tumbles in a waterfall from the pond. There is a nice picnic area on the other side along the banks of the stream. Cross over the footbridge, continue across the earthen dam to its end and then stay to the right on a narrow path that enters the woods, hugging the shoreline of the pond. The path is rocky with little hills and periodically offers views of the pond through the foliage. You will pass a trail entering from the left about two minutes into your walk but you should keep straight along the pond. Most of the trees are oak with a few small American chestnut trees growing from stumps.

After walking about fifteen minutes you will pass through an opening in a stone wall. Then you will pass another trail on the left. The boardwalk will soon be on your right and you should cross the boardwalk over the wetlands. In autumn the swamp maples here are ablaze with color. Swamp maples, or red maples, like wet feet and are among the first trees to turn color in New England, sometimes as early as the end of August. Be sure to look beneath the boardwalk for frogs and snakes hidden in the grass. Raccoons also prowl both the swamp and the shoreline looking for freshwater mussels, crayfish, frogs, salamanders, fish, snakes, and a wide range of plants. They use their extremely dexterous front feet to probe every nook and cranny.

On the opposite side of the boardwalk the trail splits. Before continuing the walk at the pond's edge, take time to go left on the trail a few feet. You'll come to power lines where you can walk to the right a few more feet and be on top of a high ledge of rock overlooking a portion of the park. The clearing beneath the power lines is a good place to see butterflies and birds, such as the kestrel, which hunts insects and small rodents. Other animals use the corridor beneath the power lines, and if you are here early you might see a white-tailed deer, red fox, or even a wild turkey. Park Ranger Jennifer Valiente frequently sees wild turkey in the northern section of the park, while Supervisor David Green says that raccoon, pheasant, and quail also live in the park, and muskrat live along the banks of the pond. He also reports there are nesting marsh hawks on the property and that several species of hawks, including red-tailed hawks and sharp-shinned hawks, are often seen near the picnic area by the pond. A fully mature sharp-shinned hawk is about 10 inches long with a wingspan of 21 inches, and it is fairly common along wood margins. It has a brown and tan pattern on its underside with a long narrow tail. They often fly above treetops in the early morning and soar higher at mid-day. Small birds are its preferred prey.

Retrace your steps back to the pond and continue northward. Soon you will pass a nice clearing with a large rock by the edge of the pond, which makes a good rest stop. Scan the water for wading birds such as great blue heron or the belted kingfisher, which does not wade but scouts from branches along the water's edge. Both birds feed primarily on small fish. Ospreys are also seen here during a brief period in the spring and fall when they stop on their migration. The pondside path continues north for another quarter mile before ending at the water's edge. Canada geese are often seen at this end of the pond, as is the occasional cormorant..

To return to the parking area retrace your steps back to the boardwalk. When you cross the boardwalk you can take a different trail back. Take the trail to the right and then make a quick left on a trail that leads eastward. This trail is fairly level, and you can really get up a head of steam on your walk. The trail passes by small oaks and gray birch. Ignore the side trails on your left that connect back with the pondside trail.

About five minutes down the path there is a rock ledge on your right that makes a good resting spot in the sun. From here it's only another five minutes back to the dam and parking area.

You can extend your walk another 2 miles by going up the east side of the pond, where the trail hugs the water's edge. You can return to the parking area by following the dirt road through the woods that also runs parallel to the pond on its east side.

## Getting There

From the intersection of Routes 18 and 123 in Abington take Route 123 west for 500 feet. Turn right on Rockland Road and go 1.2 miles to the end. Turn right on Linwood Street and follow 0.6 mile to its end and into the state park.

The park is open 10 A.M. to 6 P.M. from April to mid-June; from 8 A.M. to 8 P.M. during the summer; 10 A.M. to 6 P.M. from September to mid-October, and from 8 A.M. to 4 P.M. in the winter. No admission. Rest rooms open from mid-April to mid-October. Dogs allowed on leash. 781-857-1336

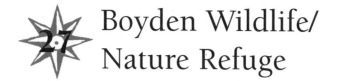

# Boyden Wildlife/ Nature Refuge

## *Taunton*

---

* 1.5 miles

* 1 hour

* Easy

* Great for children

---

### *Highlight*

- One and a half-mile loop trail with river frontage

Situated along the Three Mile River, the Boyden Wildlife/Nature Refuge has features children enjoy: water, plenty of hills and stairs for climbing, and even a log cabin in the woods. The 1.5-mile walk is easy, so even children as young as three and four years old can complete the loop through the property.

Our walk begins near the refuge headquarters building where you will see a sign for the Pine Tree Trail. This trail is a short (four minutes) loop trail that connects with the main trail. Follow the Pine Tree Trail through the white pine grove, passing a wooden seat nailed between two trees. There is a trail to the left of the seat, but our walk continues straight and soon connects with the Main Trail at a T-intersection. Turn left onto the Main Trail where you will come to another T-intersection in a couple minutes. Turn left again and you will be at the Fragrance Garden.

A wide array of perennials grow in two rock gardens at the Fragrance Garden: nicotiana, dianthus, sage, lavender, achillea, carnation, catnip, and rosemary. Adjacent to the garden is a small orchard with a bluebird house situated at the back of the clearing. Note the small entrance to the blue-bird house and the lack of a perch. The hole is purposely small (one and a half inches in diameter) to keep larger birds from nesting in the box; the lack of a perch discourages house sparrows from moving in.

While the backs of male bluebirds are a vivid blue, the females have hues of blue, gray, and brown. Both have reddish brown under the chin and white bellies. In the summer you will often see them perched on dead branches looking for insects on the ground. They will quickly dive down to pick up a cricket, spider, grasshopper, or caterpillar, then return to their perch. In the cold-weather months

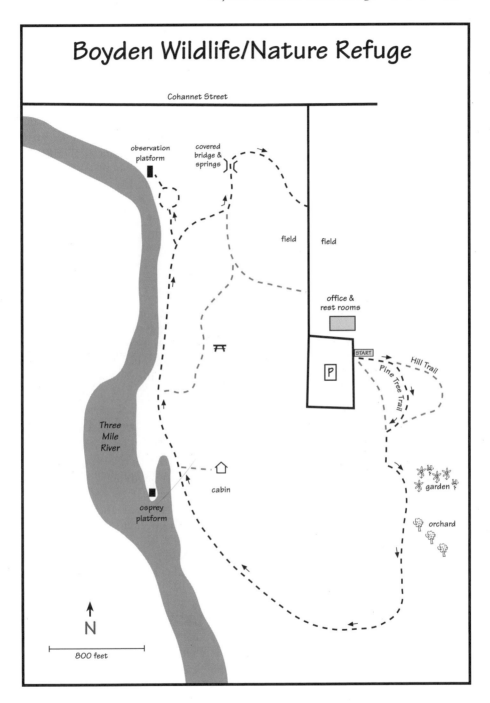

# Boyden Wildlife/Nature Refuge

Cohannet Street

observation platform

covered bridge & springs

field

field

office & rest rooms

START

Hill Trail

Pine Tree Trail

P

Three Mile River

cabin

osprey platform

garden

orchard

N

800 feet

grasshopper, or caterpillar, then return to their perch. In the cold-weather months their diet shifts to berries, such as cedar, holly, and dogwood berries.

From the garden and mini-orchard follow the wide path labeled "River Trail." Within two minutes you will be at the banks of the Three Mile River, a tributary to the Taunton River which drains into Mount Hope Bay. The marshland surrounding the Three Mile River attracts a wide array of birds such as night herons, great blue herons, wood ducks, and osprey. Note the wood duck house with the wide entrance hole, constructed to duplicate the hollow trees wood ducks prefer to nest in. When their young are born, both mother and fledglings soon leave the nest and head for the safety of the water.

You will also see a platform at the top of a tall pole situated out in the marsh. This was constructed for osprey to build their large nests of sticks on. Osprey will usually arrive in March from the south, and build (or rebuild) nests to lay their eggs. Sometimes great horned owls arrive at an existing nest earlier than the osprey, and commandeer it for their own use. If you ever spot an empty osprey nest, be sure to scan it with binoculars—more than once I've seen the "ears" of a great horned owl sticking out the top.

Osprey are primarily coastal birds that live on a steady diet of fish. From the air they scan the water for fish, which they swoop down and grab with their sharp talons. Osprey suffered greatly from the effects of the pesticide DDT.

There is a bench by the river, which is an ideal spot to sit quietly and scan the water for bird life. Nailed to one of the trees is a bat house, a shelter for these nocturnal mammals. The entrance to the bat house is at the bottom of the shelter rather than in the front. Bats come out in the evening and consume an enormous quantity of insects. Of all the mammals in the world bats are the only ones that can truly fly ("flying squirrels" can only glide). They also have a keen sense of hearing which guides them in the dark. By making a series of high-pitched noises, these sound waves bounce off objects, echoing back to the ears of the bat.

As you follow the river you will note openings in the wooden rail fence that runs between the path and the river. These openings were created so that anglers can try their skill in the Three Mile River. Like most rivers in southeastern Massachusetts, the Three Mile River is relatively warm and slow moving because of the flat terrain. It supports warm-water species such as bluegill, largemouth bass, and pickerel. Try casting out a black rubber worm, bouncing it slowly on the bottom to attract bass.

You will see a set of stairs on your right just a couple minutes down the trail from where you first saw the river. The stairs lead up the ridge to a log cabin set on a fieldstone foundation. It was built in memory of Arthur Cleveland Bent, author of *Life History of American Birds*. He was known to frequent the marshes along the Three Mile River because of the good birding found here. The cabin makes a nice spot to rest and have a snack—something essential when walking with young children.

If you are traveling with children, take a moment to explain how logs were cut and notched to form the frame of the cabin, and how the spaces between logs

*An immature night heron stalks the river bank for minnows.*

were filled with sod, wood, or plaster to keep out cold air in the winter and bugs in the summer. Explain that before glass became inexpensive enough for the settlers to buy, windows were either wooden slabs on hinges or oiled paper.

Continuing on the River Trail, you will pass two good-sized beech trees identified by their smooth gray bark. If it is winter, notice how a few brown leaves cling stubbornly to the beech trees when other deciduous trees are bare. Other trees you will see include pine and oak, with a few mountain laurel growing in the understory.

After walking about three minutes from the cabin you will see another set of stairs on the right. These lead up to a picnic area near the parking lot. Our walk continues on the river trail, passing some very large oak trees that grow next to the path. The reason you do not see large numbers of trees this size is because the forests in New England are largely second or third growth, with most of the virgin trees having been cut for timber or to make room for pastureland. The clearing of the land primarily took place in the 1700s and early 1800s, before many farmers went west for the richer soil of the plains states. Today the trees are reclaiming the land, and we now have more forested acres than cleared acres in the state—the opposite of Massachusetts two hundred years ago. Three or four more minutes on the river will lead you to a boardwalk on the left. Bear left here, following the elevated walkway through a small swamp to an observation platform overlooking the

Three Mile River. This is another good resting spot. Look for kingfishers. It is a handsome bird with a large crested head that hunts rivers, lakes and marshes for minnows, which it captures in its bill.

Retrace your steps back to the River Trail and continue in a northeasterly direction, away from the water. After about three minutes of walking you will be at a T-intersection where you should bear left onto another boardwalk. This one carries you over wetlands where there are freshwater springs, and leads to a tiny covered bridge with a bench inside. The boardwalk ends just beyond the covered bridge and the trail loops around to the southeast, leading you into a field adjacent to the entrance road into the refuge. Look for birds that prefer the open field habitat such as bluebirds or perhaps the kestrel, a small falcon that hunts in open spaces for insects or small birds.

To return to your car, just walk down the entrance road to the south which leads back to the parking lot.

## Getting There

From Route 24 take Exit 13 and go on Route 44 West into Taunton Center. From the town center (you will see the town green) continue to follow the signs for Route 44 West. Travel 1.6 miles on Route 44 West from the town center to Joseph Warner Boulevard on the left at a stop light. Take the left onto Warner Boulevard and go 0.3 mile to a blinking light. Turn right here onto Cohannet Street. Go 0.5 mile to entrance to Boyden Wildlife/Nature Refuge on the left (there is a large sign) and follow entrance road to parking lot.

Open year-round, 9:00 A.M. to sunset, seven days a week. No admission; rest rooms available; dogs allowed on leash. 508-821-1676

# Camp Titicut Reservation

## Bridgewater

---

* 33 acres
* 1.5 miles
* 1 hour
* Easy
* Great for children

---

## Highlights

* Walk along the Taunton River
* Huge white pines
* Good cross-country skiing
* Canoeing

Camp Titicut Reservation is a small but scenic conservation area situated along the banks of Taunton River. The name Titicut is derived from the Wampanoag Indian name for the Taunton River, "Seip-teih-tuk-qut," which means "the long waterway used by all." A Wampanoag village was once situated next to the river for access to the waterway and also because the river was low enough to wade across at one point. Later, in the early 1800s, the Titicut area was the site of shipbuilding activities, and a number of schooners were built here and floated down the river during the high water of springtime.

Begin your walk by following the dirt road by the gate and entrance sign. White pines line the road before it leads you to an open field. Notice the opportunistic trees such as pine, cedar, and popple that are beginning to reclaim the field. They are all sun-loving species and fairly quick growers that establish themselves in disturbed areas that receive sunlight. Look for rabbit, deer, and fox in the field, and scan the treeline for hawks and owls.

Deer are quite populous in Eastern Massachusetts because many towns have hunting restrictions and natural predators such as the wolf and mountain lion have been eliminated. Whenever you explore areas where deer live be sure to take precaution against deer ticks, which carry Lyme disease. Never wear short pants in grassy areas or fields, and pull your socks up over the bottom of your trousers.

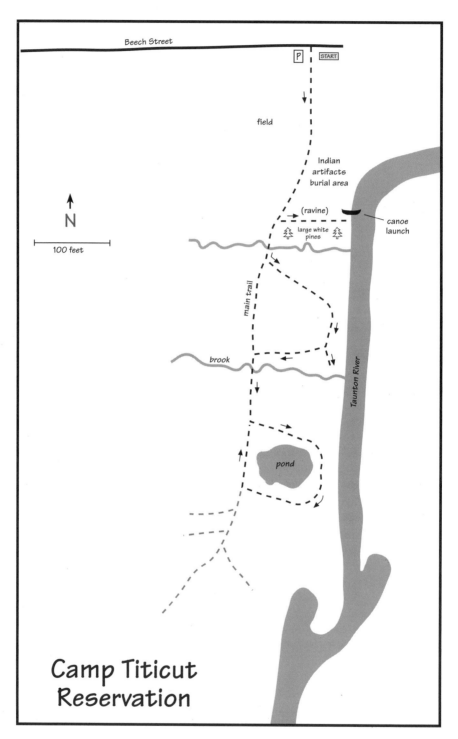

Beech Street

P  START

field

Indian
artifacts
burial area

(ravine)

canoe
launch

N

100 feet

large white
pines

main trail

brook

Taunton River

pond

# Camp Titicut
# Reservation

When you get home, give yourself a "tick check" and be sure to see your doctor if you develop a rash that is shaped like a bull's eye, one of the early warning signs.

Just beyond the field, only a five-minute walk from your car, you will see a ravine and trail on your left that leads to the river. There are two enormous white pines growing at the right side of the ravine. These large pines attracted the attention of shipbuilders, who used the timber for ship masts. In fact the trees were often blazed with an arrow, a mark of the British, that designated the pines as the property of the King, to be used by the British Admiralty. The size of these pines is somewhat unusual as most older growth trees have either been logged or cleared by farmers. Be sure to search the base of the tree for pellets from owls that perch in pines such as these.

Take a moment to watch the slow brown waters of the Taunton flow by. Great blue herons, wood ducks, and green-backed herons and night herons are sometimes seen along the shoreline, as are a variety of ducks. The mud along the river may hold the tracks of mink, raccoon, and otter that prowl the shoreline for food. Raccoons are primarily nocturnal creatures so the best time to see one is in the late afternoon or evening when they begin to prowl about. They are quite at home on the Taunton, searching for crayfish, frogs, snakes, turtle and birds eggs, grubs, and crickets. Baby raccoons are born in the spring and generally stay with the mother that first year. Many birdwatchers have mixed emotions about raccoons; while they are fascinating creatures and they play an important roll in the natural world, they can wreak havoc on birds by stealing eggs.

This section of the Taunton has a good buffer of open space along its banks and the entire upper portion of the river offers a peaceful float. You can launch canoes from this site, but you will have to drag them the short distance from the entrance gate to the shore. Taunton River has a rich history. In the eighteenth century one of the major sea ports in the world was located in the town of Taunton, even though it is about fifteen miles from the ocean. Because the river is tidal all the way to Taunton, large ships could come up the river when it rose with the high tide. In fact if you canoe down the river today, you can see the tidal effect at Taunton: during high tide the water is forced back upstream, and the river actually goes "backward" at a slow pace.

On the ridge to the left of the ravine is a spot where Indian artifacts and a burial area was found. Clay pottery, arrow heads, and human remains were found here, ranging in age from several thousand to several hundred years old. The area appealed to Native Americans because the river served as both a transportation route and a source of food, where herring could be gathered and ducks, muskrat, and other birds and animals hunted. The slopes along the river were high enough to allow protection from spring flooding and were sheltered from cold northwest winds, while streams in the area provided drinking water. Southeastern New England once had among the highest concentration of Native Americans found anywhere and Taunton was the land of the Wampanoag. Massasoit, who helped the Pilgrims survive their early winters, was the sachem of the tribe and it was his son, Metacom (Philip), who later fought to regain the tribal land from the English.

*At the site of an old shipyard, a trail leads down to the Taunton River.*

Much of the action during King Philip's War took place on the banks of the Taunton River.

After examining the river and shoreline, walk back up the ravine and continue south on the main trail. You will pass over a tiny stream that trickles into the river. Beech trees line the streambed, and during my March trip the beige paper-thin leaves of the trees were still clinging stubbornly to branches, creating a handsome contrast to the snow. Beech trees have smooth gray trunks, and have been likened to the legs of an elephant. The beech nut is consumed by many birds and animals, and up north it is a favorite mast crop of the black bear. Just beyond the stream the trail splits. Bear left. You will pass a cellar hole largely hidden by vegetation on your right.

This is a beautiful trail, especially the section that hugs the ridge alongside the river. Where the trail starts to bend away from the river you will see another small stream ahead. It's possible to walk along the ridge, bushwhacking off the main trail for about fifty feet to a spot where the ridge drops away to a gully where the stream enters into the Taunton. Fish might be attracted to the mouth of the stream because of its cool waters; in turn, they may attract wading birds such as the great blue heron.

As you retrace your steps back to the trail and turn away from the river, take a moment to admire a couple of mountain laurel bushes growing beneath the beech trees. They are an understory plant, preferring shade from the sun, and can be identified by shiny green leaves that stay on the plant all winter.

Follow the trail west, paralleling the stream, to where you will intersect with the main trail. Turn left here, cross over the stream, and then a couple minutes farther down the trail turn left again. You will soon see a small pond on your right that appears to be man-made. The trail curls around this pond and then reconnects with the main trail. By turning right on the main trail you can reach your car in about twenty minutes. The total walk is an easy one-hour stroll, which most children should be able to handle without difficulty.

## Getting There

From Route 495 exit onto Route 28 North. Go 2.7 miles to Plymouth Street on the left. Follow Plymouth Street 1.7 miles to where it turns into Green Street and then follow Green 0.3 mile to Beech Street on the left. Follow Beech Street for 0.2 mile and park at entrance gate on the left.

From Route 24 exit onto Route 44 and go 2.8 miles east to Richmond Street. Turn left onto Richmond Street and follow 2.4 miles to its end. Turn left onto Green Street and proceed 0.1 mile, then turn left onto Beech Street. Follow Beech Street for 0.2 mile and park at entrance gate on the left.

Open dawn to dusk, seven days a week. No admission; no facilities; dogs allowed on leash.

# Caratunk
# Wildlife Refuge

## *Seekonk*

---

* 195 acres
* Two Walks :
* Monument Rock: 2 miles/1 hour (easy, great for children)
* Hemlock Grove: 2.5 miles/1.5 hours (moderate)

---

## *Highlights*

- Pond
- Fields and diverse forest
- Excellent wildlife habitat

Caratunk Wildlife Refuge is often overlooked by Massachusetts residents because it is managed by the Audubon Society of Rhode Island. Set on 195 acres with ponds, fields, streams, a small bog area, and boulder-strewn woodlands, Caratunk is a hidden gem just waiting to be discovered. Deer, grouse, muskrat, woodcock, fox, and groundhog are just some of the animals you can see in addition to a diversity of birds. There is a small nature center in the barn adjacent to the parking lot that houses bird exhibits. Behind the nature center is a large field with picnic tables, butterfly garden, bird feeders, and birdhouses.

To begin your walk, face the field behind the barn/nature center and walk at an angle across it toward the left side where there is a break in a stone wall. The field you are walking through is covered with wildflowers, especially Queen Anne's lace in the summer. Queen Anne's lace is a member of the parsley family and is also called wild carrot. It has delicate white clusters of flowers that form a lace-like pattern growing flat on a two- to-three foot stem. Look for butterflies, bluebirds, and tree swallows flying above the field of flowers. The stone wall is especially handsome, but was originally created for practical reasons rather than aesthetics. When farmers cleared the land of trees in past centuries they also had to remove the many rocks from the soil. These were dragged from the field in stone boats and then fitted into walls that either marked property boundaries or kept sheep and cattle within the pastures.

Follow the trail that heads beyond the stone wall, designated by a blue arrow. The path hugs the edge of the field next to woodlands of white pine, red

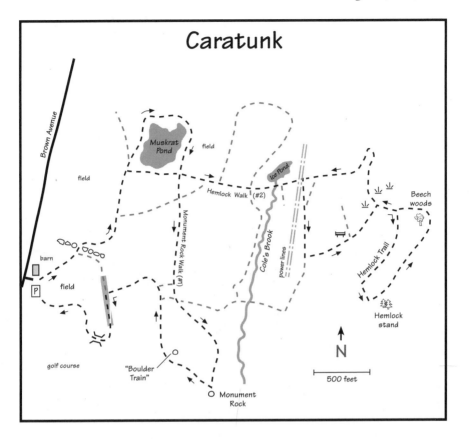

oak, dogwood, birch, and a few large willows. You will pass a trail with a yellow arrow on the right; then a little farther you will arrive at a trail with a blue arrow. Go just a few feet past the trail with the blue arrow and bear to the right where the trail splits. The trail is lined by grape vines, jewel weed, crab apple and poison ivy, and leads in a northern direction along the edge of a shallow pond with a couple small islands. This is Muskrat Pond, home to muskrat, ducks, and turtles.

On my last walk in March, I enjoyed the "konkaree" sound of red-winged blackbirds that had recently arrived on their spring migration. The male red-winged blackbird has a distinctive red shoulder patch, while the females resemble large sparrows but are long-billed and more heavily streaked. They feed, fly, and roost in huge flocks, usually near open fields or marsh. I also saw mallards sail overhead then skim the ponds surface as they landed. In the summer look for cat-birds, cardinals, and herons along the pond's edge.

The trail then continues its loop of the pond first turning to the east (pass-ing a wooden dock that leads into the water). In the warm-weather months, have your children lie on the dock and peer into the water. They might spot minnows or perhaps a sunfish scooping out its nest in the shallow pond bottom. Swamp

*Cottontail rabbits are usually seen at dawn and dusk.*

maples grow around the pond, whereas cedars begin to appear where the ground rises away toward a field at the pond's eastern end. With binoculars you can scan the field for deer, groundhog, or birds such as kestrel that hunt here. In September, woodcocks can sometimes be seen flying south just above tree level in the evening. They prefer to breed in areas where there are low wet thickets adjacent to fields, like the area here at Caratunk.

The trail now turns to the south, passing a stand of popple trees and a few old oaks before it intersects with another trail at the southeast corner of the pond. Take a moment to look back at the pond and admire the island filled with white birch.

From this point the walk to Monument Rock is perfect for first-time visitors. (At the end of this section the walk to the hemlock stand at the far eastern end of the property is discussed.) At the trail intersection at the end of Muskrat Pond turn left, go ten feet and then turn right on the next trail, which is marked by yellow paint dots on trees farther down. Proceed south on this path, which passes through immature woodlands and fields reverting back to woods. About two minutes down this trail go straight through a trail intersection and then in five more minutes pass a trail on the right. (Follow the sign straight toward Monument Rock.) In just one more minute of walking you will reach a T-intersection. Go left, crossing over a ridge of boulders. The trail forks after this ridge to the right. The trail now passes through more mature trees, primarily oaks. Within five minutes you will reach Monument Rock, a ten-foot-high boulder resting against a tree. This narrow slab of rock looks something like a giant tombstone.

Take the trail to the right of the rock and follow it as it parallels a stone wall for about seven or eight minutes, passing a trail on the right. In another minute you'll come to an intersection with another trail. To return to the parking area, bear left here onto the trail marked by red dots. Follow it a short distance to a T-intersection at a boardwalk. Go left here, passing a pleasant area where ferns grow beneath white pines, then over a small stream on two separate bridges. The trail ends at the field behind the nature center and parking lot.

The second hike is a good one for the fall, when you can see the gold colors in a beech grove. It is not a good trail during summer, as it passes through wet areas and dense woods with many mosquitoes. Begin this hike back at the southeast edge of Muskrat Pond and follow the trail that goes uphill in a southeast direction. You will pass trails on your left and right, then in about ten minutes cross Cole's Brook on a granite bridge. On your left will be a small marsh where a pond was once located. (Before the days of electric refrigeration ice was cut from such ponds and stored in shaded, insulated spots to last into the summer.)

Just after the marsh and former ice pond you will reach power lines where you should turn right. The open area beneath the power lines attracts birds and small animals, which in turn attract raccoons and foxes, so be on the lookout if you are here in the early morning. Follow the trail beneath the power lines for about four minutes then turn left at a narrow path marked by blue paint dots on the trees, ignoring the wider unmarked path that also goes into the woods. The path you are following winds through the woods and has many rocks and exposed roots. Be careful if you're with young children. You'll soon come to a bench and side trail where you should bear right. The ground beneath you is wet in the spring, and boards have been laid to assist your footing. In a short distance you will see a sign for a bog pointing to a side trail on the left. You can detour here to see the bog, but it is rather small.

After viewing the bog, go back to the trail you were on and continue another couple minutes to where it forks at a sign for the Hemlock Trail. This is the beginning of a loop that takes you to the south and a stand of hemlocks, first passing through a beech grove. The variety of trees at Caratunk is one of the reasons a walk in the autumn is special. You can go either way at this fork and it takes about fifteen to twenty minutes to complete the loop. After you've admired the hemlock and beech trees simply retrace your steps back to the parking area.

## Getting There

From I-95 take Exit 3A onto Route 123. Follow Route 123 eastward for 1.3 miles to a light. Just after the light Route 123 bears to the left, but go straight onto Thatcher Street. Follow Thatcher Street 1 mile to its end and then turn right onto Route 152. Follow Route 152 south for 5.5 miles then turn left onto Brown Street and go 0.8 mile to the Caratunk sign and parking lot on the right.

Open dawn to dusk, Tuesday through Sunday. Small fee for nonmembers of Audubon Society of Rhode Island; no dogs; rest rooms in Nature Center. 401-231-6444

# Wheaton Farm Conservation Area

## *Easton*

---

* 718 acres
* 2.5 miles
* 1.5 hours
* Easy
* Great for children

---

## *Highlights*

* White pine forest
* Pond for fishing and canoeing
* Good birding

Wheaton Farm offers the walker a relatively easy ramble through level terrain that features a white pine forest, shallow ponds, and open fields. It is the largest conservation area in Easton, and is a great place for walking with children or cross-country skiing in the winter. Some of the property is still actively farmed, but the majority of acres serves to protect the source of Easton's public water supply.

To begin your walk from the parking area, take the trail to your left as you face the woods. (The trail is alongside a wooden fence and cuts behind the pumping station.) There is a gentle descent as you walk a few feet into the woods, then the trail crosses an earthen dike, separated by two shallow ponds. The dike is a good spot to look for wood ducks, muskrat, and other wildlife that makes it's home on fresh water. Wood duck houses have been erected on poles to duplicate the hollow cavity of trees where wood ducks prefer to nest. Almost right after they hatch, the young jump from the nest into the water where they travel through the pond behind their mother. The male wood duck is one of the most handsome ducks seen in New England, with multicolored feathers on the body and a distinctive head with a red eye ring, iridescent green crest, white chin patch, and black and white markings on the cheeks. The female is grayish with a broad white eye ring. They prefer wooded rivers and ponds, and can be seen in groups in the fall in freshwater marshes. In the winter they head south, rarely staying farther north than New Jersey.

One unwelcome visitor seen on the pond is the mute swan, an exotic brought to the U.S. from Europe that now breeds in the wild. Mute swans are quite

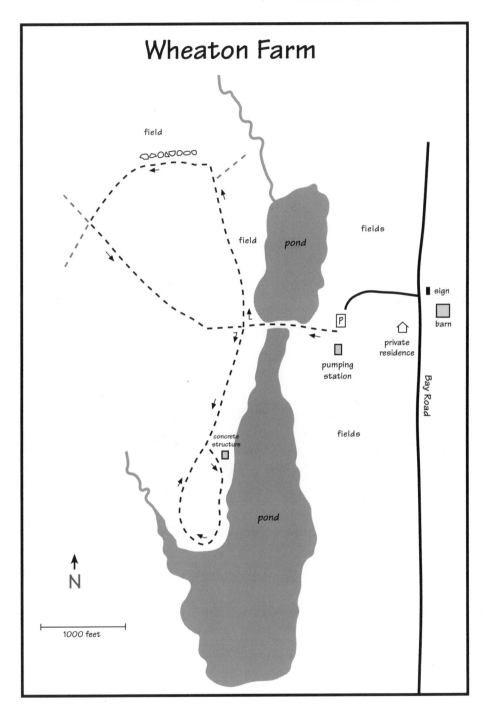

# Wheaton Farm

field

field

pond

fields

sign

barn

P

private
residence

pumping
station

fields

concrete
structure

pond

N

1000 feet

Bay Road

large, and almost pure white with a graceful S-curved neck. Despite their graceful appearance, they are very aggressive birds and extremely territorial, driving out native birds like the wood duck from preferred nesting areas. They also have large appetites, ripping up vegetation from the bottom of ponds.

When you cross the dike, turn left where a trail intersects the one you are on. You will enter a forest almost totally comprised of white pines, some of them quite large. The pines block out most of the sun. In the summer the pine needles make for a soft cushion on the trail, and there's nothing quite like the scent of green pine needles.

After walking ten minutes on the trail you'll intersect a trail on your left. Turn left here, following the trail past a small concrete building housing a well. Continue along the edge of the water. On your left will be a large dead tree. Hawks often use such trees as perches because they offer views, unobstructed by foliage, of the forest floor. Woodpeckers peck at the rotting wood for insects, and animals such as raccoons will use the hollow areas of such trees for shelter.

Within five minutes you will reach a small point of land where the pond has broadened. The shallow waters provide good hunting grounds for great blue herons, which stalk the pond for fish and frogs to snatch with their long bills. Once the prey is caught the heron tips its head and swallows the prey whole. With a wing-span of forty-four inches, black-crowned night herons are smaller than great blue herons. The black-crowned night heron has a short wing with gray wings and white

*Walkers and cross-country skiers alike will enjoy snow-covered trails winding through pine groves at Wheaton Farm.*

underparts, and as the name implies it is mostly nocturnal, roosting in trees in the days. Populations have been gradually dropping over the last 40 years due to the effects of pesticides and loss of habitat. Yellow-crowned night herons also get as far north as Massachusetts, and the adults are slate gray with black head and white cheeks. The yellow-crowned night heron is not seen as often at the black-crowned, and most sightings are in the eastern part of the state and occur in late summer.

The trail loops around to the right, heading back the way you came. It takes about fifteen minutes to return to the trail intersection by the dike. Extend your walk by walking straight through the intersection heading north. There will be a small field on the right, so be sure to approach quietly in case there is a deer feeding. Often deer will wait by the edge of open space until dusk falls.

Along the trail a few pitch pines mix in with the white pines that dominate the woods of Wheaton Farm. Notice how the pitch pine's bark is more furrowed than the white pine. Other differences between the two are that the pitch pine needles are more rigid, its cones more rounded, and the overall size of the tree is smaller than the white pine. By walking about five minutes down the trail you will reach another field, this one a bit larger than the last. For a look at the stream that feeds the pond, you can backtrack about twenty feet and there will be a small path on the east side that cuts into the woods and leads to a red maple swamp. Look for the tracks of raccoon, mink, muskrat, and otter in the mud along the streambed.

Continue your walk from the larger field by turning left and following the trail that runs parallel to the stone wall. Chipmunks like to burrow beneath the rocks, and often you will see them running along top of the wall then disappear into one of their holes. You may want to also scan the trees for signs of possum, which are often seen here.

Just five minutes of walking this trail will bring you to a four-way intersection where you should turn left. About ten more minutes of walking will bring you back to the main intersection by the pond near the beginning of your walk. (Local residents say the ponds have good bass fishing.) Cross the dike to return to the parking area.

Before leaving, be sure to take a brief walk along the edge of the fields. This is prime habitat for bluebirds and kestrels.

## Getting There

From Route 495, take Exit 9 (Bay Road) and go north toward Easton. Watch your odometer carefully and travel 3.2 miles. On the right side of Bay Street look for the Wheaton Farm sign by a brown barn and on the left side of Bay Street look for a beautiful old Federal-style house set behind evergreens. The entrance road to Wheaton Farm will be just after this house on the left. Turn into the road and follow to parking area.

(From the intersection of Route 106 and Bay Street in Easton, take Bay Street to the south and follow 1.2 miles to the entrance road on your right.)

Open year-round, dawn to dusk. No admission; no facilities; dogs allowed on leash.

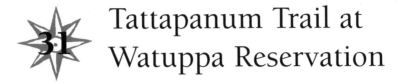

# Tattapanum Trail at Watuppa Reservation

## Fall River

---

* 1 mile
* 45 minutes
* Easy (more walking available on the causeway)
* Great for children

---

## Highlights

* Woodland loop trail
* Marsh
* Granite outcrops
* Good wildlife viewing

For many years the Watuppa Reservation was strictly used to protect the purity of Fall River's water supply, North Watuppa Pond, and the public was prohibited from walking in the forest. In 1995 a portion of the reservation, called the Tattapanum Trail, was opened to the public for walking. It was Fall River's first municipal nature trail. It was named Tattapanum after a Pocasset Indian woman whose signature granted title of the "Pocasset Purchase," which includes much of present-day Fall River, to a small group of European settlers in 1659. The trail area, located just minutes from downtown Fall River, is a wonderful natural resource surrounded by 2,800 acres of forest, marsh, and North Watuppa Pond.

Begin your hike at the Tattapanum Trail sign on Wilson Road. The stone path leads about fifty feet into the woods where it splits at another sign, this one a large map of the trail. Follow the path to the right. (Some of the trees have small numbers nailed to them, which correspond to an interpretive trail map and text produced by the Fall River Water Department. It is free to the public by calling 508-324-2330.) The trail is fairly level and well maintained, making this a great walk to take with young children, with plenty of diverse points of interest to capture their attention.

The woods are dominated by oak, white pine, birch, spruce, and ash. Other trees, however, have also established themselves, such as sassafras, which can be seen at intervals all along the trail. It is identified by the thumb and mitten outline

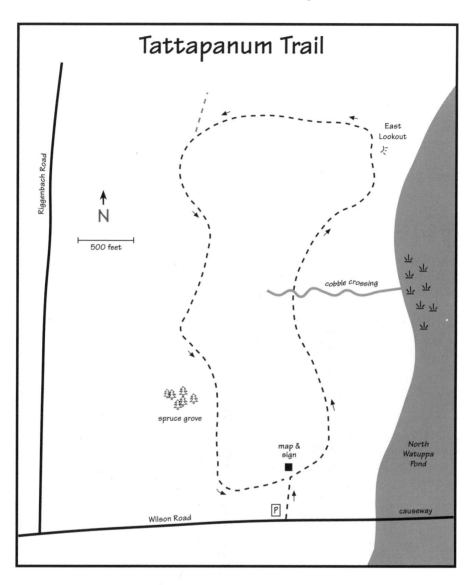

# Tattapanum Trail

Riggenbach Road

N

500 feet

East
Lookout

cobble crossing

spruce grove

map &
sign

North
Watuppa
Pond

P

Wilson Road

causeway

of its leaves. The green twigs and smooth leaves have a spicy fragrance when crushed. You will also see black birch (tree marker #1), pignut hickory (#2), and red pine (#3) located about a hundred feet off the trail to the left. Marker #4 is on a small American chestnut sprouting from an old stump. Since the 1940s the mature trees die off when attacked by the fungus known as Chestnut Blight.

About ten minutes into your walk you'll pass over a cobble crossing across a drainage area. The cobbles, or rounded fragments of rock, were placed here amidst the mud and larger rocks to improve footing for domestic animals. After walking over the cobble crossing, you will pass through a gap in a thick stone wall, yet another reminder of when this land was farm and pasture. It is estimated that the land was farmed until the Civil War, after which it reverted back to forest, as local farms were abandoned when the migration to the Great Plains began. Most of the forest in New England is relatively young, under 150 years old, and there are only a few acres of trees left in the state that have never been disturbed by man.

A short distance down the trail is a large granite outcrop on the left that children will enjoy climbing. Two features that make a hike fun for children are rocks to climb and water to investigate. Just beyond the granite outcrop on the left is the East Overlook on the right. A small granite ledge provides you with a partial view of the north end of North Watuppa Pond, which is quite shallow and perfect for wading birds to stalk the water for small fish and frogs. Scan the water for great

*Grandfather and granddaughter pause at the marsh overlook.*

blue heron and night heron. Many people think that great blue heron spear fish with their long pointed bills, but they actually grab the fish with their beak and then tip their head back and swallow it whole. Heron numbers are on the rise because we are cleaning up our rivers and because there are more beavers making ponds, which creates dead timber for the heron to nest in.

Continue on the trail, and it will begin its loop back toward the parking area. Where the trail turns south it passes an area of conifers. The shade from the evergreens give the feeling of entering a mysterious woodland. There are even a few holly trees, identified by their shiny green leaves with numerous points around the edges. The holly, a broad-leafed evergreen, keeps its leaves through the winter and its red berries are eaten by birds. They make nice specimen plants in the yard, but be sure to plant them in a protected location with a little shade and out of the wind.

Soon you will pass through an opening in a stone wall: Be on the lookout for a very old oak tree that grows just off the right of the trail. The core of the tree is hollowed out and there is an opening in the bottom—the perfect entrance for animals such as raccoons to enter and use the inside of the tree for shelter. Within five more minutes you are back at the parking area and have completed this one-mile circular trail.

You can extend your walk by following the road over the causeway that separates North Watuppa Pond from a swamp. With binoculars you can scan the swamp for wading birds such as egret, great blue heron, and night heron. Ducks and osprey are also seen. During the early part of June you might get lucky and see a snapping turtle coming out of the swamp to lay its eggs in the sand near the dike. Please do not disturb the turtles; the snappers have enough to worry about with skunks and raccoons digging up their eggs.

## Getting There

From Route 24 take Exit 8. Turn east onto Airport Road into the Industrial Park and proceed just about 1.5 miles to Riggenbach Road. Turn right, go 0.7 mile to end, then take left onto Wilson Road. Tattapanum Trail entrance is 1000 feet down the hill on the left. (Warning: This last section of Wilson Road is very rough so drive carefully.)

From Route 79 take the North Main Street exit. Go toward the north (sign will read "Steep Brook"). Follow North Main for 1.8 miles then turn right onto Wilson Road and follow for 1.4 miles to entrance on the left.

Open year-round, dawn to dusk. No facilities; no dogs allowed.

# Whitney and Thayer Woods

## Cohasset/Hingham

---

* 808 acres
* 3 miles
* 1.75 hours
* Easy

---

### Highlights

* Glacial erratics
* Large forested property
* Rhododendron-lined path
* Boulder Lane is great for children

Quiet woodland trails, and plenty of them, are the primary features of this large reservation that straddles the towns of Cohasset and Hingham. A large stand of giant rhododendrons and azaleas located on the southern border of the property, provide an attractive contrast to the thickly forested hills and glacial boulders.

The last two times I visited the property the trails were in great shape, allowing for excellent hiking and cross-country skiing. We often don't think of the maintenance involved on reservations, but I was so impressed I called Tom Foster, District Supervisor for the Trustees of Reservations, and asked him about the trails. "Over the past few years," said Tom, "we have worked to rebuild the trail system. We even used a back hoe to work on mudholes, installing concrete culverts and placing gravel on muddy parts of the path."

When asked about wildlife in the reservation, Tom told me the habitat was good for woodland birds, such as grouse. He also mentioned that the native American holly found here could be the northernmost stand in the U.S. The hollies are easiest to see in the forest during the winter, because its prickly green evergreen leaves are still on the tree. The distinctive red fruits are also on the tree in the winter, if not first consumed by wildlife such as songbirds, wild turkey, and bobwhite.

The following walk is a ramble that takes a little under two hours and makes a loop of the eastern portion of the property leading you through the rhododendrons and azaleas. From the parking area follow the wide gravel road near the signboard and beneath the telephone wires that leads into the woods. Follow the trail through pines and hardwoods for about three minutes then turn right on the first

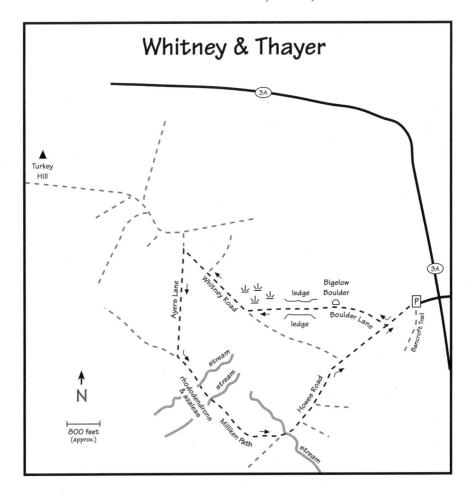

trail you come to. This is appropriately named Boulder Lane. Children will love playing on the many glacial erratics that were deposited by the retreating glaciers and they will also enjoy climbing on sections of exposed bedrock. For families traveling with young children, limit your walk to Boulder Lane, or you may soon be carrying your child for part of the way on the long loop walk highlighted here.

This is a good section of trail to see the holly tree's shiny green foliage in the understory of the larger oaks, pines, and maples. About ten to fifteen minutes into your walk you will see Bigelow Boulder on your right. This boulder weighs about 200 tons. Another couple minutes down the trail is a second boulder, which has little nooks and crannies in the jumble of rocks around it that children will love to explore. These glacial erratics are so named because they were deposited haphazardly by the retreating glaciers.

The trail passes a scattering of beech trees that brighten up the forest with their light gray trunks. Even in the winter they add a touch of color because the

*The Bigelow Boulder lies adjacent to a woodland path at Whitney and Thayer.*

papery golden-brown leaves on the lower limbs often stay on the tree until new growth pushes them off in the spring. Large outcroppings of rock line the trail on the right and left before the trail crosses through a small swamp and arrives at the intersection with the Whitney Road Trail, about a half hour into your walk. Stay to the right at the intersection and continue walking for another ten minutes. You will come to another intersection. Turn left here on Ayer's Lane.

Coyotes probably roam these woods but seeing one is difficult because they are stealthy, nocturnal animals. They moved into the state in the 1950s and have been slowly expanding. It is estimated that there are roughly three thousand in the state and their numbers continue to grow because their predator, the wolf, has been exterminated. Coyotes are very adaptable, and have found a ready food source of mice, carrion, birds, rabbits, domestic animals (such as ducks and geese and even cats), and berries.

We often look straight ahead while hiking, but it's a good idea to look down to see what's growing on the forest floor. On this section of trail you might spot sarsaparilla, partridgeberry, and club mosses. About fifteen minutes down this trail will bring you to an intersection at the Milliken Memorial Path. Turn left here to complete your loop back toward the parking lot. Rhododendrons and azaleas line the path, with hollies and hemlock trees growing nearby. All this greenery crowding the path gives it a mysterious and enchanting feeling, even in winter. But in late spring and early summer the scene is truly magnificent when the pinks and whites of thousands of flowers from the azaleas and rhododendrons brighten the woods. Rhododendrons grow up to thirty feet and sometimes the branches from several different trees interlace them and form an impenetrable jungle. Its evergreen leaves are large and leathery, sometimes reaching a length of ten inches. Flowers are often white or pink and grow in showy clusters. The bark is reddish brown, and the new twigs are green. While rhododendron flourishes in southern New England it is very rare in the northern states.

Old stone walls crisscross the woods, indicating the area was once used for pasture or farming—hard to believe with some large white pines towering overhead. Settlers called their annual harvest of stones "New England potatoes," because the frost pushed up stones at such a great rate. If you look closely at stone walls they yield clues: Walls with lots of little stones mixed with the bigger ones means that adjacent land was probably cultivated, but if there are only large rocks in the wall the land was probably used for grazing livestock or mowing for hay.

The Milliken Memorial Path narrows in some spots, and the rhododendrons along the trail's edge give it a tunnel appearance. During wet periods this trail can be very muddy, and there are a couple of small streams to pick your way across. At about the twenty-minute mark down the trail you will come to an intersection; bear left as the Milliken Memorial Path turns into Howes Road, which crosses over a stream on a bridge. Stay on the main trail, passing by various entrances to the narrower Bancroft Trail. About fifteen minutes of walking will bring you to a point where Whitney Road comes in on the left, but continue straight ahead. Within a couple minutes you will come to a chain barrier that looks like private property, but is still part of the reservation. Step over the chain and pass a private residence on the right. The trail, which turns into a gravel road, will lead you back to the parking lot in ten minutes.

If you are interested in a longer walk on your next visit, try exploring Turkey Hill at the northwest end of the property (shown on the map). From the summit there is a nice view of Cohasset Harbor. Visit World's End Peninsula and Whitney/Thayer on the same day if you are driving from a long visit. World's End is a very special Trustee's property: two glacial drumlins jutting into Boston Harbor. Old carriage roads laid out by Fredrick Law Olmstead, a noted landscape architect, wind through the hilly terrain with great water views. The park can be crowded during the warm weather and on the weekends, so consider a visit in the winter or during mid-week.

## Getting There
From Route 3 take Exit 14 to Route 228 north. Follow Route 228 north for 6.6 miles, then go right (southeast) on Route 3A. Follow Route 3A 2.1 miles to parking area on right across from Sohier Street.

Open dawn to dusk, seven days a week, year-round. No admission but donations accepted; no facilities; dogs allowed on leash.

# Ellisville Harbor State Park

## Plymouth

* 101 acres
* 3 miles
* 1.75 hours
* Easy
* Great for children

## Highlights

* Secluded beach with birding and seals
* Woods and meadow

Ellisville Harbor State Park is one of the lesser-known parks in Massachusetts, but if you love beachcombing and watching seals it will soon become one of your favorites. Located at the southern end of the town of Plymouth, the park spans 101 acres of meadow, woodlands, salt marsh, and shore. This combination of terrain attracts birds of all varieties so be sure to bring your binoculars.

Begin your walk by following the only trail, which leads through a meadow scattered with cedars. About fifty feet from the parking lot the trail splits and you should go left, following blue triangular markers. On your right is a large oak tree with enormous spreading branches looking like groping arms. About 300 feet farther down, the trail intersects with a dirt road and you should turn right and walk along the road, which heads directly toward the ocean. On the left will be a patch of woods with scrub pine and oak, and on the right is the meadow where staghorn sumac grows among the cedars. Both the cedars and sumac are opportunistic trees, among the first species to colonize abandoned fields. The staghorn sumac gets its name for the smooth velvet that covers its outer branches, much like that of a deer's antlers. The field is a good spot to look for kestrels which hunt in open areas for insects and small rodents. Sometimes they can be seen perched at the top of a cedar tree. Other wildlife that visit the field include white-tailed deer, red fox, and cottontail rabbits.

About five minutes down the trail you will see an abandoned Christmas tree farm on the left, where the blue-green color of Colorado blue spruce mix with the uniformly green colored balsam fir. You might want to take a few moments and

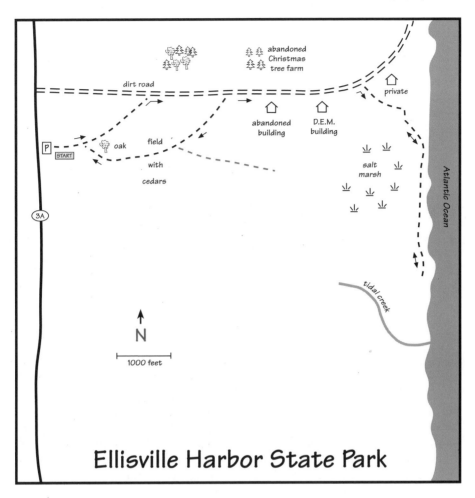

# Ellisville Harbor State Park

walk the perimeter of this field looking for wildlife, since few people detour from the road you are on. The common crow is one bird you are likely to see here. The other common creature you may see in the field or in the abandoned Christmas tree farm is the groundhog or woodchuck. It makes burrows in the ground and when in danger will make a beeline for its hole.

Continue down the road and within five minutes you will pass an abandoned house on the right and a Department of Environmental Management building also on the right. Soon you will come to a sign announcing that the rest of the road leads to private homes (one is directly ahead). At this point a footpath leads away from the road on the right. Follow this. Within a couple minutes the trail descends to the beach and you are rewarded with a deserted shoreline and the blue waters of Cape Cod Bay. To the left the coast has a considerable amount of rocks and to the right shoreline is more sandy.

With binoculars scan all the exposed rocks jutting from the water for seals. The best viewing for seals is at low tide when more rocks are exposed. You may also see a loon, two cormorant, and buffleheads bobbing beyond the breakers.

It wasn't too long ago that seals were unwelcome in the Bay State. During the late nineteenth and much of the twentieth century there was a bounty on seals, and fishermen would kill them, fearing that they were eating too many fish. But humans were depleting the fish stocks by overfishing, while seals were feeding primarily on sandlance, a small fish with virtually no commercial value. The killing of seals was finally halted in 1972 with the passage of the Marine Mammal Protection Act.

The seals often seen at Ellisville Harbor are harbor seals, which migrate each winter, heading down from Canada and Maine to Massachusetts. They arrive in October and leave in the early spring. During low tide they sun themselves on the rocks where they are safe from humans on the beach. Known as dog-faced seals because of their pug noses and dog-like looks, they can grow to five or six feet and weigh as much as 250 pounds. Perhaps one of the best places to see seals in Massachusetts is at Monomoy Island off Chatham. (Both Massachusetts Audubon (508-349-2615) and the Cape Cod Museum of Natural History (508-896-3867) offer seal watching trips.)

Continuing about four hundred feet down on your right you will be able to see the salt marsh, where wading birds such as great blue heron can be seen stalking the shallows. In October the autumnal tints of the marsh offer soft hues of gold, rust, yellows, and shades of brown. Be sure to soak up the sounds and smells of the ocean as well as its sights.

By walking the beach for about three quarters of a mile you will arrive at the mouth of the creek that drains and fills the marsh. During low tide the creek carries food such as small fish out to the ocean, and both birds and seals are often stationed just off the creek mouth. Be sure to bring your camera as the combination of marsh and ocean offer many photo opportunities. To the south the cliffs along the beach are also interesting to view. Scan the water for cormorants diving beneath the surface as they hunt for fish. In the winter, another diving bird, the common loon, is sometimes seen here. The loon's underwater feats are legendary, but their flight is equally impressive—they are surprisingly fast for such a large, heavy bird. (The distinctive summertime black-and-white coloring of the loon is replaced in winter by brownish gray feathers.)

To return to the parking lot retrace your steps. You can alter your path opposite the abandoned Christmas tree farm by exiting the dirt road on a trail just beyond the abandoned house. This will take you through the field of cedar trees and on the opposite side of the lone oak tree mentioned earlier.

## Getting There

From Route 3 take Exit 2 and follow signs to Route 3A North. Take Route 3A north about 2.2 miles and turn into parking area on the right at State Park sign.

Open dawn to dusk, seven days a week, year-round. No admission fee; no facilities; dogs allowed on leash.

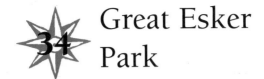

# Great Esker Park

## *Weymouth*

---

* 237 acres
* 1.5 miles
* 1 hour
* Easy
* Great for children

---

## *Highlights*

* Large esker (a glacial ridge-shaped mound) overlooking salt marsh and woods
* Great birding

With a little imagination a walk on top of the glacial esker at Great Esker Park can be compared to walking on the back of a giant snake. Formed by glacial deposits during the last ice age (12,000 years ago), the mile and a quarter long esker rises above the woodlands and the marsh, reaching a height of 90 feet. The fact that the esker runs parallel to a salt marsh makes it all the more interesting for exploring, and offers an excellent opportunity to see a wide variety of birds. (The esker could have been lost to development, but the town of Weymouth acquired the acreage in 1966 from the federal government, which owned the area, using it as a buffer zone to an ammunition depot located on the other side of the Weymouth Back River.)

Two walks are described here: the first goes through an area south of the parking lot (which can have wet spots at high tide), and the second is a short half-hour walk that goes through the northern portion the park.

From the parking area follow the paved road (closed to vehicles) that begins to the right of the maintenance buildings and climbs the esker. In three minutes you reach the top at an intersection with another paved road that follows the contours of the esker. (Eskers are shaped when rivers within the retreating glaciers filled with debris, which was left behind as the glacier melted.) Turn left here and walk along the top of the esker in a northerly direction passing beneath oaks (red oaks have bristle-tipped lobes and white oaks have rounded lobes) and maples. In the understory are gray birch and staghorn sumac. The staghorn sumac gets its name from the velvet covering its stems that look like the velvet on a stags antlers. It is non-poisonous and especially colorful in the autumn when the leaves are a

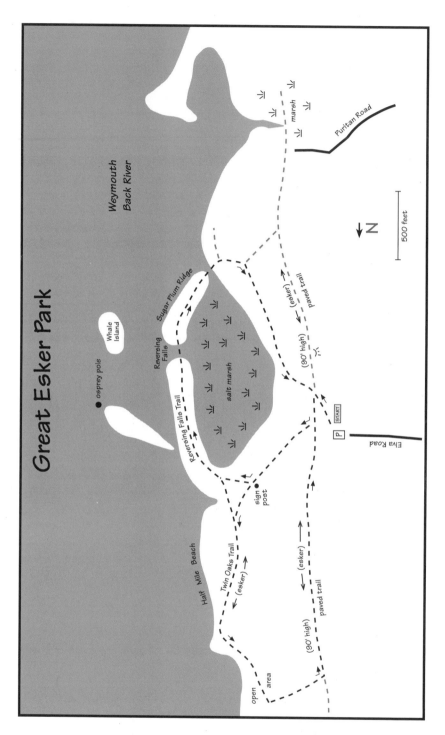

Great Esker Park

dark crimson. In roughly two hundred feet you will come to a sign for the Reversing Falls, and you should turn right at a dirt trail. The trail leads down off the esker toward the salt marsh and after three or four minutes of walking you arrive at another sign (for Twin Oaks). Bear right toward the reversing falls.

Walk along the edge of the marsh and look through the trees to spot birds feeding in the marsh grass. Park Ranger Mike Doyle told me that he often sees wood ducks, snowy egrets, great egrets, and even an occasional little blue heron in the marsh. The little blue heron is usually seen in coastal areas, migrating north to Massachusetts in the spring after the first real warm fronts. Adults have a slate-blue back and wings, with a brown-colored neck and head. Immature birds are white with dark-tipped bills and greenish legs. On my last walk at Great Esker I saw a kingfisher, osprey, cormorant, and egret, so be sure to bring your binoculars.

The salt marsh and estuary at Great Esker is quite large and is a critical link in the food chain, second only to rain forests as productive habitats. More than thirty species of fish can be found here including flounder, bluefish, striped bass, eel, herring, and smelt. Many young fish and invertebrates grow up here, finding shelter in the dense grasses. Beneath the water's surface, oysters and shrimp feed on top of the mud while sea cucumbers and worms live beneath the mud. Crabs use the tides to their advantage, burrowing in the mud at low tide for protection and scavenging along the bottom at high tide. In the spring there is an annual herring run up the Weymouth Back River and into Whitman Pond where the fish spawn in the fresh water. And in the last couple of years as Boston Harbor has become cleaner, seals have been seen in the Weymouth Back River in the springtime.

The trail climbs a smaller esker and at the top of the ridge turn right. There are good views of the marsh from both sides of the trail, and if you look to your left you will see an osprey pole used by these magnificent birds as a nesting platform. There have been a breeding pair of osprey here since 1992, and many young ospreys have been raised at the site. "The osprey," said Ranger Doyle, "catch fish in the Back River and upstream at Whitman's Pond. You can expect to see the osprey arriving about the same time as the herring run."

After four or five minutes of walking you will descend the hill and arrive at Reversing Falls. Not exactly Niagara (or even a waterfall for that matter), but a passageway between two sections of the marsh where the water rushes in at high tide and exits at low tide. (Look for hermit crabs and other marine life in the estuary.) A series of stepping stones cross the passage, making it possible to pick your way across at low tide. At high tide you may have to remove your shoes and carefully wade across. On the other side of the passage, follow the narrow trail that passes over Sugar Plum Ridge, offering nice views of the Weymouth Back River and Whale Island. Look for the pure white coloring of mute swans floating out on the water.

Low-bush blueberries are scattered about the woods beneath the oaks. At the end of Sugar Plum Ridge, cross a low-lying area (where you need to remove your shoes at high tide) and follow the trail straight into the woods, bypassing a side trail on your left. In a couple minutes bear to the right passing beneath a power line. Then at the next fork stay right (if you go straight it leads directly to the paved trail on top of the esker). You will be walking through a grove of beech trees with smooth gray trunks then passing beneath the power lines again. (The esker will be on your left.) After walking about fifteen minutes the trail swings left, and climbs the esker to the top where it intersects the paved road. You are at the spot where the paved road from the parking lot meets the paved road on top of the esker. There is a partial view of the Boston skyline from the top of the esker if you turn left and follow the top of the esker south for five minutes.

You can extend your walk an additional half hour by following the top paved road on top of the esker in a northerly direction. Retrace your original steps along the paved road then go right on the side trail which will bring you to the Twin Oaks sign. Follow the arrow toward Twin Oaks, climbing up the hill. In a couple minutes you will arrive at an intersection where you should bear left. Follow this trail for five minutes, first passing some birch trees and then by edge of the salt marsh. (Take time to explore the shoreline, examining the driftwood and shells.) In about ten minutes you will arrive at an open area. Cross the open area (comprised of wood chips and grass) and follow a dirt road to the left that brings you back to the paved road on top of the esker. To return to your car just go left on the paved road for about fifteen minutes. There will be a bench for resting along the way, offering a fine view of the salt marsh. Wildflowers line the paved road here making it a good place to see butterflies, particularly in the fall when the monarchs are passing through.

## Getting There

From Route 3 take Exit 28S (Route 18). At the first traffic light turn left onto Middle Street. At the end of Middle Street (2.9 miles) turn left onto Commercial Street and proceed 0.4 mile to the first traffic light. Turn right onto Green Street and go 0.6 mile to the triangular divider. Bear right on Elva Road and go uphill 0.2 mile to end and park in large lot.

No admission fee; no facilities; dogs allowed on leash.

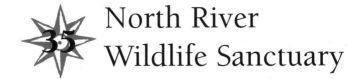

# North River Wildlife Sanctuary

## *Marshfield*

---

* 175 acres
* Walk #1: 1 mile/45 minutes
* Walk #2: 1.25 miles/45 minutes
* Easy (both walks)
* Great for children

---

## *Highlights*

* Loop trail through field along North River
* Woodland Loop Trail

The North River, so rich in history and natural history, is the jewel of this 175-acre reservation which includes meadows, wetlands, and woodlands. Two loop trails with short boardwalks circle the property. Birding is excellent here. One boardwalk leads out over the salt marsh to the edge of the river, offering splendid views.

The first walk begins by the parking area near the sanctuary's office building. A butterfly garden featuring such butterfly-attracting plants as evening primrose, bee balm, foxglove, and Siberian iris, grow along the base of a handsome stone wall. The plants were chosen for the nectar in the flowers, which the butterflies drink, or because they are sources of food for caterpillars. A good time to see butterflies is in late September when monarch butterflies begin their migration southward.

The trail you are following passes in front of the office and butterfly garden, heading east, then forks near the woods. If you go right you will head into the woods; if you go left you will cross Summer Street where the trail resumes through a field. This is the trail to follow, and from the field you can get a glimpse of the North River and gold-green salt marsh. Look for meadow-loving birds such as bluebirds and kestrels. The kestrel is a member of the falcon family, measuring only eight inches in length. It has a rust-colored back and black markings on a white face. The male is quite colorful, with touches of blue in its wings. Although it primarily hunts insects, I have seen a kestrel swoop down and kill a blackbird in a spray of feathers. Their call is a sharp, *Killy, killy, killy.* They are most frequently seen in the spring when they migrate along the coast. Another interesting bird that frequents fields is the bobolink, which begins arriving in Massachusetts during

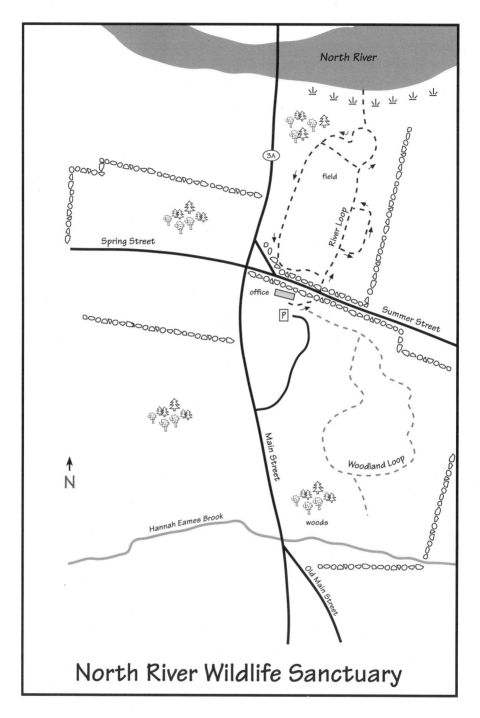

# North River Wildlife Sanctuary

frequents fields is the bobolink, which begins arriving in Massachusetts during early May.

Halfway through the field and just five minutes after crossing Summer Street a sign points to the Red Maple Loop Trail on the right. Take this trail into the shade of the woods where red maples (also known as swamp maples) thrive in the moist soil. A short boardwalk leads over the wettest sections of the woods, where the swamp maples soon grow alongside white pines. Look for chipmunks, squirrels, rabbits, and woodland birds such as titmice and nuthatch. You might even see the enormous outline of a great horned owl before it glides silently from its perch in one of the tall pines. Even if you don't see wildlife you might see their signs—like the pile of empty seed shells beneath a pine tree where a squirrel or chipmunk had been feeding.

After walking approximately five minutes on the Red Maple Loop Trail, it emerges from the woods into the field where you turn right to continue on your way to the river. In a short distance of about 75 feet a sign points the way to the river where the trail reenters the woods on the right. A short boardwalk leads through more red maples and then over the salt marsh to a small observation platform at the river's edge.

The North River is an estuarine waterway where the tidal flow from the sea mixes with the river's own fresh water. The river is tidal all the way to its source at the Herring and Indian Rivers. It has been designated a National Natural Landmark and became the first Scenic River in Massachusetts in 1979. Along the banks of the river are stands of rice cut-grass, woolgrass and salt-marsh cordgrass (especially in the lower river). Blue flag iris, yellow iris, cattails, and arrowhead are found in the upper reaches.

Waterfowl live along the river and the broad margin of salt marsh along its banks, while birds of prey such as the osprey use the river as their hunting grounds. Osprey can be identified by the crook in their wings, a white face with a black marking, and the way they dive into the water to snatch fish with their talons. From the end of the boardwalk you can see an osprey nesting platform to your right.

Another bird to look for is the harrier hawk. This slim hawk feeds primarily on rodents, and you might see one hovering above the edges of the marsh before it pounces on its prey. The male's back is light gray with a light underbelly, while the female's back is brown with white and brown markings beneath. Some of the best birding on the river is from a canoe seat, but because the river is tidal you should consult a tide chart so the tide assists your paddling rather than working against you. The Norwell section and upstream is good for paddling. Lower sections of river can be dangerous for canoeists due to the tidal currents. A launching spot recommended by the *AMC River Guide to Massachusetts, Connecticut and Rhode Island* is Bridge Street in Norwell, and from here you can paddle upstream through beautiful marshlands.

Thousands of ships were built along the banks of the North River from 1650 to 1871, because of the abundance of timber (primarily white pine and oak) and because at high tide, large boats (such as brigs and schooners weighing several tons) could be floated out to sea. (On nearby Cornhill Lane a large cast-iron sign from 1919 marks the exact location of the famed Rogers Shipyards where master shipwrights built vessels weighing between 20 and 221 tons.) Several ironworks also lined the river, and the anchor used by "Old Ironsides," the U.S.S. *Constitution,* was forged in Hanover.

After observing the river, retrace your steps off the section of boardwalk over the salt marsh and then turn right to continue the loop walk. The boardwalk now passes through scrubby woods of briars, grapevines and sumac. It soon ends and you'll walk a short distance on a trail that brings you back to the field. Follow the trail along the west side of the field before it curls to the left hooking up with the path you came in on when you crossed Summer Street and passed the butterfly garden.

You can double the length of your walk by taking the Woodland Loop Trail into the woods. This is the trail we passed earlier near the sanctuary office and butterfly garden. Cedars, oaks, maples, and small white pines comprise the majority of trees here. Stone walls crisscross the woods, and at the southern end of the trail there is a small stream called Hannah Eames Brook.

Another great walk in Marshfield is the Daniel Webster Wildlife Sanctuary. It too has exceptional birding and has a blind overlooking a pond that children will enjoy. Much of the trail traverses open meadow similar to the one at the North River Wildlife Sanctuary, giving the walker spacious vistas.

## Getting There

From Route 3 take Exit 12 and go east on Route 139 for 1.7 miles to Furnace Street on the left. Follow Furnace Street 0.7 mile and turn left on Route 3A (north). Go 3.4 miles to the sanctuary entrance marked by a sign on the right.

Open dawn to dusk, year-round. Closed Mondays except major holidays. Fee for non-Audubon members. Nature center, programs, and rest rooms. No dogs. 781-837-9400

# Allen's Pond Wildlife Refuge

## *Dartmouth*

* 186 acres
* 1.5 miles
* 1 hour
* Easy
* Great for children

## Highlights

* Coastal walk
* Osprey
* Ducks
* Rocks for children to climb

Allen's Pond Wildlife Refuge, owned by the Massachusetts Audubon Society, offers a coastal walk with Allen's Pond on one side and Buzzards Bay on the other. There are rocks to climb, tidal flats to explore, a barrier beach for brisk walking, and salt marsh habitat with excellent birding. Children will enjoy beachcombing and running along the edge of the surf. In addition to the 186 protected acres shown on its map, the Dartmouth Natural Resources Trust and Massachusetts Audubon Society have placed another 300 acres surrounding the pond under conservation restriction, making this a significant undeveloped coastal ecosystem.

    The best time to visit Allen's Pond is in the spring and fall during bird migrations, and the warm, beachcombing weather. If you come in the winter pick a day of moderate temperatures because cold winds whip off the water. Should you come in the summer choose an overcast day because the walk is entirely in the open. (In the summer, there is considerable traffic for Horseneck Beach and the town beaches. Because the town beach is next to Allen's Pond, much of the parking spaces are reserved for local residents in the summer.)

    To begin your walk from the parking area, follow the path that begins by the Allen's Pond sign. On your right is the ocean and on your left a rocky shoreline with fields beyond. Notice how the surf has rounded the rock edges closest to the water. After five minutes of walking you reach Quanset Rock, a rocky bluff with a

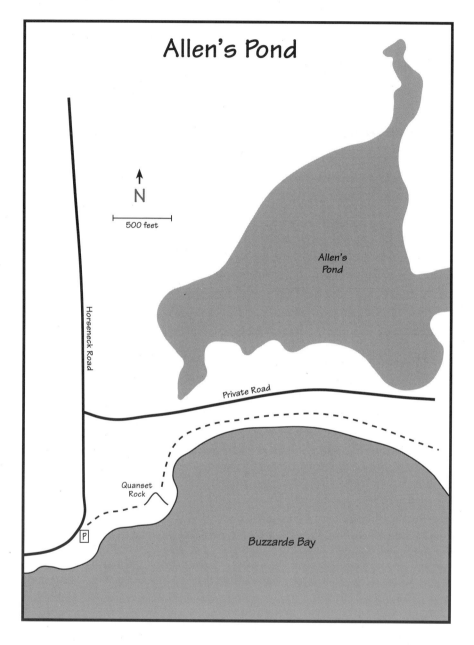

few small cedar trees growing in patches of soil within the rocks. The view from the rock is superb; you can see Allen's Pond to the left and the crescent-shaped shoreline stretching eastward. Children seem to love hikes with water or with climbing rocks and here they can enjoy both.

*A crescent-shaped beach separates the ocean from Allen's Pond.*

From Quanset Rock, walk along the beach in an easterly direction. Scan the pond with binoculars for bird life such as cormorants, geese, and mute swans. Allen's Pond is also the northernmost breeding site for the seaside sparrow, and sightings of such rare birds as the little egret (normally found only in Africa and Eurasia) have also occurred here.

The mute swan, a large white swan with a long curving neck, is an Old World species that had been introduced to North America and is now breeding in the wild. They are an aggressive bird that will actually drive out native species from ponds. The population of mute swans are increasing at an alarming 30 to 40 percent annually, and biologists are trying to limit the population.

Continue walking along the beach for about twenty minutes until you reach some private homes and then turn around and begin the walk back. If you're walking with children, stop and examine the shells, flotsam, and little pieces of driftwood. And keep an eye on the ocean, just beyond the breaking waves, for various ocean birds. There are two rocks rising from the ocean that often are used as resting spots for cormorants. You might see eiders, mergansers, buffleheads, ruddy ducks, and green-winged teal bobbing in the surf. The common eider, a short-necked diving sea duck, often flock together in the winter in groups called rafts. They fly in lines just a few feet above the ocean, using slow deliberate wing beats with head held low. The male has a touch of green on the back of the head, black on the top of the head, and white sides with a black belly. Eiders are excellent divers, often staying underwater for two minutes. Federally protected piping plovers nest on the beach during the summer months, so be careful when walking. (Sections of the beach could be closed during nesting season.)

After you make your way back to your car, you might want to explore nearby Goosebury Island (managed by the Department of Environmental Management), which offers some nice trails. (See "Getting There" for directions to this island which can be reached via a causeway.) Wide gravel paths run through the center of the island leading toward concrete observation towers used in World War II at the outer end of the island. On the east shore there is a nice bluff overlooking the ocean. There is good beachcombing here as well. A round-trip walk out to the towers takes about an hour.

## Getting There

From Route 195 take Exit 10/Route 88 South. Follow Route 88 southward for about 12 miles to where it crosses the Westport River and turns eastward. Proceed about 2 miles, passing Horseneck Beach, to a stop light. If you go right about 0.8 mile you will reach the causeway to Goosebury Island and parking at the end. To reach Allen's Pond from the stop light, go left about a mile and look for the blue Massachusetts Audubon sign on the right where there is parking along the shoulder of the road adjacent to the ocean. (In the summer there is traffic around Horseneck Beach and the town beaches. Because the town beach is next to Allen's Pond, many of the parking spaces are reserved for locals. The best time to visit is in the off-season.)

Open year-round, dawn to dusk. No admission fee; no facilities; no dogs allowed.

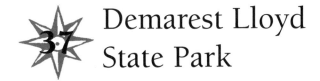

# 37 Demarest Lloyd State Park

## South Dartmouth

* 220 acres
* 1.5 miles
* 1 hour
* Easy
* Great for children

### Highlights

* Coastal walk
* Salt marsh
* Shore birds

Situated where the mouth of the Slocum River meets the ocean, Demarest Lloyd State Park offers a fine ramble along the shore and a salt marsh. Although the park is officially open from Memorial Day to Labor Day (when there is swimming at the beach), walkers can explore the park year-round, but they must park at the entrance gate and walk the half-mile entrance road to reach the shore. In the summer, the beach is a fine spot for families with small children because there is little surf or undertow. At high tide the beach is quite narrow; at low tide a walk along the beach is great for beachcombing, with shells and marine life scattered among the rocks. Walkers who go on a summer weekend may want to consider arriving early to walk, then swim later in the morning.

From the lower parking lot, begin your outing by following the dirt and grass road that runs south from the parking lot, passing between the rest rooms and the maintenance sheds. (If you plan on walking here with young children, you may want to shorten the walk and only explore the northern end of the property.) The landscape is primarily open, with scattered pitch pines, cedars, and white oak. Few people walk down this old road, so you might see a rabbit or fox moving from the thickets of vegetation. Red fox are one of nature's most handsome and graceful animals. They follow regular hunting routes on their search for mice, rabbits, and birds. Fox dens are used primarily for the protection of their young, which are born in late March and April in litters of 1 to 10. (To distinguish fox dens from groundhog holes look for bones scattered about the opening from the meals fox

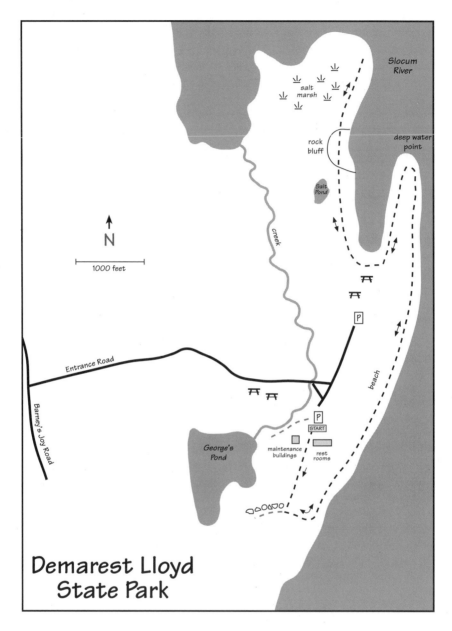

Slocum
River

salt
marsh

deep water
point

rock
bluff

Salt
Pond

↑
N

creek

├──────────┤
1000 feet

P

beach

Entrance Road

Barney's Joy Road

P
START

George's
Pond

maintenance
buildings

rest
rooms

# Demarest Lloyd
# State Park

have eaten. Fox dens tend to have a large mound of sand and dirt near their entrances.) Although not as common as the red fox, the gray fox can be seen here. Besides being smaller than the red fox, the gray fox can climb trees.

Continue following this dirt and grass road for ten minutes to where the road ends by a stone wall. Go left, and in fifty feet you will be at the ocean's edge. Football-size rocks lay about the shore and there are shells for children to discover. Piping plover (an endangered species) nest on the beach in May and June and lay eggs there, making them difficult to distinguish from surrounding pebbles. Plovers are small shorebirds with short necks and dark markings about the head. They have yellow legs and feet, and these endangered birds are seen on dry sandy portions of the beach. Another shorebird seen here is the killdeer, larger than the plover (about eight inches long), with orange on the upper tail and lower back and a white underside and brown upper back. Killdeer repeats its name as its call, and is often found far from water in fields and pastures.

The walk continues by following the shoreline northward, past the bathing area to deep water point, and narrow point of sandy beach near the mouth of the Slocum River. The shoreline here is still evolving, with sandbars appearing and then disappearing, caused by underwater currents and waves washing over low shoreline. Such plants as beach grass, dusty miller, and beach pea try to colonize exposed sandy areas and help prevent such erosion.

There is an open spacious feel here, making it a good walk in the early springtime when cabin fever will have you dreaming of warmer days. Turn back to the south and cross a creek that feeds into the lagoon, and head north again along the edge of the lagoon. You will reach an outcropping of rock in about ten minutes. This is a fine place to rest, as the rock is about thirty feet high, and there is a good view to the east. Children can try to catch minnows and hermit crabs in the pools of water just below the rock. Keep a pair of binoculars handy because osprey

*Sandy beaches at Demarest Lloyd are perfect for beachcombing.*

(identified by the crook in their wings and black markings near this crook) are seen here. They are large birds, with a length of twenty-two inches and wingspan of fifty-four inches. When hunting they swoop down to the waters surface and grab a fish with their sharp talons.

During low tide you can walk beyond the rock outcrop along the edge of the lagoon and salt marsh to the mouth of the Slocum River. In the summer months there is usually a small boat or two fishing in the river. Striped bass are the prized catch. The stripers had been over-fished, but strict laws regarding size limits and the catch and release practice of many anglers has brought this fishery back to a healthy state. When you are finished with your exploration retrace your steps past the rock to the northern end of the parking area and reward yourself with a picnic in the shade. In the fall, swallows often congregate in this vicinity before migrating south.

Before leaving you might want to take a look at George's Pond (if you don't mind trekking through a bit of mud). A narrow trail begins from the picnic area near the lower parking lot, located to the right of the rest rooms and maintenance buildings. The trail starts by crossing a ditch. Then you should bear right and walk about fifty feet to reach Giles Creek. Follow the creek to the left for about a hundred feet for a view of the pond. There are usually a pair of mute swans on the pond, as well as cormorants. Sometimes osprey can be seen circling overhead. The mute swan is a large white swan whose neck is held in a graceful S curve when swimming. Originally an Old World species introduced into North America to decorate the pond of estates in Long Island, some of the swans escaped and now breed in the wild. Although pretty to look at, the mute swan, like so many exotic species, is causing its share of problems. It is an aggressive bird and can drive away native species.

## Getting There

From Route 195 take Exit 12A and go south on Faunce Corner Road. Proceed 1 mile to stop light and intersection of Route 6. Cross Route 6 and continue on Chase Road (Brown State Park signs mark the rest of the way). Go 4.3 miles on Chase Road to its end, then turn right on Russel Mills Road and follow that 1 mile to Russel Mills Village. At intersection at Russel Mills Village continue straight (following State Park signs) and you will be on Horseneck Road. Follow Horseneck Road 2.3 miles to where it forks, and bear left onto Barney's Joy Road. Proceed 0.6 mile to T-intersection and go left (still on Barney's Joy Road). Go 1 mile to park entrance on the left.

Entrance road open from Memorial Day to Labor Day, seven days a week. Weekdays from 10:00 A.M. to 6:00 P.M., weekends from 8:00 A.M. to 6:00 P.M. Rest rooms, shower, and changing facilities. Admission charged. No dogs allowed when beach is open for swimming. Walkers can visit the park year-round but must park on the shoulder of the road near the entrance gate and walk down the entrance road 0.5 mile to reach the shore. 508-636-8816

# Cape Cod

## Sandwich Boardwalk/ Town Beach

### *Sandwich*

---

* (Also recommended walk at Greenbriar Nature Trail)
* 1.5 miles
* 45 minutes
* Easy
* Great for children
* (Special parking regulations: A sticker is required from 10:00 A.M. to 4:00 P.M. during the summer months.)

---

### *Highlights*

* Long boardwalk along salt marsh
* Shoreline walk along Cape Cod Bay

This is one walk where you might find yourself looking at the boardwalk more than the surrounding salt marsh. When the town of Sandwich needed to rebuild their boardwalk they used a novel idea to raise funds: citizens could pay for a plank and have a message carved into the wood. You'll see the names of families and lovers as well as initials, quotations, and other interesting inscriptions along this boardwalk.

Walkers who wish to use the boardwalk in the summer must plan ahead to either arrive early in the morning or in the late afternoon because of special parking regulations that require a sticker from 10:00 A.M. to 4:00 P.M. during the summer months when the town beach is open. Turn this inconvenience into an advantage. Plan ahead and enjoy the boardwalk at the best times—early morning and late afternoon when the blazing summer sun is not directly overhead. Birding is also usually better at these times.

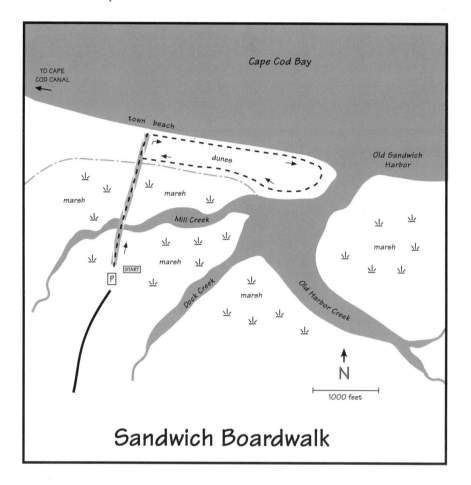

# Sandwich Boardwalk

Over a thousand feet long, the boardwalk spans Mill Creek and the salt marsh and connects to the town beach on Cape Cod Bay. The first of many board-walks here dates back to 1875 and the latest was built in 1992. A plaque at the beginning of the boardwalk calls the reconstruction a "labor of love," and judging from the messages on the planks it certainly appears so.

The boardwalk soon crosses over Mill Creek, a tidal creek that ebbs and flows with tide. (Highest tides occur just after a new moon and full moon.) The salt marsh is a nursery for shellfish and fish, and many birds are attracted by these food sources. Terns dive for minnows while herons stand motionless waiting to ambush a passing fish. Green herons, yellowlegs, sandpipers, snowy egrets, and great blue herons are just some of the birds you might see. The greater yellowlegs is a wading bird with long yellow legs, grayish back, and white underparts. It measures four-teen inches from its long straight bill to the tip of its tail. Semi-palmated Sandpiper is a small, six inch bird, that is on the Cape from May to October, when it flies vir-

tually non-stop to South America. Identification marks include black legs and bill,
light streaks on the breast, grayish brown on the back with a white belly.
Occasionally a harrier hawk is seen hovering above the marsh. The pole you see out
in the marsh to the right of the boardwalk is an osprey-nesting platforms.

As you continue to cross the salt marsh, consider the salt marsh a food factory, where the food chain starts from microscopic organisms. Even our best agricultural fields cannot produce the food per acre that the marsh can. Oysters, clams,
scallops, flounder, and striped bass are some of the species that benefit from, clean,
protected marshes.

You will reach the end of the boardwalk in ten minutes. There is a bench for
resting at the crest of the dunes. The widespreading roots of the beach grass hold
sand and thrust new roots to the surface as more sand collects, helping to build the
height of the dune. The grass is narrow and rolled at the sides to reduce surface
evaporation by the ocean winds. Do not step on the grass as this will damage it and
cause the dunes to blow away, which could lead to the destruction of the marsh they
protect. The dunes at Town Beach were strengthened in 1991 when more sand
dredged from the Cape Cod Canal was added along with more beach grass.

At the end of the boardwalk take the stairs down to the beach, where count-
less pebbles are strewn across the shore. Rounded by the pounding of waves, the
colors of the pebbles are white, tan, gray, speckled, orange, and subtle shades of
pink. With each wave there is a clacking, grinding sound of receding water rolling

*The Sandwich Boardwalk leads over the salt marsh and to the shore of Cape Cod Bay.*

over the pebbles. Sometimes starfish and sea urchin shells are mixed with these stones. This is an especially beautiful spot in the winter. There is a spaciousness here, with just the flat expanse of the horizon, which makes such a walk an adventure in solitude. In *The Outermost House*, author Henry Beston, described the Cape's shore as "solitary and elemental, unsullied and remote, visited and possessed by the outer sea, these sands might be the end or the beginning of a world."

Looking out to sea, there is usually a large boat or two in the distance, because the entrance to the Cape Cod Canal is just off to your left, marked by a stone jetty. The canal was completed in 1914 and is the world's widest sea-level canal. Before the completion of the canal hundreds of sailors lost their lives rounding the Cape when their vessels broke apart on the sandy shoals of the outer Cape. (You can walk the beach to the canal, but it takes about two hours round-trip.)

The walk heads eastward along the beach to the mouth of Mill Creek. Dock Creek and Old Harbor Creek also empty into the ocean here and the currents are quite dangerous. On my walk there was a frothing rip where incoming waves met out-going tidal water. It looked like a good spot for striped bass to lie in wait for minnows to come out of the salt marsh. This is a good place to see ducks bobbing in the surf.

You can loop back to the boardwalk by following the edge of the creek back to the west. A hundred years ago the three creeks were lined with wharves, and boats would come into the creeks to load and unload their cargo. Total time on the walk is about forty-five minutes, but plan on allowing more time to sit and soak up the salt air.

Before leaving Sandwich, be sure to explore more nearby walks and the center of town. Lowell Holly Reservation, by the Sandwich/Mashpee line is a good walk. The holly and beech trees at Lowell Holly Reservation are worth the visit, and the entire reservation is surrounded by beautiful Mashpee and Wakeby Ponds. Greenbriar Nature Center and Trails is located just 1.7 miles farther east (toward Barnstable) off Route 6A from the traffic light where you made the turn on Jarvis Road. Look for Discovery Hill Road on your right and Greenbriar is just up the road a short distance. The nature center, with its natural history exhibits, is wonderful for children. Adults will enjoy the Jam Kitchen and the resource library.

The handsome center of Sandwich is home of many attractions, including the Dexter Gristmill (a restored seventeenth-century mill); Yesteryears Doll Museum; Sandwich Glass Museum; Thornton Burgess Museum; the 1637 Hoxie House; and, just outside the center of town, Heritage Plantation (museum and gardens).

## Getting There

Where Route 6A intersects with Jarvis Street, turn east on Jarvis Street heading away from the center of Sandwich. (There will be a large sign for Sandwich Center on Route 6A near Jarvis Street.) Cross the railroad tracks and go straight, turning left on Factory Road a couple hundred feet beyond the tracks, then turn right on Boardwalk Road after traveling just a couple hundred more feet. Follow Boardwalk Road to the end (about half a mile) where there is parking (sticker required from 10:00 A.M. to 4:00 P.M. during the summer).

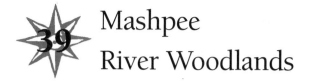

# Mashpee River Woodlands

## *Mashpee*

---

* Mashpee River Woodlands
* 250 + acres at the Woodlands
* 1.5 miles
* 1 hour
* Easy
* Great for children

---

## Highlights

* Good views of the river
* Woodland trail along undeveloped shore
* Beach walks with salt-water ponds

The Trustees of Reservations and the Mashpee Conservation Commission together own more than 250 acres, protecting the pure waters of the Mashpee River. The river supports a wide variety of fish such as sea-run trout and herring. The healthy fish population helps support the area's many birds that feed on fish, such as great blue heron and osprey. The walk is a gentle one, and is primarily shaded.

From the parking lot walk on the wide entrance trail that heads west into the woods. About a hundred feet down the trail you'll reach an intersection and a signboard. Go straight through the intersection and onto the Chickadee Trail that leads through woods of white pine, scrub oak, and pitch pine.

Examine the needles of the pine trees to differentiate between the white pine and pitch pine. The white pine's needles are slender and flexible, from three to five inches long growing in clusters of five. The pitch pine needles are rigid, flattened, and usually curving, grouped in bundles of three. The pitch pine is able to reseed after a fire, and this natural resistance actually makes controlled burning a way to retain the pitch pines and prevent the natural change to the wider diversity of trees in the forest. Because of its ability to grow in dry, barren soils the pitch pine flourishes in windswept areas of the Cape where few other trees can grow.

In fifteen minutes you will see parts of the Mashpee River, and the Partridge Berry Trail will be on your left. You should bear right, continuing on the Chickadee Trail. The trail parallels the river, and there are openings in the trees for good river

# Mashpee River Woodlands

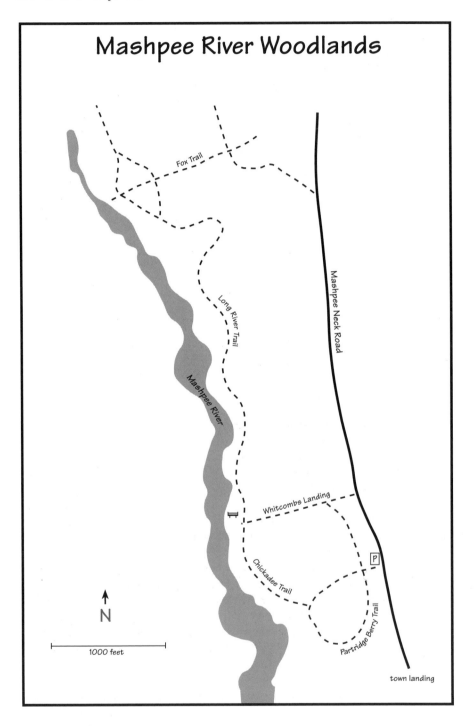

Fox Trail

Long River Trail

Mashpee Neck Road

Mashpee River

Whitcombs Landing

Chickadee Trail

Partridge Berry Trail

N

1000 feet

town landing

views. Ducks are often on the river even in the winter, because ice rarely seals the river from shore to shore. The river is about five-hundred feet wide here and is less than a mile from the ocean. It may look like a large river, but it's source is just six miles north at Mashpee-Wakeby Pond, an eighty-seven foot deep "kettle-hole" pond formed by glacial ice. The river is a combination of fresh and salt water, and the salt water extends roughly one mile upstream to the "edge" where the salt water intruding from the bay first meets the fresh water flowing down the river.

Besides "salters" or sea-run brook trout, the river has stocked rainbow and brown trout, warm-water species such as pickerel, and herring, which run up the river from the ocean each spring to spawn. The herring has long been an important food source, first for the Native Americans and later for the early European settlers. The Native Americans would construct weirs, made of sticks or rocks, in the river into which fish would swim but could not escape.

One of my recent walks here was on a cold January day, and I had the reservation to myself. I didn't see so much as a squirrel until I reached the river, where I was rewarded for my efforts by an up-close sighting of a red-tailed hawk. The hawk was perched on the branch of an oak that overlooked the river. The best field marks for identifying this hawk is the dark belly band, and uniformly colored tail: reddish above and light pinkish-tan beneath. Red-tailed hawks prey on rabbits and rodents; listen for the hawk's high pitched scream when in the woods. New England also has another similar species of hawk, the red-shouldered hawk, which

*The Mashpee River mixes with salt water and spreads into marshes near its delta at the Mashpee River Woodlands.*

is slightly smaller and slimmer than the red-tailed hawk. Red-shouldered hawks have red-barred chests, banded black and white tails; look for their chestnut-colored shoulders when they perch. This declining species prefers wetlands away from human development and preys on reptiles, amphibians, and rodents.

As you walk along the river the plants in the shallows, such as salt meadow grass and black grass, are all able to tolerate salt water. Mussels, quahogs, and soft-shell clams are just some of the shellfish species that spend part of their lives in the salt marsh. Look for bayberry along the wood edge, identified by waxy gray berries that are used to make scented candles. On the forest floor pink lady's slippers add color to woods in the spring, as does wintergreen with red berries in the fall and winter. The wintergreen is a low, creeping plant with shiny evergreen leaves that are fragrant from the plant's oils.

After about fifteen minutes of walking adjacent to the river you will reach the intersection with Whitcomb's Landing Trail, which is on your right. There will be a bench overlooking the river. Begin your return walk to the parking lot by turning right on Whitcomb's Landing Trail. After eight or nine minutes take another right (an unmarked trail) to return to the sign-board by the parking lot where you first started your walk. This last trail is a relatively short one, which you will cover in about six or seven minutes. For those who want a long outing from the bench at Whitcomb's Landing, continue north along the river—the Chickadee Trail now turns into the Long River Trail—and follow approximately one mile to a fork in the trail. Bearing right to reach the Fox Trail. Turn right on the Fox Trail and then go right again at the next intersection. You will arrive back on Mashpee Neck Road, where you can follow the road south about a mile to the parking lot.

## Getting There

Mashpee River Woodlands: From the Mashpee Rotary on Route 28, follow Route 28 northeast for 0.4 mile to Quinaquisett Road on the right. Follow Quinaquisett Road for 0.6 mile (passing the North Parking Lot for Mashpee River Woodlands) to Mashpee Neck Road on the right. Take a right at Mashpee Neck Road and go 1.1 miles to the parking area on the right at conservation area sign.

No admission; no rest rooms; dogs allowed.

The Mashpee Conservation Commission offers free, naturalist-guided tours of the woodlands. Call 508-539-1414.

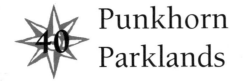

# Punkhorn Parklands

## *Brewster*

---

* 835 acres
* 1.5 miles
* 45 minutes
* Easy (additional trails for extended walks)

### Highlight

• Loop walk partially along pond with excellent birding

According to the Brewster Conservation Commission, "punkhorn" means "a place of sponge wood." Punkhorn Parklands is one of the Cape's larger conservation areas, rich in wildlife and diverse terrain. Eagle Point trail, which runs along upper Millpond, is one of several trails at Punkhorn. This is a good choice for a summer morning walk because breezes come off the water and most of the trail is in the shade.

Begin your walk from the parking area by following Run Hill Road one hundred feet south to a conservation sign and trail map box on the right near the boat launch. The Eagle Point Trail begins here, heading into the woods toward Upper Millpond. (There are numbered markers along the path that correspond with a trail guide issued by the Brewster Conservation Commission.) Catbrier, a common thorny plant on the Cape, grows beneath pitch pines and oaks. The eastern wood pee-wee, a member of the flycatcher family of insect-eating birds, is seen and heard here in the spring and summer. Listen to its plaintive call of "pee-wee, pee-wee." Other birds that frequent these woods include the white-breasted nuthatch (they usually are facing downward on the tree trunk as they search for insects in the bark), the black-capped chickadee (a social bird that will let you approach quite close), tufted titmice (slate gray color), and warblers (small active birds that flock together during migration).

Within five minutes of walking you'll pass by an old bog on the left. This was once a cultivated cranberry bog. In New England, there are three different forms of cranberries: the mountain cranberry, which is small and spreading and can grow on rocky slopes; the large cranberry, which is often the cultivated cranberry; and the small cranberry, which is best identified by its nodding pink flowers. Just beyond the bog, the trail hugs the edge of Upper Millpond, with openings in the

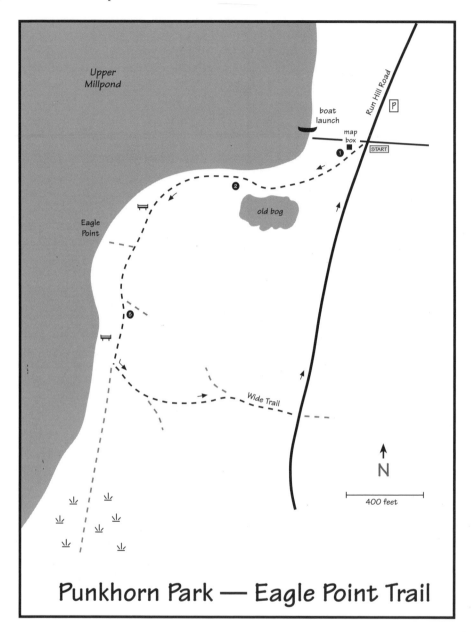

Upper
Millpond

boat
launch

map
box

❶

❷

Run Hill Road

P

START

old bog

Eagle
Point

❺

Wide Trail

↑
N

400 feet

# Punkhorn Park — Eagle Point Trail

trees for views of the water. In the winter look for bufflehead, ring-necked and rare canvasbacks on the water. In the warmer months look for night herons hunting the pond edge or roosting in the pines.

The pond has an average depth of eighteen feet and is connected to Walkers Pond to the south and Lower Millpond to the north. All three drain into Paines

Creek and Cape Cod Bay. Herring or alewifes make their way from the ocean and up the creek into the ponds each spring to spawn in the fresh water. (To see if the herring are running, visit the Stony Brook Grist Mill at Stony Brook Road which you passed to reach Punkhorn.) The yearly migration takes place when the temperature of the outflow of the pond is warmer than the bay waters, usually close to the vernal equinox (when day and night are of equal length). When the young herring reach about three inches they begin to move back toward the sea where they'll grow up to fifteen inches long. In three or four years the survivors will return to the same water to spawn. (The age of a herring can be told by the markings on their scales because they change patterns each time they enter and exit salt water.)

Continue walking parallel to the pond, ignoring small trails to the left and right. See if you can spot the beech trees with their smooth gray bark. Their autumn foliage is a vivid gold, which turns tan as the season progresses. The leaves

*A bench offers a resting spot overlooking Upper Millpond.*

on the lower branches stay on the tree well into the winter. Beechnuts are eaten by an assortment of birds, including grouse, blue jay, and the wild turkey.

After a couple more minutes of walking, the trail climbs a hills. At its crest is a bench overlooking the pond and there is a nice sunny area for a picnic. This hill, which curves toward the water, is called Eagle Point (immature bald eagles have been sighted off the point). There is a marker here which reads "We don't inherit the earth from our parents, we borrow it from our children." Let's hope that when we turn the earth over to our children we have done our best to keep it open and green like the acres at Punkhorn.

Frequent walkers at Punkhorn say there are lots of white-tailed deer here. One of the reasons deer antlers are rarely found in the woods is because the mice eat the antlers before they are found. The antlers are not bone, but are bone-like structures that are shed each season. They begin to grow on male white-tailed deer in the spring, and at their fastest growing time are covered in velvet, or hairy skin that supplies nutrients to the growing antlers. In the fall the dried velvet is rubbed off against saplings, shrubs, and even rocks. Then, in late winter, the antlers begin to loosen and fall off.

You are as likely to see snakes as you are deer at Punkhorn, and you might get lucky and see a black racer, which can grow up to sixty inches long. It is a non-poisonous snake, (as are all snakes on the Cape), that is important in keeping the rodent population under control. Another Punkhorn denizen adept at controlling the rodent population is the great horned owl. They nest and roost in the tallest pine trees, swooping from the trees at night to grab rabbits and skunks.

At marker #5 the trail splits but you should stay straight, paralleling the shoreline and passing by another bench. About hundred feet from this bench the trail forks again, and you should bear left. (If you go straight the trail follows the pond, but goes through a swampy area where the trail is often flooded.) By bearing left at this fork you stay to the high ground, heading in a southeasterly direction. Soon the trail forks again and you should bear left into woods dominated by oak. Box turtles, which are becoming rare are sometimes seen on the woodland path. Admire their yellow, orange, and black high-domed shell, but do not touch them. (Should you ever see one on a road with traffic, move it off the road in the direction it was traveling in.) In about a hundred feet the trail becomes wider. Stay to the right and you will soon be at the intersection of a dirt road.

Go left on the dirt road and you will be back at the parking lot in ten to fifteen minutes.

## Getting There

From the intersection of Routes 6A and 134 in Dennis take Route 6A east 1.1 miles into Brewster to Stony Brook Road on the right. Follow Stony Brook Road 1.5 miles to end and go left on Setucket Road for 0.2 mile. Turn right on Run Hill Road, and go 1.3 miles to large parking lot on the left.

No admission fee; no facilities; dogs must be leashed. The Brewster Conservation Commission offers a trail map to all 835 acres. Call 508-896-3701.

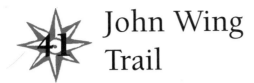

# John Wing Trail

## Brewster

---

* 140 acres
* 2 miles
* 1.5 hours
* Easy
* Great for children

---

## Highlights

* Salt marsh
* Tidal flats
* Upland woods, island, coastal dunes
* Nature museum

  (*Note:* The John Wing Trail floods at high tide—check the tide chart in the museum.)

Wing Island, near Cape Cod Bay, is a small island covered with red cedar and beach plum. It is a peaceful place, to be sure, but its history is tied to a settler who was forced to flee here. John Wing was a Quaker living in Sandwich, when the ill winds of religious persecution descended on his family in 1656. At the time the middle section of Cape Cod was still a relatively wild place, and it was here John Wing came, the first white settler of Harwich's North Parish, which would later be incorporated as Brewster.

Today, Wing Island, along with almost 140 acres of salt marsh, woodland, and coastal beach are managed by the Cape Cod Museum of Natural History and the Brewster Conservation Commission. (Stop in the museum and borrow the trail guide which explains in detail the natural history of Wing Island.) Complete with turtles, snakes, and a wide assortment of fish, the museum is fun for both children and parents.

The John Wing Trail, traversing the salt marsh, the island and the sandy coast, is a wonderful place for a family outing. The outing starts to the left of the museum on the path that heads to the north through pine woods in the direction of Cape Cod Bay. Also seen in the thickets are highbush blueberry, bayberry, choke-

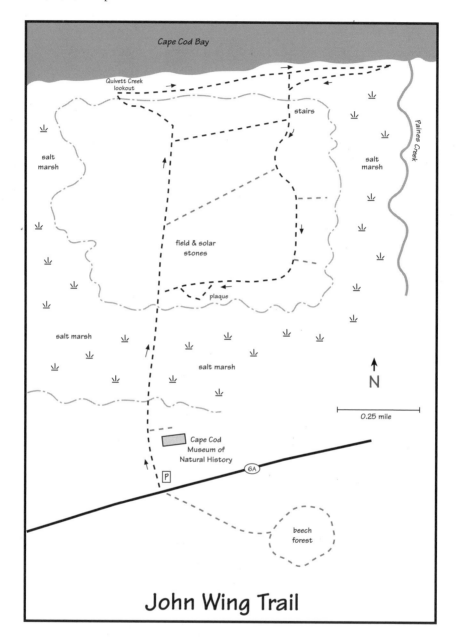

# John Wing Trail

berry, and honeysuckle. Within a couple of minutes you will enter the salt marsh where wooden boards have been laid over the wet areas to keep your feet dry during slack and low tide. (At high tide there are sections of the trail that can become wet.) Be on the lookout for wading birds, such as great blue herons and green herons, that stalk the marsh for crabs and small fish. Look for harrier hawks circling the marsh for small mammals, and kestrels perched in trees at the edge of the wetlands as they survey the ground for small birds and insects.

Glasswort, seaside goldenrod, bulrush, marsh elder, and salt meadow hay are just some of the plants found in the upper section of the marsh. Only the very high tides and storms flood this section of the marsh. The ground here is comprised of partially decomposed plants and fine sediments, and the buildup of salt marsh peat is said to be as deep as twenty feet in some sections. In the days of John Wing, the salt hay was cut and piled into wagons, then dried on Wing Island before farmers gathered it for cattle feed. Today, the scene is one of absolute beauty, particularly in autumn when the marsh grass becomes a golden hue, the low-lying vegetation a maroon with the green evergreens rising from Wing Island beyond. Bluebird houses have been erected on poles set in the marsh. They have small entrance holes to keep out larger, unwanted birds, while letting bluebirds and tree swallows inhabit the houses.

When you reach the far side of the marsh, after about a fifteen-minute walk from the parking lot, you will be on Wing Island. The low-lying vegetation is thick, and your view is limited to perhaps twenty-five feet—quite a contrast from the open marsh. Stay straight on the trail, passing a path on the right. Eastern red cedar, oak, and a few pitch pines line the trail. A few hundred feet ahead is an abandoned field where beach plum, aster, and wildflowers named starry false Solomon's-seal and New England blazing star grow. The blazing star blooms in August and September and has pushy pink and purple flowers on three-foot stalks. Listen for catbirds, chickadees, and mockingbirds calling from the trees. Also in the field is a solar calendar made from stone posts, and an interpretive sign, explaining how to track the sun in the different seasons.

*A killdeer hides in the grass on the John Wing Trail. The mother bird will often feign injury to lure predators away from its nest.*

Continue ahead, staying straight, and passing the two trails on the right. After ten minutes of traversing the island and another marsh area you arrive at the sandy beach, with its dunes, inlets, and ocean views. Children will love looking through the flotsam of crab shells, driftwood, and snail shells. Shallow pools of water left at low tide are a good place to see hermit crabs that occupy shells left behind by snails. You can also see periwinkle, sand shrimp, green crabs, and moon snails. Sandpipers, killdeer, and black-bellied plovers hunt the beach and dunes, while terns plunge into the water in search of small fish. Killdeer and black plovers are members of the greater plover family of birds. Both birds nest right on the ground, making it difficult to see their eggs because they look just like pebbles. Should you see a killdeer acting injured, it is trying to draw you away from its eggs. Walk carefully, to avoid stepping on the eggs.

Walk along the beach in an easterly direction for about fifteen minutes until you reach the mouth of Paines Creek. Then turn right for a few feet and head back west on a wide sandy trail where a dune of sand separates you and the ocean on your right. Be careful to walk on the sand and not to trample the beach grass that holds the sand in place. On your left will be the marsh. Follow this sandy path for about five minutes until you see a green sign ahead. Turn left by the sign, crossing a tiny wooden bridge over a drainage ditch. (Take time to read the sign which gives the natural history of the salt marsh.) On the other side of the ditch are stairs leading up to Wing Island. Be on the lookout for beach plum near the edge of the island. In May it will have white flowers and in September it will have fruit.

Once you climb the stairs continue directly ahead and follow the narrow path into the interior of the island, staying straight where another path enters on the right in a few hundred feet. Then after walking another three minutes you will pass interpretive marker # 6 on the right, followed a minute later by a trail on the right. You should stay straight. Continue for another couple minutes, passing a trail on the left that leads to an overlook of the creek. Then after walking a few hundred feet you should bear right, where the trail forks. You will soon come to the historic plaque on your left where the trail makes a little ten-foot loop. (The plaque is on a stone and it explains how John Wing settled near this spot.) Continue on the trail fifty feet and you will intersect the main trail. Go left to return to the parking lot.

## Getting There

The John Wing Trail is located off Route 6A in Brewster at the Cape Cod Museum of Natural History. From Route 6 heading to the outer Cape, take the Route 138 exit for Dennis and follow that north to Route 6A. Turn right (east) on Route 6A and continue for 2.6 miles to the signs for the Cape Cod Museum of Natural History on the left.

From the outer Cape at the intersection of Route 137 and Route 6A in Brewster, the parking lot is located 1.6 miles to the west on Route 6A.

Open year-round, dawn to dusk. Admission fee; rest rooms in the museum; dogs allowed. Cape Cod Museum of Natural History: 508-869-3867.

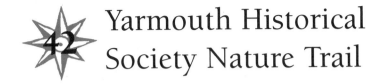

# Yarmouth Historical Society Nature Trail

## *Yarmouth*

---

* ❋ 50 acres
* ❋ 2 miles
* ❋ 1.1 hours
* ❋ Easy

---

### *Highlights*

- Secluded pond
- Holly trees, giant beech tree, Norway spruce

The winding hilly path through woodlands at the Yarmouth Historical Society Nature Trail provides a pleasant walk to a small pond. A bench overlooking the pond offers a nice resting spot where it's possible to see waterfowl, kingfisher, and maybe a deer. The Kelley Chapel and the historic Captain Bangs Hallet House on the property are worthy of a visit.

From the parking area adjacent to the post office, follow the entrance road about thirty feet to the sign for the nature trail and turn right onto the trail. Rhododendrons are scattered about so you may want to time your walk with their late-spring bloom. When not blooming they are best identified by their large (six to nine inch), evergreen leaves clustered at the end of branches, and by the bark which is thin-reddish brown. The trail forks in about fifty feet and you should bear left following the black arrow, passing through woodlands of red cedar, pitch pine (three needles per bundle), and small oak. Pitch pines require sun for the seedlings to grow, and in time the oak will shade all the woods and become the dominant tree. Honeysuckle, cherry, bayberry, and sumac also compete for the sun. The bayberry has small gray aromatic berries growing in clusters on short twigs. Although bayberry can grow as large as six feet tall they rarely exceed three feet. Early settlers boiled the fruit to get wax from which to make fragrant bayberry candles.

The thick undergrowth along the trail is a good habitat for rabbits, providing them both shelter from the wind and predators as well as food. If you hear a rustling in the leaves it might be a rabbit, or possibly a rufous-sided towhee, a brown-sided bird with white belly and white spots on the tail. The towhee scratches dead leaves on the ground to unearth insects.

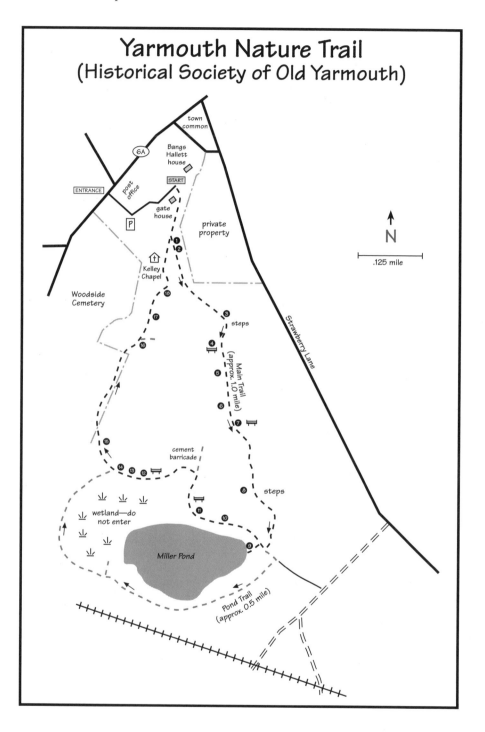

# Yarmouth Nature Trail
## (Historical Society of Old Yarmouth)

*The pointed, shiny evergreen leaves of the holly*
*tree add color to winter woodlands.*

In five minutes the trail climbs wooden steps into more mature woods of pitch pine and oak, with rhododendrons and some holly trees growing beneath the canopy. The holly tree has bright shiny leaves, with sharp points that remain on the tree all year. Pink lady's slippers also grow here. (The single petal looks like the toe of a slipper.) These members of the orchid family often are found beneath pines in acidic soil. In five more minutes you will descend a hill and head toward the pond. The trail then forks and you should go left to extend your walk around the south side of the pond. You might want to get a better glimpse of the pond on the short trail ahead. Miller Pond was formed by the pressure and melting of a huge chunk of ice left by the retreating glacier. Its shape and glacial formation give it the label "kettle-hole pond."

Back on the pond trail which circles the southern end of the pond, look for mountain laurel, hollies, and catbrier, a green-stemmed plant with nasty thorns. There are also two small hemlocks (quarter-inch needles) that normally grow in more hilly areas like the Berkshires. A fork appears about fifty feet from where you first entered the pond trail. Stay to the right to continue circling the pond. You will soon pass a little trail on the right that brings you to the water's edge where you can scan the shoreline of the pond for visiting ducks, or resident kingfisher. The belted kingfisher is the most common kingfisher. They perch motionless over open water. When they spot a fish they dive into the pond and catch the fish with their long sharp beaks. With large head, short tail, and white band around the neck, these gray birds of twelve-inch size are easy to identify. In flight they have an irregular wing beat and make a rattling call. Deer and raccoon frequent the pond, as evidenced by the tracks along the pond's edge.

On this back end of the pond there are railroad tracks to your left, wetlands along the pond edge to the right, and large pitch pines shading the path. Pitch pines do well on the Cape because they can grow in sandy soils and can withstand strong winds. The trail now curls to the right, circling the west side of the pond. A cemetery can be seen through the trees on your left. You will soon reach a T-intersection. Left leads to the parking lot and right leads to the north end of the pond. Go to the right to arrive at a bench overlooking the pond. This is a nice rest stop, with holly trees and mountain laurel growing alongside the bench. Along the way you pass a large evergreen on your left, a Norway spruce. This is the only spruce with drooping branches and the only one in our region with large cones, up to six inches long. Its needles are dark green and about three-quarters inch long. Although a European tree, it may spread from plantings into the wild.

After resting on the bench, return to the T-intersection and bear right to head back toward the parking area. Soon, a cement marker with the number 15 on it appears next to the trail. This identifies an old clay pit, now covered with blueberries, bayberry, small oak, and pine. Just beyond is cement marker #16, which marks the location of a former golf course. It too is now reclaimed by the trees. There is an open area farther down the path to the right where a lone white birch grows. Signpost #18 directs your attention to an English oak, an exotic species with small, rounded lobe leaves. Beyond that is a blue spruce and another Norway Spruce, both planted here years ago. The trail passes the charming Kelley Chapel (built in 1873, complete with whitewashed pews, wood stove, and pulpit) then connects with the entrance road. The parking lot will be just to the left.

After your walk be sure to take a look at the gardens and the Captain Bangs Hallet House, now the home of the Historical Society of Old Yarmouth, which also maintains the hiking trail. The front of the house is Greek Revival, but the back side dates back to 1740. The house, with authentic nineteenth-century pieces, is open Sunday afternoons from June through September. Adjacent to the house is a two-hundred year old weeping beech tree.

## Getting There

From Route 6 take Exit 7 and go north on Willow Street toward Route 6A. Follow Willow Street for 1 mile to its end and go right on Route 6A for 0.6 mile. There will be a sign for the Yarmouth Historical Society Nature Trail on the right just before the post office. Turn here and park in the lot.

No facilities. Small donation requested.

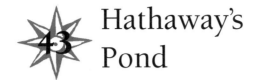

# Hathaway's Pond

## Barnstable

* 94 acres
* 1.2 miles
* 1 hour
* Easy

### Highlights

* A lesser known reservation with a circular walk around pond
* Fishing
* Picnicking

Hathaway's Pond, in Barnstable, is an undeveloped glacial pond with a wonderful loop trail around its border. Managed by the Barnstable Conservation Commission, the trail is quite hilly, passing through woodlands with an occasional opening in the trees, providing views of the water. From mid-June to mid-August a beach sticker, or daily beach fee, is required to hike the trails and swim. Other seasons are free. There is a sandy beach and picnic tables beneath the pitch pines.

The trailhead is to the left side of the pond as you face the water from the parking area. The beginning of the trail is wide and well maintained. It heads in a northwest direction through red oak (pointed leaf lobes), white oak (rounded leaf lobes), and pitch pines (needles grouped in threes). The pitch pine is well suited to the area's sandy soil and was planted all over Cape Cod to stabilize the soil that was literally blowing away because settlers had cleared the land of trees for farmland and pasture. In Thoreau's book *Cape Cod*, he discusses this problem and the importance of vegetation and beach grass: "Thus Cape Cod is anchored to the heavens, as it were, by a myriad little cables of beach-grass, and if they should fail, would become a total wreck, and ere long go to the bottom." Laws were passed in the 1800s such that cattle could not wander freely to eat and trample vegetation and inhabitants were prohibited from cutting brush.

Underneath the oaks and pines, greenbrier, a thorny vine, lines the trail. While a scourge to hikers, it produces blue-black berries that are eaten by a variety of birds. Its tangled thickets also provide safe nesting spots. Other plants you will see are red cedar, black locust, honeysuckle, and staghorn sumac, so named because their outer branch coverings resemble the velvet on a stag's antlers.

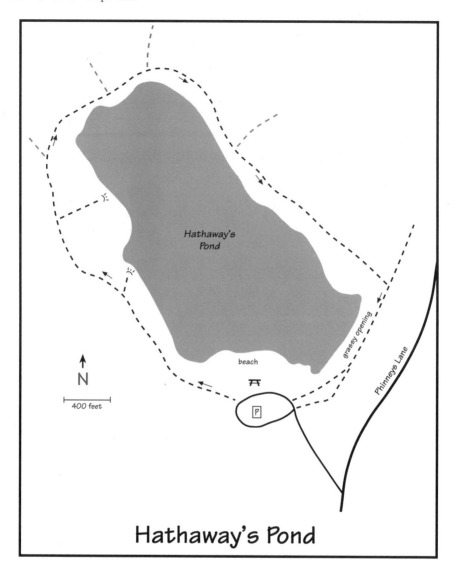

# Hathaway's Pond

About ten minutes into your walk the trail forks, with an overlook just a short distance down the trail to your right. The pond was formed during the glacial period, roughly 15,000 years ago, when huge blocks of ice formed a depression that was filled with meltwater and surrounded by rock debris deposited by the glacier. The water now in the pond is fed from the Cape's single aquifer, and fluctuations in the water level are tied to the changes in the amount of groundwater. Most kettle-hole ponds do not have surface inlets or outlets, and because of the surrounding permeable soil, the influence of surface water after rain or snow has minimal effect on the pond. Encompassing 20 acres, the pond

*The mottled color of tree frogs helps them blend in with the tree trunk and foliage.*

has an average depth of twenty-seven feet and maximum depth of fifty-six feet, thus ensuring an excellent cold-water fishery. It has been managed as a trout fishery since 1952 by the Massachusetts Division of Fisheries and Wildlife. The best time to fish the pond is in the spring and fall, when the trout are near the surface. Otherwise, in the summer, you will most likely need a canoe to fish the deep sections of the pond where the fish are holding during the heat of summer.

After about ten minutes on the main trail it curls a little to the left, away from the pond. On your left is a steep-sided hollow. In the spring it is filled with water, and is called a vernal pool because it eventually dries up during the heat of summer. While vernal pools may just appear to be waterlogged depressions, they are critically important to the natural world. Because fish are absent from such pools, amphibians can breed here with less threat of being eaten. These unique pools are used by wood frogs, tree frogs, and various salamanders as breeding sites. Invertebrates such as fairy shrimp spend their entire lives here. Tree frogs are seldom seen because they spend most of their lives high up in the trees, but they are heard on summer evenings when they make a peeping sound. With sticky pads on their feet they are well equipped for climbing and catching insects. Salamanders also live in forests that have vernal pools. During the breeding season in spring, they lay their eggs at the bottom of vernal pools; during the rest of the year they live underground, burrowing beneath the leaf litter of the woods. Bring along a magnifying glass if you are here in the spring so children can explore the vernal pools with you.

Continue on the trail and in another five minutes you'll reach a second overlook on a short trail to your left. There is an old foundation on this bluff, and some black locust, red cedar, and staghorn sumac. The dominant trees, however, are still the pitch pine and oak. The pitch was planted on the Cape in the 1800s to stabilize erosion and it then spread naturally. Besides the needles in groups of threes, you can identify it by its cones with sharp prickles and its overall scraggly appearance. Shade-tolerant oak trees are gradually replacing the sun-loving pitch pines as the forest matures.

Continue on the main path for another couple minutes to a fork in the trail by two small boulders, and bear right. The boulders are glacial erratics plucked from rock outcrops from the north and carried and dropped here by the glaciers. While most of the rocks carried by the glaciers were ground into sand by the shifting of glacial till, a few rocks such as these escaped intact.

In two or three more minutes the path forks again. You should stay to the right, closest to the pond. There are numerous resting spots here that face the pond where you can soak up some of the winter sun, which will be low in the southern horizon at the far end of the pond. It's a good place to observe rufous-sided towhee, cardinal, tufted titmouse, downy woodpecker, white-breasted nuthatch, and perhaps a kingfisher perched along the edge of the pond giving its rapid-fire rattle call. Mammals seen here include white-tailed deer, raccoon, red fox, skunk, gray squirrel, chipmunk, and opossum.

After your rest, continue to loop the pond, now heading in a southerly direction back toward the parking lot. Heath shrubs, which grow well in sandy, acidic soil, can be seen under the forest canopy. The Barnstable Conservation Commission has identified four different members of the heath family growing here, including low-bush blueberry, teaberry, huckleberry, and sheep laurel. In the summer be on the lookout for sweet pepperbush, a tall leafy shrub that grows by the pond and has upright clusters of small white flowers that are incredibly fragrant. The dry fruit capsules remain on the plant long after flowering, and help you to identify the shrub even in winter. A scattering of holly trees can also be seen along this east side of the pond. Just look for their shiny green leaves that twinkle in the sun.

It takes about twenty minutes to walk the back side of the pond, passing by two trails that lead off to the left while you stay closest to the pond. A grassy opening at the pond's southwest corner makes another good resting spot, or you could go a little farther to the beach and parking area where there are picnic tables.

## Getting There

From Route 6 take Exit 6 (Route 132) and go south on Route 132 for about a mile to Phinney's Lane on the left. Go north on Phinney's Lane and the entrance road to Hathaway's Pond will be on the left after traveling 0.3 mile.

Fee from mid-June to mid-August, none in the off-season. Rest rooms open in the summer but not in the off-season. Dogs are allowed. Open dawn to dusk. Hunting is allowed in season so be sure to wear orange. Barnstable Conservation Commission: 508-790-6245.

# 44 Fort Hill

## Eastham

---

* Part of the Cape Cod National Seashore
* 2 miles
* 1 hour
* Easy
* Great for children

---

## Highlights

- Spectacular views of ocean and salt marsh
- Open fields
- Boardwalk through red maple swamp

Treat yourself to a sunrise from the top of Fort Hill, and it will be an experience you won't soon forget. Then top it off with a leisurely walk through the hillside fields along Nauset Marsh and return to the hill via the boardwalk that winds through a red maple swamp. You can extend your walk by viewing the historic Penniman House, once owned by a whale-ship captain, and continue back to the parking lot on the trail that runs behind the Penniman House. It's a great way to spend a morning on Cape Cod's National Seashore. The combination of water, boardwalk, and expansive views make this walk a favorite of children. Bring your camera for the spectacular views.

Our walk begins from the upper parking lot at the summit of Fort Hill, a small hill with a big view. To the right is Town Cove, which separates Eastham from Orleans; straight ahead is Nauset Marsh, barrier beach; and the Atlantic Ocean lies in the distance. Henry Beston wrote the *Outermost House,* chronicling the natural year, while living in a cottage on the barrier beach. For nature lovers, the book is a must-read.

A path of crushed shells leads through the field for a few hundred yards toward the marsh directly in front of the parking lot, beckoning you to follow. The open fields are great for picnicking, kite flying, and bird watching. You might spot a snow bunting, a small bird that looks a bit like a large sparrow until it reveals a belly that is almost pure white. This ground bird is about six inches long, and is seen on tundra, dunes, and open fields. Other birds you might see are harrier

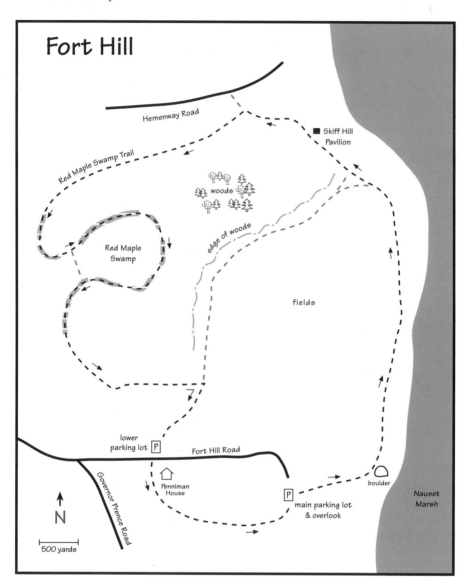

# Fort Hill

hawks hovering above the salt marsh, searching for prey; and herons or greater yellowlegs feeding in the mudflats.

A trail of shells leads down to the marsh where a huge glacial boulder makes the perfect place to climb and rest. The boulder here is a glacial erratic, deposited during the last ice age. Look closely at its south side and you will see a spike embedded in the rock, perhaps used as an anchor for small boats or to pull bales of salt hay out of the marsh. Bayberry, black cherry, honeysuckle, and salt-spray rose grow along the edge of the marsh. Autumnal tints here are subtle but pleasing to the eye, with golden marsh grass ringed by russet vegetation.

Follow the trail to the left in a northward direction for about ten minutes until you reach the woods comprised primarily of cedar trees. Bear right and into the woods. In a couple minutes you will arrive at a pavilion with a fine view. In the pavilion is Indian Rock, a boulder used by Nauset Indians to sharpen fish hooks and tools. The abrasive qualities of this fine-grained metamorphic rock were perfect for grinding and polishing implements. Let children run their fingers over the grooves in the rock, and explain how the Indians sharpened their tools in those same grooves. This glacial boulder was originally farther out in the marsh, but was moved here for viewing.

About three-hundred yards farther along the trail is the beginning of the Red Maple Swamp Trail on the left. A series of interspersed boardwalks help keep the feet dry and children will love the winding wooden paths. (Don't be surprised if your child gets a burst of energy here and takes a run on the boardwalk!) The standing water here is fresh water not salt water, and the swamp maple, or red maple, can tolerate having wet feet and is an extremely adaptable tree.

Follow the trail about a half mile and then at an intersection bear left to enter the darkest recesses of the swamp. The contrast in this dark and shaded wetland from the sunny fields at the beginning of the walk is one of the features that

*An artist captures the beauty of Nauset Marsh at Fort Hill.*

makes this walk special. Interpretive signs along the trail identify plants such as highbush blueberry, netted chain fern, and fox grapes. There is also winterberry (a low plant with bright red berries eaten by birds) and sweet pepperbush (which gives off a fragrant aroma from its flowers in August).

In about fifteen more minutes you will reach another fork. You should bear left. After another five minutes of walking you are back at the fields of Fort Hill. (Scan the fields for meadowlarks or bluebirds.) Turn right here and follow the trail to the lower parking lot, then cross the street to the Penniman House. You can't miss this historic home because at the front of the yard is an enormous archway formed by the jawbones of a whale. Captain Edward Penniman took to the sea at eleven years of age, eventually circling the world seven times. His home, built in the French Second Empire-style with cupola overlooking both the bay and sea, became a local landmark. Behind the house you can pick up the trail that will lead you in an easterly direction through low-lying woods for about a third of a mile back to the main parking lot.

## Getting There

From the rotary where Route 6 and Route 28 meet on the Eastham/Orleans border, drive north on Route 6 for 1.3 miles. Turn right onto Governor Prence Road, then about a quarter mile down bear right onto Fort Hill Road. Follow the signs to the upper parking lot a short distance ahead.

Open year-round, dawn to dusk. No admission; no facilities; no dogs allowed.

# Wellfleet Bay Wildlife Sanctuary

## *South Wellfleet*

---

* 720 acres
* 3 miles
* 1.5 hours
* Easy
* Great for children

---

## *Highlights*

- Estuary and salt marsh
- Island walk
- Shorebirds and waterfowl
- Pond

Wellfleet Bay Wildlife Sanctuary is one of the Cape's most popular outdoor destinations because of its extensive trail system along the edge of Wellfleet Bay and its salt marsh. To the north of the Nature Center is the Bay View Trail, a 1.4 mile-loop trail, and to the south is the Goose Pond Trail and Try Island Trail/Boardwalk that together cover about 3 miles. There is also a short trail along the edge of Silver Spring Brook that runs for 0.6 miles. All are worth exploring, but Goose Pond Trail and Try Island will be the focus of this walk. Both have great vistas and diverse plant life. The birding is also excellent—more than 250 species of birds have been seen at the sanctuary.

To begin your walk and exploration of the Goose Pond Trail follow the signs from the Nature Center directing you to the trail which heads in a southwesterly direction. A side trail, called the Fresh Brook Pathway, soon heads to the right, but you should stay straight. You get a glimpse of Try Island as you cross Silver Spring Brook, which has been made into a pond by the small dam you traverse. The shoreline of the pond on your left is surrounded by marsh fern, white poplar trees, swamp milkweed, and purple loosestrife, a non-indigenous plant that crowds out native vegetation. The loosestrife is easy to spot because of its bright purple flowers that bloom in the summer.

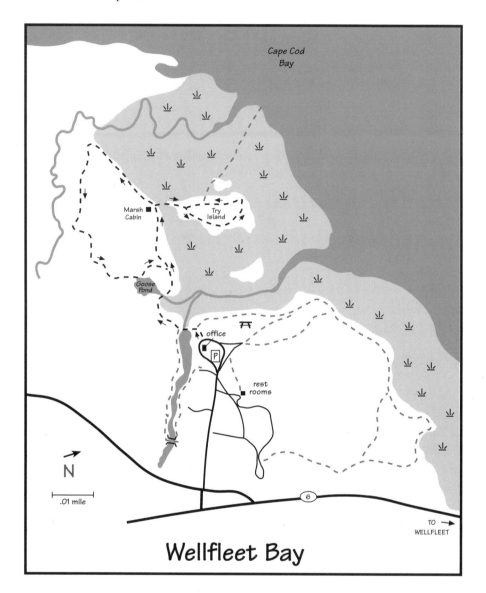

## Wellfleet Bay

If you want to see more of the pond, turn left after crossing the dike for a half-mile loop trail around the pond that will bring you back to the parking lot where you can resume your walk. The pond has red-wing blackbirds from March to October, and the male can be identified by its red shoulder patch. The females are dark brown and they nest in the wetlands, in grass and weed nests usually set in low bushes. They feed on insects and marsh plants. Warblers also visit the thickets around the pond during migratory periods. Other pond dwellers include turtles such as the snapping turtle, with its dark green-black shell with ridges, and the painted turtle, with smooth black shell and a head streaked with yellow markings.

When you cross the dam over Silver Spring Brook on the Goose Pond Trail you will emerge into an area of pines, including white pine (five clustered needles) and pitch pine (three twisted needles in a group), and red pine (long needles and reddish bark), and Scotch pine (shorter needles and orange-colored upper trunk). All were planted here to stabilize the sandy soil. It's interesting to note that when the Pilgrims landed at Cape Cod, the peninsula was covered with trees, but by the time Thoreau made his four explorations of the Cape he lamented that the Cape was literally blowing away because almost every single tree had been cut.

Follow the path through the pine woods for two or three minutes and then bear right over a small bridge. Goose Pond will be on your left. Many species of birds visit here, including the great blue heron and kingfisher. (As you face the pond there is a small bird blind set up for observation on the left side of the pond to the east.) Continue past westward on the main path past the pond and past a white spruce on the right. Keep going straight, passing a trail that comes in on the left. Red cedars will be scattered through the woods and a small observation deck will be on the right overlooking the marsh. About five minutes from Goose Pond, you will see a trail on the right opposite the "marsh cabin" that leads through the marsh and over to Try Island. Take this right and as you're walking through the marsh, have your binoculars ready. Kestrels, harrier hawks, and red-tailed hawks can all be seen in this area.

Just a minute or two through the marsh you will come to a fork in the trail. Bear right, following the sign to Try Island. Soon you will reach the island and be walking along its wooded eastern end. Follow the trail to the very end of the island where a bench has been erected on a bluff offering a great view of the bay and the salt marsh. One of the birds you might see in the marsh is the greater yellowlegs, a fourteen-inch long wading bird with long yellow legs and grayish back and white underparts. Tree swallows, which have a glistening blue-black coloring above and white below, can be seen swooping through the air, catching insects above the marsh in mid-flight. They prefer nesting boxes in open areas, often competing with bluebirds for choice boxes.

From the end of the island at the bench, turn around and follow the path on the right that runs parallel to the ocean, passing by another bench with a view. Within two or three minutes you will reach the intersection with the boardwalk. Turn right onto the boardwalk to head toward the beach. It's about a five minute walk to the shore, passing by the fine bladed high-tide grass that colonial farmers used for cattle feed, and past beach grass with narrow backs rolled at the sides to reduce area of surface evaporation from coastal winds. The beach grass has an extensive and wide-spreading root system than helps hold the sand on the dunes and beach.

After exploring the beach retrace your steps over the boardwalk and then bear right to exit Try Island. Once you cross the marsh, you will be back at the T-intersection by the marsh cabin. Turn right to complete your loop of the property.

The path is wide and sandy, with fields and woods to your left, and the salt marsh to your right. Look for viginea rose and salt spray rose with curved thorns and pale pink blossoms in the early summer. Sea lavender, also called marsh rosemary, grows at the upper edge of the marsh, staying close to the ground to conserve moisture. It has tiny white flowers that stay on the plant into the fall.

About five minutes down this path is an arrow pointing you to the left at a fork. Bear left, heading into the fields. Beach plums which have pink-white flowers in May before the leaves are fully out, grow in the sheltered spots of the field. They yield deep purple fruit in September which is eaten by red fox, raccoon, and birds. Other plants seen here include black locust, pokeweed, goldenrod, spindle tree, and golden aster. If you look closely you might be able to see the tall, green, fern-like leaves of asparagus, the wild descendants of farming that was done here more than sixty years ago. One of the dominant trees here, the oak, will carry its rusty leaves well into November when many other trees have lost their foliage.

Two reptiles that might be in your path in this upland meadow are the box turtle and the black racer. The box turtle has a high-domed shell with yellow, orange, and black markings. Be sure not to disturb box turtles as man's development has led to loss of turtle habitat and their numbers are down. The black racer is a rather large, extremely quick snake. They can grow over five feet long, and can be seen basking in the sun or hunting for small rodents. The black racer is not poisonous, as are all of the ten species of snakes that live on the Cape, and it too should be left undisturbed.

After walking through the fields and woods for five minutes you will be back at Goose Pond. Turn right to return to the parking lot which takes about another ten minutes. Before you go into the nature center to examine the many exhibits be sure to pause by the beautiful butterfly and hummingbird garden directly in front of the nature center.

## Getting There

Follow Route 6 for 0.3 mile north from the Eastham-Wellfleet town line to signs at the entrance road on the left. Follow the entrance road, crossing West Road, to the Sanctuary parking lot 0.4 mile away.

Open year-round, dawn to dusk. Admission fee; rest rooms; nature center; no dogs allowed. Closed Mondays except for certain Monday holidays. 508-349-2615

# Atlantic White Cedar Swamp Trail

## *Wellfleet*

* 1.5 miles
* 1 hour
* Easy
* Great for children

### Highlights

* Large Atlantic white cedar trees
* Boardwalk

Entering the Atlantic White Cedar Swamp is like visiting another world. The bright sunshine, sand, and open vistas of the Cape are replaced by a dark and mysterious forest of cedar trees, where you can't help but walk in hushed footsteps in respect for this beautiful and unusual swamp. Come early in the morning or in the off-season and you might have the magic of the cedar swamp all to yourself.

From the parking lot follow the sign for the Atlantic White Cedar Swamp Trail, and bear left at the intersection just a short distance from the start. The first part of the walk brings you through open heath lands and stunted pitch pines and twisted bear oak. Both species are probably the most numerous trees on the Cape because they can tolerate dry, sterile sandy soil. The bear oak is also known as the scrub oak, and in exposed areas, it rarely grows taller than ten feet. Most of the trees before you are approximately eighty years old, even though they are the height of most shrubs.

The path of pure sand gradually descends toward the swamp, passing taller pines and oaks with black huckleberry and broom crowberry in the understory. Both the huckleberry and crowberry are low-growing heaths that tolerate sandy soil. Huckleberry is best identified by its yellow, resin-spotted leaves. The oaks and pitch pines become progressively larger as the trail descends because there is less wind in the low-lying area to stunt their growth. Roots of the trees are also closer to the water table which also contributes to better growth.

About fifteen minutes into your walk the trail crosses a dirt road. This is where the boardwalk into the swamp begins. Standing water is on either side of the boardwalk, and swamp-loving plants like the highbush blueberry and sweet

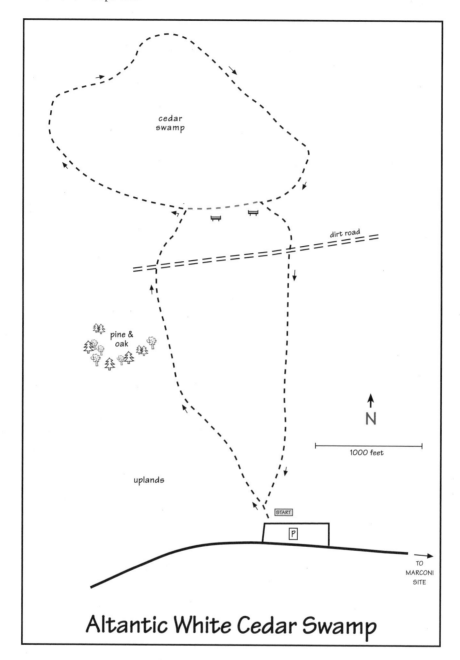

cedar
swamp

dirt road

pine &
oak

N

1000 feet

uplands

START

P

TO
MARCONI
SITE

# Altantic White Cedar Swamp

pepper-bush grow in the rich soil. But it's the cedar trees that will capture your attention, with richly textured bark and spreading branches that block out the sun. On fallen trees lichen grows on the trunk, and where an occasional shaft of light penetrates the canopy, the lichen takes on a vivid, iridescent hue.

*A boardwalk snakes through the dark recesses of
this unusual and mysterious Atlantic white cedar
swamp.*

It's hard to believe that in the 1850s this land was barren, stripped of timber
by settlers. Atlantic white cedar was a particularly prized wood, decay-resistant and
easy to shape. It was split into boards and used for joists and frames, doors, floors,
and rafters. Slats of cedar were used as boxes, woodenware, and tanks to hold whale
oil. Fence posts of cedar would last for years. Only a few small cedars survived the
logging and those trees regenerated this forest. Atlantic white cedar is a hardy tree,
sprouting up in wet areas, and even regenerates after fire and wind storms.

Just a short distance into the swamp the boardwalk forks. You should stay
left to complete a clockwise loop through the cedars. The cedars are not the only
trees in the swamp; red maples, or swamp maples, also like wet feet and are equally hardy. In autumn, the red maples are among the first trees to show color, usually a deep burgundy.

The farther you go into the swamp the stronger the feeling of peace and solitude. Still, brown pools of water reflect the image of the cedars that rise from small
hummocks. Such scenery will have you reaching for your camera. (You might

want to bring a tripod because of the lack of light.) It is said that the peat beneath the water extends some twenty-four feet. As you walk the boardwalk consider that this cedar swamp would have been obliterated by development were it not for the creation of the Cape Cod National Seashore. Public funding to protect the biodiversity of a region is not only important to plant and wildlife species, but can enhance our own lives by offering us a place of solitude and unusual beauty.

Because the swamp soil is acidic, only a few species of plants can grow beneath the cedars. One is the swamp azalea, which has white flowers in early summer, and another is the beard lichen that grows on the cedar's trunks. The protected depression that you are walking through was formed when a glacial block of ice was buried by gravel as the glaciers retreated northward. The block of ice then melted creating this depression that was later filled by a rising water table.

It takes about twenty minutes of walking to circle the swamp, but plan on taking much more time if you stop and linger. At the boardwalk's next intersection you can exit the swamp by walking to the left, but try going straight a few more minutes to reach some benches. If you are traveling with children this would be a good place to have a snack and explain how these are among the last Atlantic white cedars we have on the Cape due to development.

To leave the swamp, retrace your steps to the last intersection passed to reach the benches. Walk to the south. You will soon reach an intersection with a dirt road, but you should continue straight ahead passing through pitch pines and black oak (one of which has a fat growth near its bottom called a burl). Within ten minutes you will pass through a sunny opening with poverty grass, golden heather, and American beach grass. In five more minutes you will return to your car—but don't let your exploration stop here. Instead, walk eastward on the paved road for ten minutes toward the ocean and visit the Marconi Station Site and the Overlook Platform, both of which offer superb views of the Cape and ocean. In 1903, Italian inventor Guglielmo Marconi successfully completed the first transatlantic wireless communication between the U.S. and England from this site. (The barren site was conducive for sending wireless radio waves.)

While you are at the site, look down at the ocean's rolling breakers. This offshore area of the Cape was called the graveyard of the Atlantic, because of all the doomed ships that ran aground on offshore sandbars and then were pounded by waves. The pirate ship "The Whydah," commanded by pirate Samuel Bellamy, was wrecked here in 1717, and the Castagna was driven ashore and destroyed in 1914.

## Getting There

From Route 6 at the Cape Cod National Seashore's Salt Pond Visitor Center in Eastham, go 5 miles north on Route 6 to South Wellfleet. Turn right at the traffic lights into the Marconi area. Follow the signs to Marconi Station Site and, in about a mile, park in the paved lot at the end of the road.

Open dawn to dusk. Admission fee in summer months; seasonal facilities; no dogs allowed.

# Great Island

## *Wellfleet*

---

* 4 miles
* 2.5 hours
* Moderate

---

### Highlights

- Tidal flats, salt marsh
- Wooded island and dunes
- Historical significance

The combination of pine woodlands and coastal dunes makes Great Island a special place to walk. The estuarine tidal flats formed by the Herring River drainage are rich habitat for marine life such as fiddler crabs, quahogs, and oysters. There are no roads on the reservation; the only sound you will hear is the lapping of the waves and the call of the birds. Because the island is large and is often overlooked by visitors, you can look out over the water and enjoy Great Island in relative solitude. Be sure to bring drinking water and a hat, as the walk is relatively long and much of it is in the sunshine.

Great Island is a knob of glacial debris that is currently connected to the mainland by a narrow hill of sand. (Winds and tides have continually reshaped this area.) In the late 1600s and early 1700s, a tavern served mariners on Great Island, and the walk goes to this historic site.

From the parking lot, follow the trail next to the map and sign welcoming you to the Cape Cod National Seashore. The trail passes through a stand of pitch pine (identified by the three rigid needles) that are all about the same age due to the replanting activity here at the end of the nineteenth century. Early settlers cut most of the old timber that once covered much of the Cape, and without it's diverse covering of trees the Cape was literally blowing away, before planting efforts began to stabilize the soil.

Within three or four minutes you will arrive at the water's edge on the Wellfleet Harbor side of the island. Turn right here and follow the shore in a southerly direction. A sign tells you the mileage of the various walks on the island: 1.8 miles to Smith Tavern, 2.9 miles to Great Beach Hill, and 4.1 miles to Jeremy

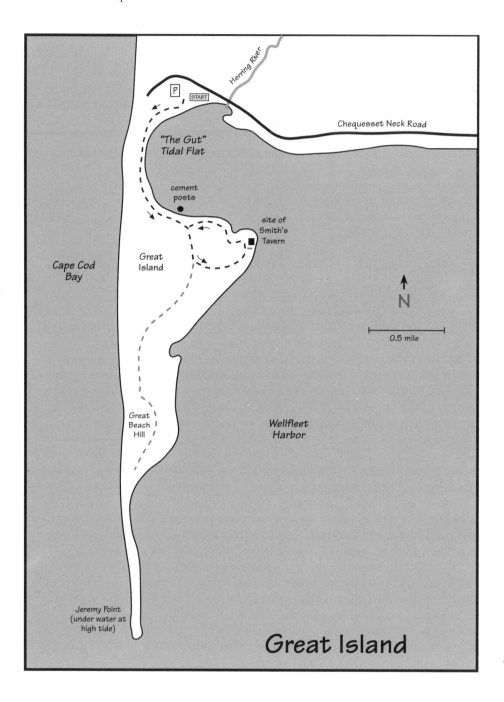

Herring River

P

START

Chequesset Neck Road

"The Gut"
Tidal Flat

cement
posts

site of
Smith's
Tavern

Cape Cod
Bay

Great
Island

N

0.5 mile

Great
Beach
Hill

Wellfleet
Harbor

Jeremy Point
(under water at
high tide)

Great Island

Point. The salt hay growing along the shore was used by early settlers as cattle feed. On a winter walk here, you might get lucky and see a harbor seal swimming in the bay or sunning on the shore.

As you walk the shore look for oyster shells. Wellfleet oysters are known for their excellent quality. Oysters were important in the diet of the Native Americans that lived here, and later to the settlers who commercially harvested them for food and used their shells to make lime. Over-harvesting, and perhaps other unknown factors, caused the disappearance of the Wellfleet oyster. In an attempt to reestablish oysters in the bay, oyster stock from the southern U.S. has been introduced.

During high tide the shoreline walk can be a bit muddy, so wear boots during cold-weather months. About fifteen minutes into the walk there is a path on the right that leads to wooden stairs spanning the dunes to the beach on the Cape Cod Bay side of Great Island. Young children will enjoy walking along the water on both sides of the island.

After you check out Cape Cod Bay, return to the Wellfleet Harbor side of Great Island and continue walking southward. Follow the curving contour of the shore around the tidal flat known as The Gut. You might see sideways-moving fiddler crabs, which burrow into the sand. The males have a large singular claw that they use in battle during mating season.

Continue along the coast for about ten more minutes and you will pass cement posts and then a sign that informs you of how many miles there are to reach various Great Island destinations. Take a right on the path that comes from the interior of the island. On hot days the pitch pines in the woods provide welcoming shade.

Follow this interior path for about seven or eight minutes until you reach a fork in the trail. Go left on the narrow path to the east-southeast. You will find that you make better time on this woodland path because you are walking on firm ground rather than in sand. In about ten minutes you will arrive at a sign for the tavern. (There is also a short trail to the right that quickly brings you to a small bluff overlooking the water, which makes for a good resting spot.) The view before you is impressive. The sparkling blue water of Wellfleet Bay stretches north and east toward the Cape Cod mainland. (This bluff is roughly an hour and fifteen minutes into your hike, which is the halfway point.)

The Smith Tavern site is marked by a sign and boulder. It once served as a meeting place for weary mariners. A recent excavation of the site revealed more than 24,000 artifacts including wine glass stems, clay pipes, and even a lady's fan. Whalers frequently visited the tavern, both those on ship and those who were shore whalers. Using small boats equipped with harpoon and lance, shore whalers stayed close to shore, often driving the whales up on the sand where they could easily be killed and butchered.

Even before the arrival of the white man, the Native Americans were on the lookout for shore-stranded whales to use as a food source. When the Pilgrims landed on the Cape prior to settling in Plymouth, they came upon Indians butchering a whale on a beach near Great Island. Thoreau witnessed a similar scene on one of

*A trail passes through pitch pines and leads to the bay.*

his four walks through the Cape, when he saw 30 blackfish (a small whale) stranded on the beach: "They were a smooth shining black, like India-rubber, and had remarkably simple and humplike forms for animated creatures, with blunt round snout or head, whale-like, and simple, stiff looking flippers."

The whales were so plentiful here prior to the 1900s that lookouts were posted on the high ground at Great Beach Hill. The lookouts alerted the whalers who pursued the great mammals in small boats. Whale houses (in which gear was stored) and try-works (used to boil out the whale oil) were built around the perimeter of the island. The height of whaling activity in New England was reached in the 1840s, when there were more than 700 American whaling vessels at sea. But with the discovery of the mineral oil in Pennsylvania, the demand for whale oil dropped. Today, visitors to Cape Cod see whales on whale-watch excursions and concerned people are trying to protect the whales, which are still killed by some foreign countries for commercial purposes.

Retrace your steps back from the bluff to the Smith Tavern sign. Bear right to complete your loop back to The Gut and toward the parking lot. After five minutes of walking there you'll see a faint trail to the right, but you should continue through the woods heading northwest. In about five more minutes you will be back at the shore by the cement posts. From here, turn left and retrace your earlier steps along the shore and around The Gut to return to the parking lot.

If you enjoyed this four-mile walk you may want to return and try a more ambitious walk farther out on Great Island—a rise of land known as Great Beach Hill. This would be a six-mile round-trip walk. Jeremy Point, at the southern most end of Great Island is not recommended as a walk because it is under water at high tide.

## Getting There

From Route 6 take the Wellfleet Town Center exit and follow the sign toward the town center. At 0.2 mile turn left onto East Commercial Street and follow that for 0.8 mile to the town pier. Turn right onto Kendrick Road and follow it about a mile to its end. Turn left onto Chequesset Neck Road and go 1.7 miles to the Great Island parking lot on the left.

No admission; portable rest rooms provided seasonally.

# About the Author

Mike Tougias is the author of several books about New England, including *Nature Walks in Eastern Massachusetts*, and *Exploring the Hidden Charles*, both published by AMC Books. His other works include:

- *New England Wild Places*
- *Autumn Rambles of New England* (co-author)
- *Quiet Places of Massachusetts*
- *Nature Walks in Central and Western Massachusetts* (co-author)
- *Country Roads of Massachusetts*
- *A Taunton River Journey*
- *Until I Have No Country* (A Novel of King Philip's Indian War)
- *Cape Cod in the Words of Thoreau & Beston*

Tougias is a native New Englander who enjoys reading, canoeing, fishing, biking, and swimming. In his free time, he leads visually impaired people on nature walks and volunteers for conservation work in an effort to save more open spaces.

"Researching *More Nature Walks in Eastern Massachusetts* was great fun," says Tougias, "and there were some days on the trail when I really felt my spirit soar. I explored about a hundred new places since I wrote the first book, *Nature Walks in Eastern Massachusetts,* and it was difficult to narrow down the number of walks to a manageable number. The real challenge, however, was reviewing all my trail notes and actually doing the writing!"

Tougias gives narrated slide presentations for each of his books. To learn more about these presentations, please write to him at PO Box 72, Norfolk, MA 02056.

# About the AMC

**Begin a new adventure!**

Join the Appalachian Mountain Club, the oldest and largest outdoor recreation club in the United States. Since 1876, the Appalachian Mountain Club has helped people experience the majesty and solitude of the Northeast outdoors. Our mission is to promote the protection, enjoyment, and wise use of the mountains, rivers, and trails of the Northeast.

Members enjoy discounts on all AMC programs, facilities, and books:

### AMC Outdoor Adventure Programs

We offer more than 100 workshops on hiking, canoeing, cross-country skiing, biking, and rock climbing as well as guided trips for hikers, canoers, and skiers.

### AMC Facilities: Mountain Huts and Visitor Centers

The AMC maintains backcountry huts in the White Mountains of New Hampshire and visitor centers throughout the Northeast, from Maine to New Jersey.

### AMC Books & Maps

Guidebooks and maps to the mountains, streams and forests of the Northeast—from Maine to North Carolina—and outdoor skill books written by backcountry experts on topics from winter camping to fly fishing. Call 1-800-262-4455 or visit our webpage at www.outdoors.org to order AMC Books or to receive a complete catalog.

To learn more about our workshops, facilities, books, and membership benefits, contact us at:

The Appalachian Mountain Club
5 Joy Street
Boston, MA 02108
617-523-0636

Find us on the web at www.outdoors.org

# Alphabetical Listing of Areas